THE ILLUSTRATED ROCK ALMANAC

Library of Congress Cataloging in Publication Data
Marchbank, Pearce.
    The illustrated rock almanac.

    1.   Rock music—History and criticism.   2.   Music—
Almanacs, yearbooks, etc. I. Miles, Barry, joint
author. II. Title.
ML3561.R62M34   784   76-57167
ISBN 0-448-22675-8

Typeset by ABM Typographics, Hull, Yorkshire.
Printed in England by Cox & Wyman Limited, London, Reading & Fakenham

In the United States :
Paddington Press Limited,
distributed by
Grosset & Dunlap.

In the United Kingdom :
Paddington Press Limited.

In Canada :
distributed by
Random House of Canada Limited.

In Australia :
distributed by
Angus & Robertson Pty. Limited.

THE ILLUSTRATED ROCK ALMANAC

PADDINGTON PRESS LTD

NEW YORK & LONDON

Book and cover designed by Pearce Marchbank.
Cover photograph by Annie Leibovitz.

The authors would like to give special thanks to:
Janice Pober, Jacqui Bailey, Graham Keen, Roger Perry, Jonathon Green,
John May, Neil Spencer, Ingrid Von Essen,
Cornelia Bach and Music Sales Limited.

The authors would like to acknowledge the use of the following
publications in the preparation of this book:
The Encyclopaedia Of Rock, Rock File, Rock Encyclopedia,
The NME Book Of Rock, The Age Of Rock, The Illustrated History Of Pop,
The New Musical Express Annual, Rock On, The Story Of Pop,
The Country Music Encyclopedia, The Rolling Stones File,
The Rolling Stones Blue Book, The Rolling Stones: An Illustrated Record,
The Beatles Press Book, The Beatles: An Illustrated Record,
As They Were, The Beat Book, Rolling Stone Magazine and
Creem Magazine.

The following companies and organizations provided publicity
photographs for use in this book, for which the authors are very grateful:
A&M, Apple, ABC/Dunhill, Anchor, Asylum, Atlantic, Arista/Bell,
Bizarre, Blackhill Enterprises, Capitol, Charisma, Chrysalis, CBS,
Columbia, Cotillion, Decca, Elektra, EMI, Epic, Harvest, Island, Liberty,
MCA, Motown, NEMS, Phonogram, Polydor, Pye, RSO, Reprise, Rocket,
RCA, Track, Transatlantic, United Artists, Virgin and Warner Brothers.

THE ILLUSTRATED ROCK ALMANAC

Compiled, written and edited by
Pearce Marchbank and Miles.

JANUARY 1

Day of Janus, Roman God of Entrances, Christianized as St. Almanach.

Beatles first record company audition in London in 1962. "These boys won't make it. Four-groups are out. Go back to Liverpool Mr. Epstein—you have a good business there".

Country Joe McDonald born in El Monte, California in 1942. "Electric Music for the Mind and Body" was a key album of the "psychedelic era". His protest albums contributed to the anti-Vietnam war effort in the USA in the late Sixties.

Hank Williams, the country singer, dies of heart failure and too many pills in 1953. He was an influence on the whole of the country and western music field, and the folk and rock circles from Bob Dylan to the Byrds.

Morgan Fisher, organist of Love Affair, born. They had a UK No.1 hit with "Everlasting Love" in January 1968.

J. Edgar Hoover born in Washington DC in 1895. "Intellectual license and debauchery is un-American. In righteous indignation it is time to drive the debauchers of America out in the open".

Watergate John Mitchell, H R Haldeman, John Ehrlichman and R Mardian were found guilty in 1975 at the Watergate cover-up trial.

"The Sounds of Silence" by Simon and Garfunkel reaches US No. 1 in 1966.

Beatles begin tour of Scotland in 1963, and in 1964 begin three weeks at the Paris Olympia with Trini Lopez and Sylvie Vartan.

Drugs. The Single Convention on Narcotic Drugs designed to simplify machinery of international drug control adopted at a UN conference in New York City in 1971 in a session which lasted until March.

The Times newspaper founded in London in 1788.

Censorship British Board of Film Censors introduced in 1966.

JANUARY 2

Day of Harpocrates, ancient Egyptian God of Silence

Roger Miller born in Fort Worth, Texas in 1936. "Dang Me" was his first US chart entry in June 1964. He had 15 US chart entries up until 1968, the most famous of which was "King of the Road".

Chick Churchill, organist with Ten Years After born in Mold, Flintshire in 1942. Their first album chart entry in UK was with "Stonehenge" in February 1969.

Tex Ritter (Woodward Maurice Ritter) dies in 1974 of a heart attack. His "Wayward Wind" reached US No. 28 in June 1956, but he was best known for his cowboy movies. He was 67 when he died.

Che Guevara and Fidel Castro and the revolutionary army enter Havana, Cuba in triumph in 1959. Cadillacs and parking meters are smashed. Phone lines to Florida cut and casinos looted.

JANUARY 3

St. Genevieve, Janua Nova, a form of the Egyptian Isis. Has the title "Visible Index of the All Powerful".

George Martin born in London in 1926. Joined EMI Records in 1950 where he produced the comedy records of the Goons and Peter Sellers as well as commercial hits by Matt Monro and Shirley Bassey. He signed The Beatles in 1962 and produced all of their records from 1962 until 1969 sometimes playing piano or harpsichord on them and often writing the arrangements. In 1965 he left EMI to start his own production company AIR. The Beatles chose not to use him for their "Let it Be" album but after it turned into a disaster they asked him

back to produce "Abbey Road"—the last Beatles album. These two albums were released in reverse order of recording.

John Paul Jones (John Baldwin) of Led Zeppelin born in Sidcup, Kent in 1946. The group's name was invented by Who drummer Keith Moon. Their first

album was released in 1969 and they quickly became a supergroup in the USA though took much longer to gain acceptance in the UK. Famous for the length of their sets and lack of promo.

Philip Goodhand Tait born in Hull, England, in 1945. Originally a member of the underground band Circus, he then recorded four solo albums for DJM before finally joining Chysalis. His backing group left to become Camel.

J R R Tolkien born in Blomfontein, South Africa, in 1892. "Hobbits are an unobtrusive but very ancient people, more numerous formerly than they are today".

The First Acid Test was held at the Fillmore Auditorium in San Francisco in 1966. LSD was still legal.

"Darlin" by the Beach Boys enters the UK charts to stay for nine weeks in 1968.

Bob Dylan opened his 1974 American tour with a concert at The Amphitheater in Chicago. There were 660,000 tickets available on the tour for which the organizers received over 6,000,000 applications. Dylan commented: "Six million, a hundred million, it's all an illusion. It doesn't mean that much to me, really. I mean, who else is there to go and see?"

John Lennon & Yoko Ono's "Two Virgins" record sleeve, which shows them posing naked together, was declared as pornographic in New Jersey, USA. Police seized 30,000 of them in 1969.

The Psychedelic Shop is opened in 1966 on Haight Street by Ron and Jay Thelin. It opens the way for innumerable sellers of "hippie trinkets" to capitalize on the freak explosion.

Drugs. "If you can't smoke it, wear it". The slogan for an American company called Quog which produced a cologne called "Grass" in 1972. It was made from the essence of Cannabis Sativa. "Unfortunately it does not have the effect of smoking grass, but it does have a very refreshing smell."

JANUARY 4

Volker Homback of Tangerine Dream's early lineup born in Kamenz in 1944. One of the first German experimental groups to get off the ground in Britain. The first album "Electronic Meditations" was released in 1970.

First pop chart based on record sales was published in Billboard in 1936. No. 1 was Joe Venuti.

JANUARY 5

Mal Evans, ex-Beatles Road Manager shot dead in the home of his girlfriend in 1976 by the Los Angeles

police, allegedly after an argument involving a shotgun which he refused to surrender. Evans was an Honorary Sheriff of Los Angeles County.

FM radio first demonstrated in 1940.

Thom Mooney, drummer with Nazz born. A hard rock group which began in 1968 and split in 1969 after introducing Todd Rundgren to the public.

Don Hartman of Frost born 1946. A late Sixties underground group not too well known outside the New York area.

JANUARY 6

Twelfth Night
St. Befans, traditional Fairy Saint.

Syd Barrett born in Cambridge in 1946. He formed the Pink Floyd and was responsible for the band's early direction, writing their first hits such as "Arnold Layne".

Became a psychedelic casualty, though made two solo albums, "The Madcap Laughs" (1970) and "Barrett" (1971) before retiring completely from public life to live reputedly in a Cambridge cellar.

Sherlock Holmes (William Sherlock Scott Holmes) born at Mycroft, Sigerside, Yorkshire in 1845. "Mediocrity knows nothing higher than itself, but talent instantly recognises genius."

Wilbert Harrison born in 1929. His single "Kansas City" was a US No. 2 in April 1959. "Let's Stick Together" was a hit for both Canned Heat and Bryan Ferry.

The Rolling Stones begin their first tour in which they top the bill in 1964. They opened at the Harrow Granada with the Ronettes.

Tom Mix born in 1880. US Marshall who turned actor and made over 400 western B movies.

JANUARY 7

Day of Numa, Wizard King of Rome.
(Immediate successor to Romulus).

Kenny Loggins of Loggins and Messina born in Everett, Washington in 1948. He wrote "House at Pooh Corner" which was a hit for The Nitty Gritty Dirt Band. Messina first met him in the

PINK FLOYD AFTER SIGNING THEIR FIRST RECORDING CONTRACT IN 1967

role of producer but they soon teamed up and made a large number of albums. The group broke up amicably in July 1976.

Mike McGear (Michael McCartney) of the satirical fun group Scaffold and of solo album fame born in Liverpool in 1944. ''Lily The Pink'' was a UK No. 1 Christmas 1968. Brother Paul produced his solo album in 1974.
Andrew Brown of The Fortunes born in 1946. ''You've Got Your Troubles'' was No. 2 in UK in July 1965.
Danny Williams born in Port Elizabeth, South Africa in 1942. ''Moon River'' was UK No. 2 in October 1961 staying 14 weeks in the charts.
Jim West of The Innocents

born in 1941. They had two UK No. 28's with ''Honest I Do'' and ''Gee Whiz'' in the early Sixties.
Paul Revere of Paul Revere and the Raiders born in Harvard, Nebraska. A US teenybopper band that never caught on in the UK. They first reached the US charts in April 1961 and

had 5 Top Ten hits including the No. 1 ''Indian Reservation'' in April 1971.
Cyril Davies collapsed and died in 1964 of leukaemia. He was the founder member of Blues Incorporated with Alexis Korner. In 1962 he left and founded the Cyril Davies All-Stars which had been

previously operating as Screaming Lord Sutch's Savages which was a popular R & B band on the London circuit until his death. Played harmonica with Charlie Watts and Brian Jones in Blues Unlimited until they met up with Jagger and Richards and left to form The Stones.

PAUL REVERE (SECOND FROM RIGHT) AND THE RAIDERS.

JANUARY 8

Day of Amitabha : The Buddha of Boundless Light, the Western Buddha. Christianized as St. Lucian whose name derives from a root meaning "light".

Elvis Aron Presley born at 12:20pm in East Tupelo, Mississippi in 1935. Elvis said at the LA Forum, "I've got 56 gold singles and 14 gold albums and if there's anyone out there who doubts it, if you ever come through

Memphis you can come in and argue about it 'cause I've got every one of them hanging on the wall. I'm really proud of it. I've outsold The Beatles and The Stones . . . all of 'em put together !''
David Bowie (David Robert Jones) born in Brixton, London in 1947. His mother was granted a divorce five months later. He saved up £12 to hire a demo studio and cut "You've Got A Habit of Leaving Me" which was ignored. He was in the Lindsay Kemp mime troupe before finally achieving fame.
He released his first single in 1964 as one of the King Bees ("Liza Jane") and on 1st April 1966 released his first solo single, "Do anything you Say", "Good Morning Girl".
"I'm one of the World's actors. I'm an exhibitionist, a peacock. I like showing off. Freud would have had a heyday with me. You see, I'm not very mature. My basic outlook is still much the same as it was when I was fourteen".

DAVID BOWIE, LONDON, 1976 / PHOTO: CHALKIE DAVIS

Dead, born in 1943. Archetypal West Coast Acid-Rock guitarist, famed for over-long solos. Made solo recordings and guest appearances on friends' albums, including Crosby, Stills, Nash and Young.

Lee Jackson born in Newcastle in 1943. Bass player with The Nice, he formed his own group Refugee when The Nice split up in 1973.

Terry Sylvester singer with The Hollies, born in 1945. He replaced Graham Nash when he left to join Crosby and Stills.

JANUARY 9

Joan Baez born in 1941. Superstar of folk who helped bring Bob Dylan to fame by introducing him to the public at her concerts. She

Jimmy Page (James Patrick Page) born in London in 1944. In 1965 he produced John Mayall's ''I'm Your Witchdoctor'' and even produced Nico's first single for Immediate. In June 1966 he joined The Yardbirds as bass guitarist but soon changed to joint lead guitar with Jeff Beck. Beck left in Xmas 1966 and Page played lead until the group disbanded in the summer of 1968. He formed The New Yardbirds who were later renamed Led Zeppelin and became one of the most successful concert bands of all time, regarded as the originators of ''heavy metal'' rock, though Page hates the term. He is a collector of Aleister Crowley books and artifacts and bought Crowley's old Boleskine Manor in Scotland.

Bobby Kreiger (Robert Kreiger) guitarist and later vocalist with The Doors born in Los Angeles in 1946.

After Jim Morrison's death the group recorded two unsuccessful albums and then disbanded.
Shirley Bassey born in Tiger Bay, Cardiff, South Wales in 1937. ''I Who Have

Nothing'' and ''Goldfinger'' are her best known recordings.
Little Anthony (Anthony Bourdine) of Little Anthony and The Imperials born. His first big hit in the US was ''Tears On My Pillow'' in 1958.

Jerry Garcia (Jerome John Garcia), of The Grateful

and Dylan split up during his 1965 tour but were friends again on Dylan's 1975-6 ''Rolling Thunder Review''. She founded a college of pacifist studies out in California and visited Hanoi at the height of the American bombing.

Scott Walker (Scott Engel) born in Hamilton, Ohio in 1944. The Walker Brothers had two UK No. 1's with "Make It Easy On Yourself" (August 1965) and "The Sun Ain't Gonna Shine No More" (March 1966). The group split up at the peak of their fame but their solo careers were nowhere near as successful and they reformed in late 1975.

Marcus Doubleday born in Tacoma, Washington in 1943. He played trumpet with The Electric Flag before joining The Buddy Miles Express, which lasted until 1970. He has made many guest appearances on albums.

Lou Reed marries Betty, a cocktail waitress, in New York City in 1973.

Simone de Beauvoir born in 1908. "One is not born a woman—one becomes one."

Richard M. Nixon born in Yorba Linda, California in 1913. "Sincerity is the quality that comes across on television".

Eldridge Cleaver "On January the 9th of 1971, I issued an order to Field Marshall DC who works in our intercommunal section here in Algeria to go to Leary's apartment and to take Leary and his wife Rosemary, to another location and to confine them there until further notice. . . we busted Leary".

ROD STEWART IN LOS ANGELES / PHOTO: JOHN D. CONROY.

JANUARY 10

St. Agatho: Pope, magician and wonder worker.

Rod Stewart born in Highgate, London in 1945. Made a choice between football and rock music, and first came to the public's attention as vocalist with The Jeff Beck Group on their first album "Truth". Later found both fame and fortune with The Faces. During this entire period he made solo albums on a rival record label and finally, in January 1976, he split from the group to go solo. Moved to live in Los Angeles with Britt Eckland.

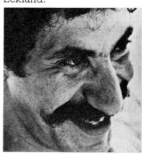

Jim Croce born in South Philadelphia in 1943. A former truck-driver, he became well-known for his narrative songs, "Bad, Bad, Leroy Brown" going to US No. 1 in 1973. He was killed in a plane crash in the same year, before his career really had a chance to develop.

Ronnie Hawkins born in Huntsville, Arkansas in 1935. "Forty Days" and "Mary Lou" were US Hits in 1959. In 1963 he cut "Bo Diddley"/"Who Do You Love" with Robbie Robertson (later of The Band) and returned to Canada with him. He now

runs a nightclub where the likes of Bob Dylan drop by and sometimes jam.

Aynsley Dunbar born. Drummer leader of the Aynsley Dunbar Retaliation after playing with the John Mayall Bluesbreakers. He formed the brass oriented band, Blue Whale after Retaliation split up and then joined Frank Zappa's Mothers of Invention for four albums. Played on David Bowie's ''Pin Ups'' album and then formed a new group Journey, largely ex-Santana members. Also featured on Nils Lofgren's solo albums

Howlin' Wolf (Chester Burnett) dies in a Chicago hospital in 1976. One of the legendary Chicago bluesmen, he was discovered in Memphis by Sun Records talent scout Ike Turner in 1951. A year later in Chicago he went electric and made many of the blues classics that formed the backbone to the early Sixties R & B revival, writing numbers such as ''Sittin' On Top Of The World'' ''Smokestack Lightnin'', & ''Spoonful''. **Martin Turner**, bass player with Wishbone Ash, born in 1947. The band formed in late 1969 and their third album ''Argus'' made No. 3 in the UK album charts. **Donny Hathaway** born in Chicago in 1945. He majored in music,

played in a jazz trio, then worked for Curtis Mayfield as a producer. Later had some chart success with Atlantic Records, both as performer and producer. **Sal Mineo** born in the Bronx, New York City in 1939. He co-starred with James Dean in ''Rebel Without A Cause'' apart

from many other film roles. He had a modest success as a singer, having a US Top Ten hit in April 1957 with ''Start Movin''. On February 12, 1975 he was found murdered in Los Angeles.

Johnny Ray (John Alvin Ray) born in 1927. Sob singer who first entered the charts with ''Cry'' in 1951. ''Yes Tonight Josephine'' was a UK No. 1 in 1975 but only made No. 16 in the US. **Buddy Johnson**, the great Thirties bandleader born in 1912. **The United Nations** first General Assembly was held in 1946 in London. **''Great Balls Of Fire''** by Jerry Lee Lewis reaches No. 1 in the US in 1958. **Rolling Stones** on tour play Walthamstow, England in 1964, and in 1965 played the Commodore, Hammersmith, London. **Bob Dylan** appears on Earl Scruggs Fanfare TV Show in 1971.

JANUARY 11

Slim Harpo born in West Baton Rouge in 1924. ''Baby Scratch My Back'' was a US No. 16 in February 1966 but he was always high in the R & B charts with numbers such as ''Rainin' In My Heart'' which was No. 1 in 1961.
Don Cherry born in 1924. ''Thinking of You'' was his first US hit in 1950. He is not to be confused with the famous jazz musician of the same name.
Karten Vogel born. For seven years he led the premier Danish rock group Burning Red Ivanhoe before joining Secret Oyster.

Votes for Women In 1918 the House of Lords pass the Representation of the People Bill giving the Suffragettes a victory and British women the vote at last.

JANUARY 12

Long John Baldry born in London in 1941. He began singing with Blues Incorporated, alternating on vocals with Cyril Davies, whose Cyril Davies All-Stars he then joined. He played with The Rolling Stones on their first ever gig under that name and had a UK No. 1 in November 1967 with ''Let The Heartaches Begin''. It made No. 88 in the US charts.

Maggie Bell born in Glasgow in 1945. Originally a founder member of Stone The Crows. The group split up in 1973 and she went solo. Known as one of the most powerful female singers in Britain.
Tex Ritter born in Panola County, East Texas in 1906. Star of endless B movies.

Sang the ballad featured in ''High Noon'' in 1952.
Charlie Gracie born in Philadelphia in 1936. ''Butterfly'' was a US hit in 1957.

Bob Dylan records a radio play, ''Madhouse On Castle Street'' for the BBC while in London in 1963. He sang two numbers : ''Blowin' In The Wind'' and ''Swan On The River''—a number which he never again recorded. He was in Britain returning from a trip to Italy to search for his girlfriend Suze Rotolo (seen with him on the sleeve of ''The Freewheelin' Bob Dylan''). **''Please Please Me''** by The Beatles released. It became their first UK No. 1 reaching the top on the 16th February 1963.

JANUARY 13

Day of Hesus or Hu, the Druidic form of Christ.

John Lees, guitarist of Barclay James Harvest, born in 1948. The band, although giving the name to their label, Harvest, have never had the big audience their classically oriented music deserved.

Stephen Foster dies in 1864 by tripping over a washbasin while drunk when he was living on The Bowery in New York City. He was the first pop composer, writing "Old Folks At Home", "Beautiful Dreamer", "Jeannie With The Light Brown Hair" and "Oh ! Suzannah !"

Eric Clapton makes a comeback from his drug addiction with a concert at the London Rainbow in 1973, helped and encouraged by Pete Townshend.

Emile Zola publishes "J'Accuse" in 1898.

Wyatt Earp dies in Los Angeles in 1929.

JANUARY 14

Alain Toussaint born in New Orleans in 1938. Cut his first album "Wild Sounds Of New Orleans" in 1958. Well known for his exceptional work as a songwriter and producer, he finally opened up a studio in New Orleans, the Sea Saint Recording Studios.

"Hey Joe", The Jimi Hendrix Experience first record, enters UK charts in 1967 at No. 24 to reach No. 6.

Bob Dylan sits in as Blind Boy Grunt on the "Dick Farina and Eric Von Schmidt" album being recorded in Dobell's basement, Charing Cross Road, London in 1963.

Bill Graham gets the lease on the San Francisco Fillmore Auditorium in 1966. His first production is a final benefit for the San Francisco Mime Troupe, whom he previously managed.

The First Be-In happened in 1967 in the polo field·of Golden Gate Park, San Francisco. Thousands of hippies came together to love each other, take drugs, hear music . . .

Tim Harris, drummer with The Foundations born in 1948. The group was launched in 1967 with "Baby Now That I've Found You" which was to be their first million seller.

Paul Gadd, who finally achieved fame under the name of Garry Glitter, performed a ceremony on board the Sloop John D on the River Thames in which Paul Raven, one of Gadd's earlier stage names, was officially drowned by lowering a coffin containing all of Paul Raven's unsuccessful records and publicity into the water, in 1973.

Phil Lesh of The Grateful Dead busted at his Fairfax, Marin County, California home in 1973 on drugs charges.

CAPTAIN BEEFHEART / PHOTO: BYRON NEWMAN

The Move had their first UK chart entry with "Night of Fear" in 1967. It reached No. 2. They were one of the major heavy-rock underground groups of the time. Roy Wood has now made a career for himself as a solo artist.

"I'm A Believer" by The Monkees enters the UK charts to reach No. 1 Written by Neil Diamond, it was later recorded in 1975 by Robert Wyatt, ex-drummer with The Soft Machine and entered the UK charts.

Jack Jones born. He had 19 US chart singles from 1962, none of which entered the UK charts. He is the husband of actress Susan George.

Albert Schweitzer born in 1875. "I too had thoughts of once being an intellectual, but I found it too difficult".

JANUARY 15

Day of Fo, an early Chinese Buddha.

Captain Beefheart (Don Van Vliet) born in Glendale, California, in 1941. Attended Antelope Valley High School with Frank Zappa who gave him his name. His first single was "Diddy Wah Diddy" followed by "Frying Pan" both in the blues-rock tradition. His first album "Safe As Milk" began his cult following. His classic Magic Band backing group were assembled for his third album, "Trout Mask Replica", a double album produced by Zappa and released on his Straight label. His Magic Band left him in 1974, renaming themselves Mallard and he retired from the business

for over a year. In 1975 he toured with Zappa, appearing on their joint album "Bongo Fury" and formed a new Magic Band.
Earl Hooker, Chicago blues guitarist, born in Clarksdale, Mississippi, in 1930. He died of TB in 1970 but not until his playing had reached a wider audience in the late Sixties due to the new interest in blues from the white teenage audience.
The Who's first single, "I Can't Explain"/"Bald Headed Woman" released on the Brunswick label in 1965. Decca pressed 1,000 copies for the first run. It reached No. 8 in the charts selling over 100,000 copies in six weeks.
Rosa Luxembourg and Karl Liebknecht shot in 1919. Leaders of the left-wing Spartacist uprising in Germany, they were captured and executed without trial. The uprising failed.
"American Pie" by Don McLean reaches US No. 1 in 1972.

JANUARY 16
Day of Commemoration of the Temple of Concord.
Sandy Denny born in 1947. She replaced Judy Dyble as vocalist in Fairport Convention. Her arrival in the group led to their "folk/rock" sound, coming as she

did from folk club roots. She left to pursue a solo career but rejoined the Fairports in 1974. She is married to Trevor Lucas who is the guitarist and vocalist with the Fairports.
William Francis, keyboards with Dr. Hook and The Medicine Show, born in California in 1942.
Damo Suzuki, one-time vocalist with the experimental German rock group Can, born in 1950.

Freedom for Timothy Leary

Timothy Leary placed under house arrest in Kabul, Afghanistan in 1973 by two armed Federal Agents of the US Government who seized his passport in the airport and transferred him to an American plane before he could launch any complaints. He had escaped from San Luis Obispo prison in California 28 months earlier with the aid of the Weather Underground.
Clara Ward, gospel singer, dies at the UCLA Medical Center after a week in a coma following a stroke in 1973. She was 48.
Paul Beaver, of Beaver and Krause, dies of a stroke in 1975. Their records created an "electronic environment" which in turn created a cult following.
Raymond Philips of The Nashville Teens born. "Tobacco Road" was a UK No. 6.
The Cavern Club opens in Matthew Street, Liverpool, in 1957. Originally a jazz club it later became world famous as the place where the Beatles first achieved fame.

Barbara Lynn (Barbara Lynn Ozen) born in Beaumont, Texas, in 1942. Her first hit, "You'll Lose A Good Thing" was a poem written when she was 16. It made No. 1 in the US R&B charts and made the US Top 10 in 1962. The Rolling Stones recorded her "Baby We've Got A Good Thing Goin'".

JANUARY 17
Day the pagans sacrificed swine to the Earth Goddess. Day of St. Anthony ; pigs are sacred to him. Horses are blessed in Rome.

Mick Taylor born in Welwyn Garden City, Hertfordshire, England, in 1948. Left school at 15 and taught himself guitar. In local group, The Gods. Deputized for Eric Clapton when he missed a John Mayall's Bluesbreakers gig, later joining the group when Clapton left. He stayed for two years. On 5 July 1969 he made his debut with The Rolling Stones before 250,000

people at a free concert in London's Hyde Park, two days after the death of his predecessor. In December 1974 he left The Stones to join the short-lived Jack Bruce Band which toured France but soon broke up.

CLAY FEEDS PREDICTIONS TO EXP[...]
April
The **RING**
BIG CHAMPIONSHIP ISSUE
AM KIN[...]

Muhammad Ali (Cassius Marcellus Clay Jr.) born in Louisville, Kentucky, in 1942. "I'm the prettiest. Look at me and I've been fighting for twenty years. I'm serious, it's hard to be humble when you're as great as I am."
Chris Montez born in 1943 in Los Angeles. "Lets Dance" was US No. 4 in August 1962 and reached No. 2 in the UK.
William Hart of The Delfonics, born in Washington in 1945. The Philly Groove label was formed for the group by

their manager, Stan Watson.

Billy Stewart and three of his band die in 1970 when car goes over the parapet of a bridge. He began singing with The Rainbows who had a hit in 1955 with "Mary

Lee''. Of his 11 US solo chart entries "Summertime" was the biggest, reaching No. 10 in 1966. He was 32 when he died.

Francoise Hardy born in Paris in 1944. The premier French singer-songwriter of the Sixties.

"The Mighty Quinn" by Manfred Mann reaches UK No. 1 in 1968. One of the demo songs on Bob Dylan's "Basement Tapes" which were themselves released in 1975. Heavily bootlegged, when asked why he waited so long before releasing the tapes Dylan replied "I thought everybody had them".

The Boston Tea Party opened in 1967. The most important rock venue in town until it closed in January 1971.

American B52 bomber carrying four atom bombs crashes off the coast of Spain in 1966.

Anton Chekhov born in Taganrog, Russia.

Patrice Lumumba, first President of the Congo (Zaire), assassinated in 1961 by the CIA as he was unpopular to American business interests.

First Jazz Concert at the New York Metropolitan Opera in 1944.

JANUARY 18

Hindu day of the sun.

Elmore James, legendary blues guitarist, born in Durant, near Canton, Mississippi in 1918. He first recorded in 1952, "Dust My Broom" being his most famous song. Cited by Eric Clapton, George Harrison and many others as a major influence.

Bobby Goldsboro born in 1941 in Florida. "Honey" was a US No. 1 in 1968.

Dave Greenslade, keyboards with Colosseum, born. After the band split in 1971 he got together with Tony Reeves to form Greenslade in November 1972.

The Rolling Stones held a benefit concert at the Los Angeles Forum in 1973 in aid of the victims of the Nicaraguan earthquake in which Bianca Jagger's mother had to crawl from the ruins. The concert raised over $200,000. On May 9, 1973 Jagger give the money to the Pan American Development Fund after topping the money up to $350,000.

David Ruffin born in Meridian, Mississippi, in 1941. With The Temptations he had such hits as "Ain't Too Proud To Beg" before going solo in 1968 and having a hit with "My Whole World Ended".

Cary Grant (Archibald Alexander Leach) born in 1904.

A. A. Milne born 1882. His "Winnie The Pooh" books were influence on late Sixties lyricists. Brian Jones bought his house and died there.

JANUARY 19

Sun enters Aquarius, ruled by Saturn but associated with Juno by the Romans.

Janis Joplin born at 9:45am in Port Arthur, Texas, in 1943. "God, how did this happen? How did I turn into this person, man?... Sometimes I look at my face and I think it looks pretty run down, but considering all I have been through, I don't look bad at all''.

Phil Everly born in Brownie, Kentucky in 1939. With his elder brother Don he formed one if the most influential acts in the formation of rock, affecting many, including The Beatles and Simon and Garfunkel. "Bye Bye Love" was their first hit in 1957, a year after their hillbilly singer father had persuaded Chet Atkins to produce them in Nashville. They met

Bordleaux Bryant who wrote many of their hits. Phil, the lighter more pop-oriented brother, performed alone

on a 1963 UK tour after Don had had a nervous breakdown. Things were never the same again and they eventually split in July 1973.

Dolly Parton born in Sevierville, Tennessee, in 1946. Her first hit was "Dumb Blonde" in 1967, but her sensitive country ballads have been well received by a much wider audience, particularly such numbers as "Jolene" and "In My Tennessee Mountain Home".

Robert Palmer, born in 1949. Originally shared the vocals in Vinegar Joe with Elkie Brooks before the group broke up in 1974. He went solo and made a number of critically acclaimed albums.
Rod Evans, with his original line-up of Deep Purple, born in Edinburgh. "Fireball" and "Machine Head" were UK No. 1 albums in 1971-2. Deep Purple split up in July 1976.
"Johnny Angel" By Shelly Fabares was US No. 1 in 1962.
Ken Kesey busted for the second time in three days in 1966 along with Mountain Girl (Carolyn Adams) on Stewart "Whole Earth Catalogue" Brand's roof in San Francisco.
Edgar Allan Poe born in 1809.
Robert E. Lee, born in 1807.

JANUARY 20
Leadbelly (Huddie Ledbetter) born in Morningsport, Louisiana in 1889. He was first recorded by Alan and John Lomax for the Library of Congress in 1933 and 1934. Best remembered for "Goodnight Irene" and having served time for murder.
Melvin Pritchard, drummer of Barclay James Harvest, born in 1948. The group never achieved the success that their perseverance deserved. They have remained a cult band, having always lived in Manchester, never moving to London. The Harvest label was named after them.
George Grantham original drummer with Poco, born in Cordell, Oklahoma, in 1947.

Alan Freed dies in 1965. The DJ who coined the term "Rock 'n' Roll" from the words to Bill Haley's "Rock A'Beatin' Boogie" in 1952: "Rock, Rock, Rock, everybody. Roll, Roll, Roll, everybody."

Bill Graham puts on his notorious three-day Trips Festival in 1966 at Longshoremens Hall in San Francisco. Large quantities of LSD ingested.

Tribute to Woody Guthrie Concert held at Carnegie Hall, New York, in 1968. Bob Dylan and the Band play an electric set amongst Woody's friends from the folk world including Joan Baez and Peter, Paul and Mary.
Federico Fellini born in 1920.
J. F. Kennedy inaugurated as the President of the USA in 1961.
US Panama Canal Zone military authorities issued circular No. 5 in 1923 declaring marijuana illegal for American soldiers there.

JANUARY 21
St. Agnes' day: the day to find a husband.
Edwin Starr (Charles Hatcher) born in Nashville in 1942. In 1965 his first solo single "Agent Double O Soul" reached the Top 30. "25 Miles" in 1969 and "War" in 1970 brought him back to charts after a slack period.

Richie Havens born in the Bedford-Stuyvesant section of New York City in 1941.

His underground mysticism of the late Sixties made his albums hits in the US. Played at Woodstock in 1969.
Jimmy Ibbotson born in 1947. Guitarist and keyboards for The Nitty Gritty Dirt Band, who managed to fuse many styles into a country-rock whole. The pinnacle of their success was the triple album "Will The Circle Be Unbroken" in 1973, featuring many country veteran guests.
Chris Britton of The Troggs born. Only when Jimi Hendrix recorded "Wild Thing" did this English West-country group achieve any underground status.
"I Feel Free" by Cream enters the UK charts in 1967. Their first chart entry.
The Rolling Stones arrive in Sydney, Australia for the Roy Orbison tour of 1965. Thousands of fans riot at the airport.

George Harrison marries Patricia Anne Boyd in 1966 at Epsom Register Office. "When we started filming I could feel George looking at me and I was a bit embarrassed. Then when he was giving me his autograph he put seven kisses under his name. I thought he must like me a little.''—Patti Harrison talking about how she met George during the filming of ''A Hard Day's Night.'' She played one of the schoolgirls in the train scene at the start of the film.

Bob Dylan plays in Atlanta, Georgia during his 1974 American tour.

George Orwell (Eric Blair) dies of pulmonary tuberculosis in 1950. ''People worship power in the form in which they are able to understand it.''

Vladimir Ilyich Lenin dies in 1924, having suffered a stroke in May, 1922.

JANUARY 22

Sam Cooke born in Chicago in 1931. ''You Send Me'' was a US chart entry in 1957 but the UK waited until ''Only Sixteen'' in October 1959. He was killed in 1964.

Brian Keenan of The Chambers Brothers born in New York City.

Ray Anthony born in Cleveland, Ohio in 1922. He had many chart instrumentals from 1950 onwards in the US. ''Peter Gun'' was in the charts in January 1959.

The Spencer Davis Group, which included Stevie Winwood, reaches UK No. 1 with ''Keep On Runnin'' in 1967.

The Rolling Stones refuse to go on the revolving stage which characterized the

finale of the British TV London Show ''Sunday Night At The London Palladium'' in 1967. It caused a great scandal at the time.

Buddy Holly makes his last recordings in 1959 in his New York apartment, using the same Ampex tape recorder that he used to record ''That'll Be The Day'', ''Peggy Sue'' and most of his other early hits.

Bloody Sunday in St. Petersburg in 1905. A march in aid of more food is mown down by soldiers and the first Russian Revolution begins.

Queen Victoria dies in 1901.

JANUARY 23

Eugene Church born in 1938. ''Pretty Girls Everywhere'' was his US Top 40 hit in 1958.

Bill Cunningham of The Box Tops born. ''The Letter'' was US No. 1 in 1967 and is a consistent oldie but goodie.

Jerry Lawson, of The Persuasions, born in Fort Lauderdale, Florida in 1944. They first got together in 1968 and have moved through a number of labels since then.

Big Maybelle, blues singer with an enormous voice, dies in Cleveland, Ohio in 1972.

Alvin Stardust makes his first appearance under that name at the Midem Festival in Cannes in 1974. For the previous 14 years he had been singing under the

name of Shane Fenton.

Sergei Eisenstein, the Russian film-maker, born in Riga, Latvia in 1898. ''Strike'' was made in 1924, ''The Battleship Potemkin'' in 1925 and his epic ''Ivan The Terrible'' from 1942 till 1946. Inventor of film montage.

Edward ''Kid'' Ory dies in Honolulu, Hawaii in 1973 of pneumonia and heart failure. He was 86. Louis Armstrong joined his band in New Orleans in 1916.

JANUARY 24

Doug Kershaw born in a houseboat in Tiel Ridge, Louisiana in 1936. A genuine Cajun, best known for his fiddle-playing, he has been recording since 1955. His early work with his brother Rusty is among his best. His autobiographical ''Louisiana Man'' has been recorded over 600 times.

Neil Diamond born in 1944 in Brooklyn, New York City. Wrote various hits for others including ''I'm A Believer'' for the Monkees. Had a long string of US hits from 1967 before, in 1970, getting into the UK charts with ''Cracklin' Rosie''. Signed to Columbia Records in 1973 at great expense. Ray Charles, Aretha Franklin, Elvis Presley, Four Tops and Robert Wyatt have all recorded Diamond songs.

Beatles sign contract in 1962 for management with Brian Epstein. ''I never signed a contract with the Beatles. I had given my word about what I intended to do, and that was enough. I abided by the terms and no one ever worried about me not signing it.''

IN WITNESS whereof the parties hereto have hereunto set their hands the day and year first before written

SIGNED by the said
BRIAN EPSTEIN in the
presence of :-
J. A. Taylor.
FLAT C. 'MEREWNDS'
THE SERPENTINE SOUTH
BLUNDELSANDS
LIVERPOOL 23.

SIGNED by the said
JOHN WINSTON LENNON
in the presence of :-
J. A. Taylor.

SIGNED by the said
GEORGE HARRISON
in the presence of :-
J. A. Taylor.

SIGNED by the said
JAMES PAUL McCARTNEY
in the presence of :-
J. A. Taylor.

Jack Scott born in Windsor, Canada in 1938. "My True Love" was an October 1958 hit in the UK.

James 'Shep' Shepherd found dead in his car on the Long Island Expressway in 1970, after having been beaten and robbed. When the Heartbeats disbanded in the late 50's he formed Shep and The Limelights, and had a hit with "Daddy's Home" in March 1961.

The Moon contacted by radar in 1946 by US Army Signal Corps.

Gold first discovered in California in 1848.

JANUARY 25

Grace Slick and Paul Kantner's baby girl born 1971 in a San Franscico hospital. The original choice of name for the child was God but they finally decided upon China.

Drugs. In the crematorium at the Mexican frontier town of Tijuana were burnt 22 tons of marijuana, 40 million assorted pills, 19 ozs of heroin and $4\frac{1}{2}$ lbs of cocaine.

Anita Pallenberg born in Germany in 1943. Originally the girlfriend of Brian Jones, she left him in favor of Keith Richard, with whom she still lives. They have a son Marlon. She co-starred with Mick Jagger in "Performance".

JANUARY 26

Corky Laing, drummer with Mountain, born in Montreal, Canada in 1948. Did two numbers as West Bruce and Laing in 1972 and 1973, before reforming Mountain in 1974 to cut the "Avalanche" album.

Angela Davis born Birmingham, Alabama in 1944. An attempt to set her up on a weapons charge failed miserably when massive international support was given her.

Buddy Holly makes his first recordings for the American Decca label (MCA) in Nashville in 1956, and appears with the Crickets on the Ed Sullivan TV Show in 1958.

Spencer Dryden, drummer with the Jefferson Airplane, married Sally Mann in the Airplane's front parlor in 1970.

Richard Neville's book "Play Power" published in 1970 in UK. A full length portrait of "The International Underground" including such gems as "the way to a girl's mind is through her cunt." Neville was editor of UK underground magazine "Oz".

John Logie Baird gives the first demonstration of his "television" to the Royal Institution at his workshops at 21a Frith Street, Soho, London in 1926. 'The Times' said the pictures were rather blurred. The rooms now comprise Bianchi's restaurant.

JANUARY 27

Nick Mason, founder member of the Pink Floyd, born in Birmingham in 1945. The Pink Floyd grew out of the Central London Polytechnic's architectural department group The Abdabs : Nick Mason, Rick Wright and Roger Waters all being architectural students. Mason provided the initial money for the group's equipment. After studying sailing and navigation, Mason developed his collection of veteran racing cars.

Bobby Bland (Robert Calvin Bland) born in Rosemark, Tennessee in 1930. Originally one of the Beale Streeters he first recorded in 1954, "Dry Up Baby". He was in the Johnny Ace Review and together with Junior Parker he led Blues Consolidated.

Nedra Talley of The Ronettes born in New York City in 1947.

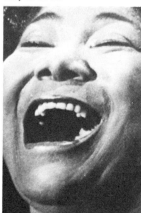

Mahalia Jackson dies of heart failure. Though born in New Orleans, she came to fame in Chicago, recording a

stream of gospel hits in the early Fifties. She became well known also for her work in civil rights and her song "We Shall Overcome".

Rudi Maugeri, baritone with The Crew Cuts born 1931. Their version of "Sh Boom" was their biggest US hit. The original version by The Chords is thought to be the first rock 'n' roll record.

Patricia Hearst, aged 21, goes on trial in San Francisco in 1976. Charged with armed robbery, after her abduction by the Symbionese Liberation Army. She faced a 25 year prison sentence.

"Ballad of Bonnie And Clyde" by Georgie Fame reached UK No. 1 in 1968.

Gary Glitter, under the name of Paul Raven, releases his first single "Alone In The Night"/"Too Proud" in 1960.

Sweet reach UK No. 1 with "Blockbuster" which stayed there for five weeks.

Wolfgang Amadeus Mozart born 1756 in Salzburg, Austria.

Lewis Carroll (The Reverend Charles Ludwidge Dodgson) born in 1832.

JANUARY 28

Zoroaster, founder of the Pavisi Religion.

Rick Allen of The Box Tops born. The group was best known for "The Letter".

Acker Bilk (Bernard Bilk) born in Pensford, Somerset in 1929. "Stranger On The Shore" was the theme of a BBC TV Series and made UK No. 1 as a 1961 Christmas record staying thirty-nine weeks in the charts.

Barbi Benton Hugh Hefner's personal bunnygirl, born in Sacramento, California.

Sacha Distel born in Paris. French ballad singer.

Roger Daltrey's wife Jacqueline sues for divorce in 1968. He had been married for four years and had a three year old son.

Gary Glitter British King of Glam Rock, announces his retirement at 31, in 1976. Glitter, real name Paul Gadd, earned £500,000 a year.

George Harrison announces in 1976 that he would participate in the planned £15 million Beatles reunion concert. The other three had already agreed.

Iceland becomes the first country to introduce abortion on medical and social grounds in 1935.

"Inside Linda Lovelace" cleared of obscenity charges at the Old Bailey by a jury of nine men and three women in 1976. The book purported to be an autobiography by the star of "Deep Throat".

JANUARY 29

David Byron, vocalist with Uriah Heep, born in Epping near London, in 1947. The group's first album "Very 'eavy, Very 'umble" was a big success both on the continent and in the US.

Germaine Greer born in 1939 near Melbourne,

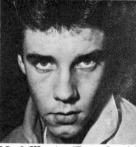

Australia. "The Female Eunuch" was published in 1970. She is a university professor and a one time editor of "Suck—The European Sex Paper".

Mark Wynter (Terry Lewis) born in Woking, Surrey in 1943. "Image Of A Girl" (August 1960), "Venus In Blue Jeans" (October 1962), "Go away Little Girl" (January 1963) and "It's Almost Tomorrow" (November 1963) were all UK hits for him.

Allen Klein, New York music business financier wheeler-dealer who once controlled both The Beatles and The Rolling Stones finances through his ABKCO company, found guilty in 1971 of ten counts

of "unlawfully failing to make and file return of Federal income taxes and FICA taxes withheld from employees wages". The conviction was upheld on appeal. Klein is generally regarded to be responsible for the break-up of Apple and The Beatles.

Bob Dylan plays his second night at the Nassau Colliseum, New York during his 1974 American tour. His wife Sarah was seated on a couch on stage.

"A Groovy Kind Of Love" by The Mindbenders enters the UK charts 1966.

P. J. Proby's trousers split on the stage in Croydon, London, in 1965.

Frederick Delius, English composer, born in 1863.

Black Dwarf, the British satirical, libertarian newspaper, founded in London in 1817. The government was forced to publish a "White Dwarf".

JANUARY 30

St. Tydie Virgin, Celtic Saint.

Marty Balin (Martyn Jere Buchwald) born in Cincinnati, Ohio, in 1945. Inventor of The Jefferson Airplane which was launched from his small San Francisco club The Matrix in August 1965.

Steve Marriott born in 1947. Former child actor, member of Small Faces, the East London "mod" band. "Whatcha Gonna Do About It" (September 1965), 'Sha La La La Lee' (February 1966) and "Itchycoo Park" (August 1967) were some of their UK hits. In 1969 Steve Marriott left to form Humble Pie.

Stephen Stills born in Dallas, Texas, in 1945. He played with Buffalo Springfield, Crosby Stills Nash and Young and the group which he led, Manassas. He also played on a variety of other people's records including Van Dyke Parks. The list of artists who have appeared on his solo albums is impressive: Booker T, Eric Clapton, Carole King, Jimi Hendrix, Steve Winwood, Ringo Starr. . . . It was through his solo albums, and particularly through the single "Love The One You're With" that he achieved his greatest success.

Joe Terranova baritone with Danny and The Juniors, born in Philadelphia in 1941. "At The Hop" was the biggest of their nine US chart entries.

Bob Dylan plays Madison Square Garden, New York City on his 1974 American tour. "Knocking On

Heaven's Door" on the "Before The Flood" album was recorded at this concert.

Ruth Brown born in Portsmouth, Virginia in 1928. Her first hit in US was "5-10-15 Hours" in 1952. She was last in US charts with "Mama, He Treats Your Daughter Mean" in 1962.

Beatles film and record on the roof of Apple in Savile Row in 1969. They played "Get Back" which was released as a single, and other tracks which appeared on the "Let It Be" album.

Watergate James W. McCord and G.Gordon Liddy convicted of plotting to spy on the Democratic Party's 1972 campaign office in the Watergate building.

Charles I King of England, publicly beheaded at Whitehall, London, in 1649.

Mahatma Gandhi shot by a Hindu extremist in 1948. Gandhi was the figurehead of the Indian independence movement, and advocate of

Ahimsa (non-violence).

"Bloody Sunday" Londonderry, Northern Ireland, in 1972. UK army troops opened fire on alleged snipers during a Civil Rights march. No snipers were ever discovered, but thirteen civilian marchers were shot dead.

JANUARY 31

St. Melangell Monacella. Patroness of hares, formerly sacrificed on this day.

Phil Manzanera, guitarist with Roxy Music, born in 1951. Has done a certain amount of solo work since the group stopped regular work, including a solo

album "Diamond Head" and the "Go" project with Stomu Yamashta.

Phil Collins, drummer of Genesis, born in 1951. From 1971 they gathered a wide following as their records

began to reflect the theatricality of their live shows.

Terry Kath, guitarist and vocalist with Chicago, born in 1946. Brought out a series of numbered albums "Chicago I to VIII" one a year since 1969.

Cyril Stapleton born in Nottingham in 1914. Had a UK No. 2 in September 1955 with "Blue Star" but best known in Britain for his thousands of radio broadcasts.

Buster Brown dies in 1976. His record "Fannie Mae" of 1959 is a golden oldie blues classic.

Norman Mailer born in Long Branch, New Jersey, in 1923. "It is not the facts that count, only the nuances."

Slim Harpo dies of a heart attack in 1970 in Port Allen, just over the Mississippi River from Baton Rouge. His "King Bee" was an important early hit for The Rolling Stones. Originally performed as Harmonica Slim.

Meher Baba the avatar of tens of thousands of followers including Peter Townshend and Ronnie Laine, dies without speaking in 1969. He was thought to be going to give a final message to his followers before dying after many years of silence.

Grateful Dead busted in New Orleans in 1970 for possession of narcotics, LSD and barbiturates. They were with Owsley Stanley, famous for his brand of LSD.

Mario Lanza (Alfred Arnold Cocozza) born 1921. He had many operatic hits in the 50's.

Bob Dylan plays Madison Square Garden, New York City. Dylan's second concert at the Garden during his 1974 American tour. He did two shows.

P. J. Proby's trousers split on stage at the Ritz Cinema, Luton, in 1965.

Guy Fawkes executed in 1606 for his part in the plot to blow-up the Houses of Parliament.

bass in The Byrds and is featured on their double album, half of which is of live recordings, "Untitled" in 1971. Battin had previously been half of the early Sixties group Skip and Flip.

Roberta Flack born in Asheville, North Carolina in 1937. A music BA, she accompanied opera singers and taught music. She was discovered singing in a jazz club and

Simon Dupree and The Big Sound before they all three left in 1969 to form Gentle Giant. Their first transatlantic success came with their "Octopus" album in 1973, at which time brother Phil left the group. Derek does the lead vocals, plays bass and alto sax.

Beatles begin touring with The Helen Shapiro Tour at the Bradford Gaumont, in 1963, and "Please Please Me" enters UK charts to reach No. 1 and stay eleven weeks.

Peter Macbeth, bass player with the Foundations, born in 1943. "Build Me Up Buttercup" and "Baby Now That I've Found You" in 1968 were the group's million sellers.

had her first solo chart success with "First Time Ever I Saw Your Face" in 1972. She has moved steadily away from soul toward more commercial material.

Derek Shulman born in Glasgow in 1947. Together with his brothers Phil and Ray he was a member of

Lonnie Johnson born in New Orleans in 1889. His bending of notes on the guitar made him a distinctive musician from the very beginning of his career. Played in Louis Armstrong's Hot Five.

Gary Glitter, under his previous stage name of Paul Raven, makes his first TV appearance on "Cool For Cats" in 1960 singing "Alone In The Night".

FEBRUARY 1

Februa of the Classical Greeks and Romans in honor of Proserpina. Day of purifications of ancient Eyptians. St. Bridget, little modified form of Brighde, Celtic Goddess having a fire shrine, served by women, never by men.

Don Everly born in Brownie, Kentucky in 1937. Together with brother Phil as The Everly Brothers has a string of country rock hits with 24 US chart entries including three No. 1's: "Wake Up Little Suzie" (September 1957) "All I Have To Do Is Dream" (April 1958) and "Cathy's Clown" (April 1960). The Everlys were one of the most important acts in early rock 'n' roll; they broke up in 1973.

Ray Sawyer, vocals and guitarist with Dr. Hook and The Medicine Show, born in Alabama in 1937.

Bob Shane of The Kingston Trio born in Hawaii in 1934. "Tom Dooley" was a big Christmas hit in 1958.

Jimmy Carl Black born in El Paso in 1938. As drummer of The Mothers Of Invention he was "The Indian of the Group".

Tommy Duffy, lead of The Echoes, born 1944. "Baby Blue" was their big US hit in 1961.

P. J. Proby banned by the massive British ABC Theatre chain in 1965 following two trouser splitting episodes in their theaters.

"I Want To Hold Your Hand" by The Beatles reaches US No. 1. It stayed there seven weeks, 1964.

Fleetwood Mac reach UK No. 1 in 1969 with "Albatross".

Elvis Presley's only child, Lisa Marie, born in 1968.

FEBRUARY 2

Ground Hog Day.

Graham Nash born in Blackpool in 1942. After a long career with The Hollies he left in December, 1968 and joined with Stephen Stills and David Crosby to form Crosby Stills and Nash. He and David Crosby have recorded and toured a number of times together.

Skip Battin born in 1934. He replaced John York on

GRAHAM NASH / PHOTO: MICK GOLD.

THE WRECK OF BUDDY HOLLY'S PLANE

FEBRUARY 3

St. Blaze. Patron of wool combers. Connected with the myth of the Golden Fleece.

Buddy Holly, Ritchie Valens and The Big Bopper die in an aircrash in 1959. The Beechcraft Bonanza light aircraft took off from Mason City, Iowa on its way to Faro, North Carolina, where its passengers had a concert booking. It crashed in the snow and darkness a few miles from Mason City in a cornfield at Ames, Iowa. Non-arrival of the artists allowed Bobbie Vee to take Buddy Holly's place and start his career.

Dave Davies of The Kinks, younger brother of Ray, born in Muswell Hill in 1947. Made some solo singles also, including "Death Of A Clown", which was in the UK charts in July 1967. Also did a solo album.

Melanie Safka born in Astoria, Long Island, New York, in 1947. Her "Brand New Key" went to US No. 1 in October 1971.

Johnny "Guitar" Watson born in Houston, Texas in 1935. Originally worked as a pianist in Los Angeles, but noted for his piercing blues guitar dynamics. The original "Gangster of Love" a great influence on Steve Miller, he has had a long string of singles released from 1953.

Angelo D'Aleo of The Belmonts born 1940. They backed Dion and then went solo.

Dennis Edwards, lead singer with The Temptations, Tamla Motown's most successful male vocal group, born.

Frankie Vaughan born in Liverpool in 1928. His first record "Strange" was released in March 1963.

Beatles, with the exception of Paul McCartney, hire Allen Klein as their business manager for Apple in 1969. "I suppose there are two things I miss. I often think it would have been nice to have had a mother when I was a little boy. And, yes, sometimes I think it would be nice to be considered a good guy . . ." Allen Klein.

Gertrude Stein born in Allegheny, Pennsylvania in 1874.

FEBRUARY 4

Japanese day dedicated to Fortune, evil spirits being exorcised by the throwing of beans.

Jerry Shirley, drummer with Humble Pie, born in 1952. Formed in 1969 by Peter Frampton, the band toured the US endlessly and enjoyed a huge reputation until they broke up in 1974.

Johnny Gambale, second tenor with The Classics, born in New York City in 1942. "Till Then" was No. 20 in US charts in June 1963.

Neal Cassidy, hero of Jack Kerouac's "On The Road"

under the name Dean Moriarty, dies of exposure in Mexico in 1968.

John Steel, drummer with the original Animals lineup born in 1941.

Patricia Hearst, who was kidnapped by the Symbionese Liberation Army in 1974, arrested in San Francisco in 1975.

Beatles appoint Eastman and Eastman, Linda Eastman's father's law firm as general council to Apple, in 1969. This was Paul McCartney's response to Allen Klein's appointment the previous day.

FEBRUARY 5

Bob Marley (Robert Nesta Marley) born at Rhoden Hall, St. Anne in the Parish of Middlesex, Jamaica in 1945. His father, Captain Norman Marley, was an English soldier from Liverpool. After starting welding as a trade, he recorded some singles having being introduced to Jimmy Cliff. The Wailers were formed in 1964, with Marley writing most of their material. "Simmer Down" was their first single, and by 1966 they were leaders of the Ska music, Kings of Trenchtown. He left for the US and worked in a car factory, returning after a while to continue with moderate success. In 1971 Chris Blackwell of Island records signed him up and the Wailers made the LP "Catch-A-Fire". By 1974 Marley had become the first Rastafarian Reggae superstar.

Alex Harvey born in The Gorbals, Glasgow in 1935. He formed The Alex Harvey Big Soul Band in 1959. In 1972 he formed The Sensational Alex Harvey Band, which gave him chart success.

Nigel Olsson, drummer, born in 1949. Originally in Spencer Davis Band with bassist Dee Murray, the two of them caused a sensation when they teamed with Elton John in 1970. They backed him on the albums and the shows that took John to superstardom.

Ron Wilson, congas, bongos and percussion with Joy Of Cooking, born in 1933. Their first album was released in 1970.

Norman Barratt, lead with Gravy Train, born in Newton-le-Willows, Lancashire in 1949.

Sven Johannson of the early line-up of Tangerine Dream born in Stockholm in 1943.

Red Buttons (Aaron Chwatt) born 1919. "The Ho Ho Song" and "Strange Things Are Happening" were his early Fifties hits.

BOB MARLEY, LONDON, 1976 / PHOTO: ADRIAN BOOT.

Chuck Winfield, trumpet and flugelhorn with Blood Sweat and Tears born in Monessen, Pennsylvania.
Cory Wells of Three Dog Night born in Buffalo, New York.
Claude King born in 1933. ''Wolverton Mountain'' reached US No. 6 in 1962

William Seward Burroughs born in St. Louis in 1914. Olympia Press first published ''The Naked Lunch'' in Paris in 1959.
T-Rex reaches UK No. 1 with ''Telegram Sam''.
''Will You Still Love Me Tomorrow'' by The Shirelles, reaches US No. 1 A classic Carole King number.

FEBRUARY 6

Mike Batt born in 1950. Producer of The Groundhogs and of the English psychedelic group Hapshash and The Coloured Coat. More recently known for writing the many Wombles' hits.

Fabian (Fabiano Forte) born in Philadelphia in 1943. ''I'm A Man'' was in US charts January 1959.
Dave Berry born in Sheffield in 1941. ''The Crying Game'' was a 1964 UK No. 5.
''You've Lost That Lovin' Feeling'', by The Righteous Brothers, produced by Phil Spector, reached US No. 1.
Mick Jagger announces that he is sung ''The News Of The World'' for libel

concerning a fictitious story about public drug-taking.

Jesse Belvin, author of ''Earth Angel'' and other classic songs dies in a car crash in 1960.

FEBRUARY 7

Hesiod, successor of Orpheus, author The Theogony, sacred book of Greek paganism.
Laurence Scott, keyboards man with Isotope born 1946 in Windsor, Berkshire. Experimental jazz-rock ensemble.
Warren Smith, early rockabilly artist, born in Louise, Mississippi, in 1933.
George Harrison has his tonsils removed at University College Hospital London, in 1965.
Beatles make first visit to the USA in 1964. They appear twice on The Ed Sullivan Show.
Charles Dickens born in 1812.

FEBRUARY 8

Pythian Games in honor of Apollo.
St. Apollonia, Virgin martyr, invoked against toothache.
St. Oncho, Celtic Saint, guardian of Tradition.
James Dean (James Byron), born in 1931. Archetypal symbol of rebel youth,

he starred in only three films. His death in 1955 in his crashed Porsche before his last, ''Giant'' was released caused an outburst of emotional necrophilia. He never heard Rock 'n' Roll.

Jim Capaldi born in 1944. He played with all the original Traffic members in Birmingham before they formed the group with Capaldi on vocals and drums. In 1972 he made a solo album at Muscle Shoals, ''Oh How We Danced''. In 1975 Traffic eventually broke up after a long and traumatic history and Capaldi launched his solo career. He had a 1976 hit with the classic, ''Love Hurts''.
Ted Turner, co-lead guitarist in Wishbone Ash, born in 1950. The band soon had success and their third album made UK No. 3, ''Argus''. Ted retired from the business in June 1974 and was replaced by Laurie Wisefield from Home.
Tom Rush born in Portsmouth, New Hampshire, in 1941. Part of the Boston/Harvard folk set, he released a number of highly regarded albums in the early sixties. He missed

the protest era but returned for folk-rock. In 1968 ''The Circle Game'' album broke with his folk roots and contained his most successful song, ''No Regrets''.

Adolpho ''Fito'' de la Parra of Canned Heat born in Mexico City in 1946.
Max Yasgur, owner of the farm that the Woodstock Festival took place at dies of heart failure in Florida.
Bob Dylan's ABC-TV film ''Eat The Document'' was finally shown at the New York Academy of Music in 1971. D A Pennebaker made the film originally for a show called ''Stage 67'' but it was never shown. Dylan edited the film. The proceeds from the screening went to a Pike County citizens group to stop strip mining.

P. J. Proby banned by ABC-TV in Britain following the ban imposed on him

by ABC theaters as a result of his splitting trousers in 1965.

"Half As Nice" Amen Corner's only UK No. 1 enters charts in 1969. They had other hits with "Bend Me, Shape Me" and "Hello Suzie".

"Blackberry Way" by The Move reaches UK No. 1 in 1969.

First execution in a gas chamber at Nevada State Prison in 1924 when Gee Jon was executed for murdering a rival tong.

Jules Verne born in 1828.

FEBRUARY 9

Carole King (Carole Klein) born 1941 in Brooklyn. She was Neil Sedaka's "Oh ! Carol !" (October 1959). Together with Jerry Goffin she wrote many of the great hits of the early Sixties. Her own solo albums are a feature of the Seventies, "Tapestry" being one of the three best selling albums of all time.

Mark Mathis born in Hahira, Georgia, in 1942. Together with Dean Mathis he had a hit in 1959 with "Tell Him No" under the name of Dean and Mark. Joined by Larry Henley they became the Newbeats and their first record "Bread and Butter" took them to US No. 2 in 1964.

Barbara Lewis born in 1944. "Hello Stranger" which reached US No. 3 in 1963 was her first hit.

Mia Farrow born 1945. Went from Peyton Place to join The Beatles with the Maharishi in India, via being Mrs. Frank Sinatra, now Mrs. Andre Previn.

Bruce Bennett, drummer with The Shadows born in Arnos Grove, London in 1941.

Gabby Hayes dies in 1969. Last of the misogynist Western heroes.

Brendan Behan born in Dublin, in 1923. "When I came back to Dublin I was court-martialled in my absence and sentenced to death in my absence, so I said they could shoot me in my absence."

Fyodor Dostoyevsky dies in 1881.

First striptease occurred in 1893, at a student rag held at the Moulin Rouge when an artist's model called Moira exposed herself on stage.

Bob Dylan plays Seattle, Washington during his 1974 American tour, closing his evening concert with the words "Thank you. Glad to be in Seattle, home of Jimi Hendrix".

FEBRUARY 10

St. Caedmon, Anglo-Saxon poet.

Ral Donner born in Chicago, in 1943. His biggest hit was "You Don't Know What You've Got" in summer 1961.

Phil Spector severely burned when his car bursts into flames and crashes in Los Angeles, in 1970.

Bertolt Brecht born in Augsburg, Germany, in 1898. "How does a man live ? Because his fellows/Are persecuted, tortured, plundered and die/Man only lives because he well knows/How to suppress his humanity/For once you must try to not shirk the facts/Man only stays alive through bestial acts."

FEBRUARY 11

St. Gobnet, Celtic Virgin.
Chinese New Year's Day.
Vision of Virgin Mary at Lourdes, 1858.

Gene Vincent (Vincent Eugene Craddock) born in Norfolk, Virginia, in 1935. Left school at 16 for a life long career at sea, but was permanently disabled by a motorcycle crash in 1955. He began singing on a C & W radio station while convalescing in Norfolk, Virginia. Eventually he was signed by Capitol as an answer to Elvis Presley and his career was launched in

1957 with "Be Bop A Lula", recorded in Nashville. But his initial impetus was dulled by bad management. His greasy, vicious image was unacceptable to clean, middle class America. After some success in Europe, Beatlemania and alcohol took their toll. He died in 1971 of a seizure.

Earl Lewis, of The Channels, born 1941. "The Closer You Are" was their 1956 hit in the US.

Josh White born in 1908. Great blues singer, noted for unusual guitar tuning.

The Beatles record all the tracks for their first album "Please Please Me" in one 12 hour session, with

George Martin at the EMI Abbey Road studios in London, in 1962. Two years later on this day they give their first concert in the USA at the Washington Colosseum.

Ringo Starr marries Maureen Cox at Caxton Hall, in 1965. They divorced ten years later.

George Washington born in 1732.

FEBRUARY 12

Diana, Virgin Goddess of Hunting. Form of the Moon Goddess.

Ray Manzarek, of the Doors, born in Chicago, in 1935. The Doors formed in 1965 when Manzarek met Jim Morrison in the film department of UCLA. They were fired from their booking at the Whisky A

Gogo in Los Angeles for performing their melodramatic song "The End". But, taken up by Elektra records, their first album was a hit and "Light My Fire", taken from it, became a No. 1 single. "Hello, I Love You" was a 1968 US No. 1; altogether they had 6 Top Twenty hits. Manzarek took the band on to make 2 more albums after Morrison's death in 1971, but they split up in 1973.

"Chicago Eight" Trial ends in 1970. Abbie Hoffman, Tom Hayden, Dave Dellinger, Rennie Davis and Jerry Rubin sentenced to maximum five years jail with $5,000 fine each. Lee Wiener and John Froines were found not guilty. Bobby Seale had been given a mis-trial already, lawyers William Kunstler and Leonard Weinglass contempt sentences of four years, thirteen days and one year, twenty-eight days respectively. All sentences successfully appealed.

Stanley Knight, guitarist with Black Oak Arkansas, born in Little Rock, Arkansas, in 1949. Though they formed in 1964 they only took the name Black Oak Arkansas in 1969, when they moved to Los Angeles which was where they found success after signing with Atlantic in 1970.

Steve Hackett born in 1950. The guitarist of Genesis. Their brand of melodramatic rock and highly theatrical stage presentations brought them success in the Seventies, especially in Europe.

Sal Mineo found murdered, in 1976, in Los Angeles, aged 37. Best known as an actor, he made a US Top Ten single "Start Movin'" in 1957.

Keith Richard's home "Redlands" in West Wittering raided for drugs by local police in 1967. Among those present were Mick Jagger, Marianne Faithfull, and art dealer Robert Fraser.

Gene McDaniels born in Kansas City, in 1935. "Chip Chip" was a 1962 hit.

Kenny Dino born in 1942. His only US hit was "Your Ma Said You Cried In Your Sleep Last Night", October 1961.

The Beatles play Carnegie Hall, New York City, in 1964.

Abraham Lincoln born in 1809.

Lady Jane Grey beheaded in 1554.

KEITH RICHARD AT REDLANDS / PHOTO: GERED MANKOWITZ.

FEBRUARY 13

St. Agabus, Patron of Soothsayers.

Peter Tork, of The Monkees born in Washington DC, in 1946. He left the Monkees to form a group called The Release.

Tennessee Ernie Ford born in 1919. He began in 1949 with "Mule Train" but his big US No. 1 was "Sixteen Tons" in September 1955.

King Floyd born in New Orleans in 1945. Had a Top 10 hit in 1970 with "Groove Me" and was also in the charts with "Baby Let Me Kiss You" in 1971, "Think About It" in 1973 and "Don't Cry No More" in 1974.

Gene Ames, of the Ames Brothers, born in 1925. They first entered US charts with "My Bonnie Lassie" in 1955.

Rolling Stones appear on Ed Sullivan show, New York City, in 1966.

Richard Wagner dies in 1883.

Bob Dylan plays The Forum in Inglewood, Los Angeles, in 1974. Many of the tracks on his "Before The Flood" album were recorded at this concert.

FEBRUARY 14

St. Valentine's Day.

Tim Buckley born in Washington, DC, in 1947. He died in 1975 in New York City. Began as a Los Angeles folk singer but his

albums soon became more experimental and personal, "Star Sailor" and "Greetings From LA" being his most challenging.

Vic Briggs, of the original Animals, born in 1945, in Twickenham, London.

Magic Sam, Chicago blues singer and guitarist, born in Mississippi, in 1937.

Eric Anderson born in Pittsburgh, in 1943. Originally brought to New York as "the new Dylan" by Tom Paxton, he has made albums for many companies but never achieved anything other than cult status.

Albert Grossman goes to court to prove that Janis Joplin's death from a drug overdose was an accident and not suicide. He had her life insured for $250,000.

"Teen Angel" by Mark Denning reaches US No. 1 in 1960.

Chris Barber's "Petite Fleur" entered UK charts in 1959. He only had one chart entry throughout the "Trad" boom but was very influential nonetheless.

Bob Dylan plays The Forum in Inglewood, Los Angeles. Many of the tracks on the "Before The Flood" were recorded live at this concert.

Muhammad Ali defeats European Heavyweight Champion Joe Bugner in 1973, at Las Vegas. Ali won every round.

"St. Valentine's Day Massacre" in 1929 seven of Bugs Moran's gang shot dead in the SMC Cartage Co. Warehouse, at 2212 North Clark Street, Chicago. The killers, disguised as policemen, were "James Morton" and "Frank Rogers", both generally assumed to be hired by Al Capone.

Sinyavsky and Daniel imprisoned in 1966 by Soviet courts, for seven years and five years in labor camps. Their "trial" was the first of attacks on Soviet dissidents and radicals.

FEBRUARY 15

Pan, God of Nature.

Brian Holland born in Detroit in 1941. He met up with Lamont Dozier in 1961, who was already working for Motown. They became a

regular writing and production team, while Brian's brother Eddie was a hit artist with Motown. Eddie joined the team in 1962. Everything the trio touched turned to gold, as they wrote and produced a long succession of hits for Marvin Gaye, Supremes, Temptations, The Four Tops, Martha and The Vandellas and the Isley Brothers. In 1968 they quit Motown and formed their own company and a law suit with Motown was settled out of court. Brian and Lamont returned to recording themselves.

Mick Avory, drummer with The Kinks born in 1944, in Hampton Court, London.

Hank Locklin born in Florida, in 1918. "Please Help Me I'm Falling" was his 1960 hit.

Nat King Cole dies of lung cancer in 1965, in Santa Monica, California.

Little Walter dies of head injuries sustained in a fight. The great Chicago blues harmonica player.

Mick Jagger and Marsha Hunt settle a long-standing paternity suit out of court.

"Get A Job" by The Silhouettes reaches US

No. 1 in 1958.

"Stagger Lee" by Lloyd Price reaches US No. 1 in 1959.

"Everyday People" reaches US No. 1 in 1969 for Sly and The Family Stone.

FEBRUARY 16

Day of Krishna, Eighth Avatar of Vishnu.

Sonny Bono (Salvatore Bono) was born in Detroit, in 1935. He touted himself around local record companies in the late Fifties as a writer. He had a few minor successes but in 1963 The Searchers had a huge hit with "Needles And Pins" which he wrote with Jack Nitzsche. He began working for Phil Spector and in 1964 he married his girl friend Cher. Under Spector's direction they began recording as Sonny and Cher and in 1965 made the

million seller "I Got You Babe", written, arranged and produced by Bono. The same year he had a solo Top Ten hit with "Laugh At Me", but this was followed by four years of chart failure and their act deteriorated into Las Vegas lounge-rock. In 1972 they began their own TV show and two years later the couple separated.

Herbie and Harold Kalin born in 1939. The Kalin Twins' "When" was a US No. 5 in June 1958. It made No. 1 in the UK.

Bill Doggett, rock and roll pianist, born in 1916. "Honky Tonk" was a US hit in July 1956.

Paul Anka marries Marie Ann Dezogheb in Paris, in 1963.

Lyn Paul, of The New Seekers, born in Melbourne, Australia, in 1949. Among their hits was the Coca-Cola jingle "I'd Like To Teach The World To Sing" in 1972. They disbanded in 1974.

FEBRUARY 17

The Flight into Egypt.
Festival of the Ass.

Tommy Edwards born in 1922. "It's All in The Game" was US No. 1 in 1958.

Bobby Lewis born in 1933. He had US No. 1 with "Tossin' And Turnin'" in March 1961.

Gene Pitney born in Hartford, Connecticut, in 1941. He had a string of US and UK hits in the mid-Sixties. "Twenty-Four Hours From Tulsa" became a minor classic.

John Leyton born in Essex, in 1939. "Johnny Remember Me" was a UK No. 1 in August 1961. "Wild Wind" reached No. 2 two months later.

"Love Makes Sweet Music" The Soft Machine's only attempt at a chart single in the UK was released in 1967. It flopped.

Joni Mitchell announces that her concert at the Royal Albert Hall in 1970 will be her last public appearance.

Jerry Lee Lewis appeared at Steve Paul's "Scene" in New York City. He received such an enthusiastic audience response he vowed to return immediately. "To hell with Carnegie Hall, I'm gonna play right here." He had been booed by a Los Angeles crowd at a Doors concert a few months earlier in 1967.

The Dylan Cash Session

Bob Dylan begins recording at Columbia Studios in Nashville with Johnny Cash in 1969, though few of the tracks laid down were ever released officially.

FEBRUARY 18

Sun enters Pisces, ruled by Jupiter, associated with Neptune

JOHN AND YOKO PLANT ACORNS FOR PEACE, 1969.

Yoko Ono Lennon born in Tokyo, Japan, in 1934. Her family sent her to study philosophy in the USA. During the early Sixties she was involved with the ''Fluxus'' group of experimental artists, film-makers and composers. She married John Lennon in 1969.

"Committee of 100" a hard-core splinter group of the Campaign for Nuclear Disarmament formed in 1961. Led by Bertrand Russell, it included playwright John Osborne, Vanessa Redgrave and novelist John Braine. It was pledged to illegal activities to stop the spread of nuclear weapons.

FEBRUARY 19

William "Smokey" Robinson born in Detroit, in 1940. Bob Dylan's favorite poet, he formed The Miracles in 1957. ''Tracks Of My Tears'' in 1969 was their only UK entry but they had had over 40 US chart entries, including a No. 1 with ''Tears Of A Clown'' in 1970.
Lou Christie (Lugee Sacco) born in Glen Willard, Pennsylvania, in 1943. ''Lightnin' Strikes'' was a US No. 1 in December 1965.
Pierre Van Der Linden, drummer of Focus, born in 1946. This Dutch group met with some success in Britain, having two Top Twenty hits in 1973, and a number of notable albums. They were formed for the Amsterdam version of ''Hair''

Tony Iommi, guitarist of Black Sabbath, born in 1948. The band represent the ultimate in negative, doom-laden heavy metal, appealing almost entirely to a young male audience.

Andy Powell, guitarist with Wishbone Ash, born in 1950. He replaced Glen Turner. They achieved UK No. 3 with their album ''Argus'' in 1972.

America's ''A Horse With No Name'', English Underground DJ Jeff Dexter's discovery, entered US charts to reach No. 1 in 1972.
Phil Cracolici, leader of The Mystics, born in 1937. Had US hit in May 1959 with ''Hushabye''. Later recorded ''All Through The Night'' with Jerry of Tom and Jerry (real name Paul Simon).
Harry Nilsson reaches No. 1 in US in 1972 with ''Without You''.

Dr. Timothy Leary convicted in 1970, in the Orange County Superior Court, of being in possession of two joints. His trial lasted four to five weeks, was ignored by the press, and stemmed from his arrest on December 26th, 1968 in Laguna Beach, California. He was held without bail.

Wes Wilson's poster style sets the tone for the ''psychedelic art'' that typified newspapers, posters and general printed ephemera in the Haight Ashbury. Wilson's first poster was used in 1966 for a Fillmore dance. The style never really altered.

FEBRUARY 20

Johnny Cash Day in the City of Los Angeles as from 1975.

Buffy Sainte-Marie born in Maine, of Cree Indian stock, in 1941. An important figure on the New York City folk scene of the early Sixties.

She wrote ''Universal Soldier'', a hit for Donovan. Her first album was released in 1964 and since 1968 she has experimented with many musical styles, including electronics, country and western and mainstream rock.
Patricia Campbell Hearst born in San Francisco, in 1954. Grand-daughter of ''Citizen Kane'' and member of the Symbionese Liberation Army.
Randy California, guitarist, born in Los Angeles. When Spirit folded, he formed

Kaptain Kopter and the Twirlybirds. Spirit then re·formed in 1974.

Alan Hull born in Newcastle in 1945. A member of the all-Newcastle band Lindisfarne, who reached their peak in 1972 with the album "Fog On The Tyne", the year's best-selling record in Britain. They never managed to find success in America. "Lady Eleanor" is their best-known hit.

Louis Soloff, ex-trumpet with Blood Sweat and Tears, born in New York City.

Barbara Ellis, of The Fleetwoods, born in Olympia, Washington. Originally called Two Girls and A Guy, they changed to The Fleetwoods and had hits with "Come Softly To Me" and "Mr. Blue" both in 1959.

Dr. Timothy Leary, international laureate of LSD and candidate for California Governor, is sentenced to ten years for possession of marijuana in 1970.

Yes sold out at Madison Square Gardens in a couple of days in 1974, without any advertisements, ticket outlet listings being the only information available to fans.

Ringo Starr plays a Mexican gardener in the film "Candy", which had its world premier on this date in 1969.

FEBRUARY 21

Florence Ballard, one of the original Supremes, dies in a Detroit hospital, in 1976. She left The Supremes in 1967, having made eight gold records with them in less than two years, and owned a pink Cadillac Eldorado and a golden Fleetwood. She died in total poverty, never having received any royalties. She received only a weekly

allowance during her time with the group.

Nina Simone (Eunice Waymon) born in North Carolina, in 1933. Her Black Liberation songs were a powerful contribution to the Civil Rights Movement, such as "Backlash Blues" and "Go To Hell" (1969-1970).

David Geffen born in New York City in 1943. Founded Asylum Records in 1971 with $400,000 and sold it to Warner Brothers the next year for five million.

Rolling Stones play Adelaide, Australia in 1963. 5,000 fans clash with police. Second single "Not Fade Away"/"Little By Little" released in the UK.

Simon and Garfunkel's album "Bridge Over Troubled Water" enter UK charts in 1970 to reach No. 1 and stay in charts for 130 weeks. One of the top three selling albums of all time.

The Beatles return to London in 1964 after their first US visit.

Malcolm X (Malcolm Little ; El-Hajj Malik el-Shabazz) assassinated in 1966, at the Audubon Ballroom, New York City. His murderers, Norman 3X Butler and Thomas 15X Johnson were members of Elijah Muhammad's mainstream Black Muslims from whom Malcolm had broken away.

W. H. Auden, poet, born in 1907.

Watergate Ehrlichman, Haldeman and company sentenced to imprisonment in 1975.

Patricia Nixon born in Whittier, California in 1946.

Nixon arrives in China in 1972 as president of USA and again, four years later to the day.

FEBRUARY 22

Pagan festival of Charistes.
Poya Day in Sri Lanka (Ceylon).

Bobby Hendricks born in 1938. He was with The Five Crowns, The Swallows, lead with The Drifters for eight months and went solo when he made "Itchy Twitchy Feeling" which was a US hit in 1958.

Elvis Presley in 1956, enters US charts for the first time. "Heartbreak Hotel" went to No. 1.

The Beatles began filming "Help!" in The Bahamas. They stayed until March 12, 1965. "'Help!' was great fun but it wasn't our film. We were sort of guest stars. It was fun, but basically as an idea for a film it was a bit wrong for us'."
– Paul McCartney

Luis Bunuel, film maker born in 1900. "Un Chien Andalou" was made with Salvador Dali in 1928. More recent classics include

"Viridiana" (1961), "Belle de Jour" (1966) and "The Discreet Charm Of The Bourgeoise" (1973).

FEBRUARY 23

Day of Atisha, reformer of Tibetan Buddhism.

Johnny Winter born in Beaumont, Texas, in 1944. Steve Paul, owner of The Scene nightclub in New York City "discovered" him in Texas after reading about him in "Rolling Stone".

Rusty Young, pedal steel guitar player of Poco, born in Long Beach, California, in 1964. This good-time country-rock group used to be called Pogo until Walt Kelly sued.

The Russian Revolution starts in 1917, in St. Petersburg (later Leningrad), with the storming of the Winter Palace. Kerensky's Menshevik government took power, but in October Lenin's more extreme Bolsheviks confirmed the rule of the proletariat.

George Frederick Handel born in 1658.

FEBRUARY 24

Nicky Hopkins born in London, in 1944. Began with Screaming Lord Sutch's Savages and in 1962 joined the Cyril Davies All-Stars. Has played with almost all top groups: The Who, The Rolling Stones, Steve Miller Band, Quicksilver Messenger Service, The Jeff Beck

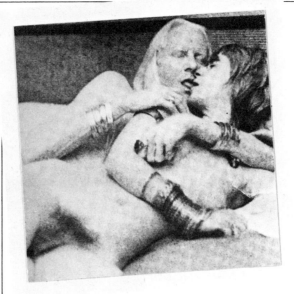

Group, Jefferson Airplane as well as sessionman on albums by George Harrison, John Lennon and many others. His keyboard work was finally given a solo album in 1973 with "The Tin Man Was A Dreamer".

Paul Jones (Paul Pond) born in Portsmouth, in 1942. At first with Manfred Mann, he reached UK No. 5 in February 1964 with "5-4-3-2-1". He left in 1966 and had solo hits with "High Time" and "I've Been A Bad Bad Boy". Since then has pursued an acting career, having starred in the film "Privilege" with model Jean Shrimpton in 1967.

P. J. Proby banned by BBC TV, following his trouser splitting and subsequent ban by other TV companies and theaters, in 1965.

"Tolpuddle Martyrs" arrested in 1834. Six laborers in a Devon village attempted to form an illegal trades union. They were transported to the convict settlement in Australia. Later, when laws changed, they were reprieved.

King Birendra of Nepal, crowned in Katmandu in 1975, in the presence of many dignitaries, including Prince Charles, who consistently refused the tea.

FEBRUARY 25

George Harrison born in Speke, Liverpool, in 1943. "I declare that the Beatles are mutants. Prototypes of evolutionary agents sent by God, endowed with a mysterious power to create a new human species— a young race of laughing freemen."—Timothy Leary.

Faron Young born in Shreveport, Louisiana, in 1932. Began recording back in 1952, having a hit with "Goin' Steady" in 1953. In 1971 he was still going strong with "Four In The Morning".

Elkie Brooks born in Manchester in 1945. Originally a jazz singer with Humphrey Littleton she moved on to Dada, a jazz-rock combo and then to Vinegar Joe. After three albums they disbanded in 1974 and she went solo.

The Beatles "Penny Lane"/ "Strawberry Fields Forever" enters UK charts in 1967 to reach No. 2. It

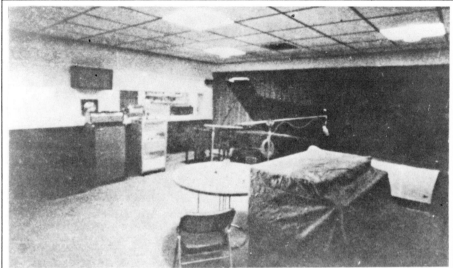

was recorded at the beginning of the mammoth four hundred hours of sessions at Abbey Road Studios, which resulted in ''Sgt. Pepper''.

Buddy Holly records ''That'll Be The Day'' at Norman Petty's studio in Clovis, New Mexico, in 1957, after weeks of rehearsal.

Drugs. Heaviest bust ever near St. Louis, France, in 1971. Thirty-five tons of unprocessed morphine, opium, heroin and hashish discovered in floating bales.

Cassius Clay becomes World Heavyweight Champion, in 1964, by defeating the ''Great Ugly Bear'' Sonny Liston, in Miami Beach, Florida. Liston retired in the seventh round with an injured tendon.

FEBRUARY 26

Antoine ''Fats'' Domino born in New Orleans, in 1928. The most successful of the New Orleans rock and rollers, he has sold over sixty million records beginning with ''The Fat Man'' which was a US hit in 1950. Among his classics are ''Blueberry Hill'' (1956), ''Blue Monday'' (1956), ''I Want To Walk You Home'' (1959) and ''Walking To New Orleans'' (1960).

Johnny Cash born in Dyess, Arkansas, in 1932. He began with the country–

rock Sun label in Memphis and entered the US charts eleven times with them, beginning with the famous ''I Walk The Line'' in 1956. He later had a string of hits for Columbia including ''A Boy Named Sue'' which reached US No. 2 in 1969. He sang a duet with Bob Dylan on ''Girl From The North Country'', on his ''Nashville Skyline'' album.

Sandy Shaw (Sandra Goodrich) born in 1947, in Dagenham, Essex. Bare-footed mid-Sixties sound. ''There's Always Something There To Remind Me'' was UK No. 1 in October 1964, ''Long Live Love'' (May 1965) and ''Puppet On A String'' (March 1967) were her other UK No. 1 hits.

Bob ''The Bear'' Hite, of Canned Heat, born in Torrance, California. Lead singer and discographer. Their first album ''Canned Heat'' was a hit in 1967. They appeared in the ''Woodstock'' movie and

had a hit single in 1968 with ''On The Road Again''.

''Barbara Ann'' by the Beach Boys entered the UK charts 1966 to reach No. 3.

Buffalo Bill (W. F. Cody) born in 1845.

Cassius Marcellus Clay, Jr. becomes Muhammad Ali, denouncing his slave name, and becoming a Black Muslim, immediately after becoming the World Champion in 1964. Muhammad means ''praiseworthy'', Ali means ''the most high''.

FEBRUARY 27

Noah's Ark Day, Egress from the Ark. Procession of Animals.

P. J. Proby's record ''I Apologise'' appears in the UK charts in 1965, following his almost total ban from the British entertainment media as a result of his trouser splitting.

''Come And Stay With Me'' by Marianne Faithfull enters UK charts in 1965.

Gene Chandler reaches US No. 1 with ''Duke Of Earl'' in 1962.

Ralph Nader born in 1934. Champion of consumer-protection.

Mick Jagger, together with a girl friend, reported in 1976 to have entered hospital in New York City with a drug overdose under the names of Mercedes and Benz. Two weeks later apologies appear stating that he was suffering from a respiratory infection and apologising to Mr and Mrs Jagger for any embarrassment.

Elizabeth Taylor born in London, in 1932. Her first film was ''Lassie Come Home'' in 1943. One of her five husbands was singer Eddie Fisher who left Debbie Reynolds for her. She married Richard Burton twice.

FEBRUARY 28

Brian Jones born in Cheltenham Spa, in 1942. The Rolling Stones were his original concept and lost a vital element when he died. ''We've always had a wild image. We built ourselves on the fact. Groups like The Hollies envy our image—I know Allen Clarke does . . .''

John Fahey, the blues guitarist, born in Takoma Park, Maryland, in 1939.

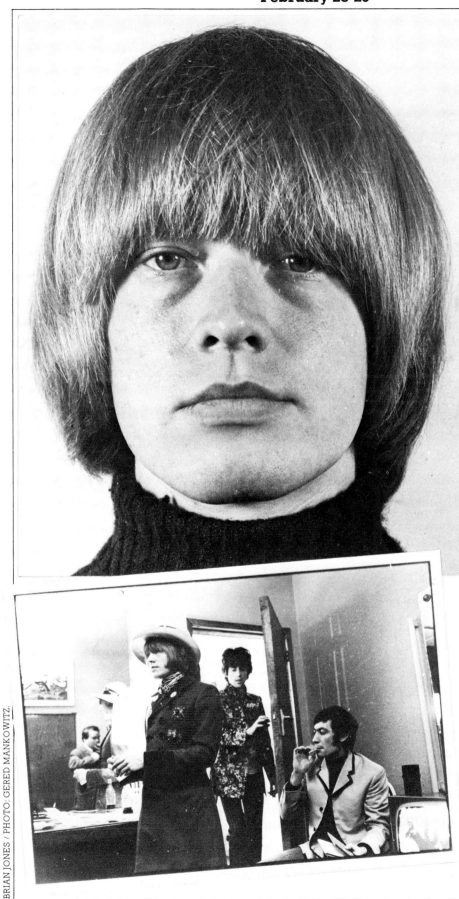

BRIAN JONES / PHOTO: GERED MANKOWITZ.

He wrote a biography of bluesman Charley Patton and started his own record label to release largely ethnic albums, including some of his own. His best-known album is from this period before he joined a major label, "The Transfiguration Of Blind Joe Death".

Joe South born in Atlanta, Georgia, in 1940. Had a 1958 hit with "The Purple People Eater Meets The Witch Doctor", worked on Dylan's "Blonde On Blonde" ("Joe South? He played real pretty") and had two Top Ten hits with "Games People Play" and "Rose Garden".

Bobby Bloom shoots himself through the head with a Derringer, in a West Hollywood motel in 1974. "Montego Bay" was a US No. 8 in September 1970. He wrote "Heavy Makes Happy" for the Staple Singers.

The Cavern Club in Liverpool closes in 1966, with debts of £10,000. The stage was sawn up into small sections and sold.

Drugs. Most valuable bust ever in 1972. 937 lbs of pure heroin worth $100 million retail seized on board a shrimp boat at Marseilles.

FEBRUARY 29

Jimmy Dorsey, great bandleader, born in Pennsylvania in 1904.

Gretchen Christopher, of The Fleetwoods, born in Olympia, Washington. "Come Softly To Me" was their big hit.

PHOTO: BOB GRUEN.

John Lennon's US immigration visa expired in 1972 and he then began his struggle to obtain a resident's permit, which was granted in September 1976.

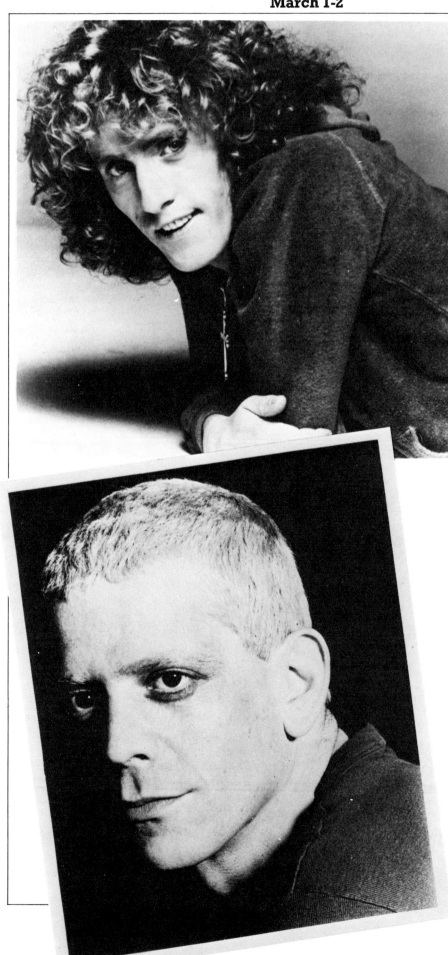

MARCH 1

Matronalia, classical festival dedicated to Mars and his mother, Juno. (Mothering Sunday sometimes falls on this day. 4th Sunday in Lent.)

Roger Daltrey born in 1944. The vocalist of The Detours, who changed their name to The High Numbers and later to The Who. ''Tommy'' brought The Who international fame, and when Ken Russell filmed it in 1975, inevitably Daltrey played the lead he had sung on stage for the previous six years. He starred in Russell's next excess ''Lisztomania'' and recorded two solo albums, produced by ex-UK teen idol Adam Faith.

Harry Belafonte born in 1927. His first UK chart entry was exactly thirty years later when ''Banana Boat Song'' entered to reach No. 2. It reached No. 5 in the US. Bob Dylan made his first ever recorded appearance on one of Belafonte's albums.

Mike D'Abo, vocalist with Manfred Mann, born, in 1944. Ex-Etonian who replaced Paul Jones as vocalist, originally with the Etonian group The Band of Angels.

Jim Edward Brown, of the Browns, born in Pine Bluff, Arkansas in 1934. ''The Three Bells'' was US No. 1 in August 1959.

Sonny James born in 1929. ''Young Love'' reached No. 2 in US in 1956.

"Where Do You Go To My Lovely?" by Peter Sarstedt reaches UK No. 1 in 1969.

Timothy Davey, the young Briton, is sentenced to six years and three months imprisonment by Turkish court for conspiring to smuggle hashish in 1972. Finally released May 20, 1974.

Chopin born in 1809.

MARCH 2

St. Chad, Anglo-Saxon saint.

Lou Reed born in New York City, in 1944. He met John Cale in New York in 1964, who was on a Leonard Bernstein fellowship. They began playing clubs with Sterling Morrison and Maureen Tucker as The Velvet Underground. Andy Warhol put them on in his Exploding Plastic Inevitable show in 1966, which toured the US and Canada, adding singer Nico. Reed's fascination with the more unpleasant sides of urban life, tempered with a true pop sensibility, dominated their first album. They made four more and Reed left in 1971. David Bowie produced his second solo album, and among his releases are two tight live albums. His solo success in the Seventies has spotlighted The Velvets, the most influential New York group of the Sixties.

Rory Gallagher born in Ballyshannon, Ireland in 1949. In 1965 performed with his first trio in Hamburg, but his guitar playing first came to public attention in 1968 in Taste, where he developed his blues style. When Taste disbanded, he went solo, being one of the few guitarists to successfully continue playing blues into the Seventies.

Karen Carpenter born in New Haven, Connecticut in 1950. With her brother Richard she comprises The Carpenters, who have had an unbroken string of hit singles and albums featuring their sweetened versions of songs such as "Ticket To Ride" and "Please Mister Postman".

The Doors play in Miami, Florida in 1969, resulting in six charges being made against Jim Morrison for "lewd behavior".

Willie Chambers, of the Chambers Brothers, born in Flora, Mississippi, in 1938. **Paul Dino** born in 1939. His only US hit was "Ginnie Bell" in January 1961.

MARCH 3

Tony S. McPhee born. Originally with The John Dummer Blues Band, he joined The Groundhogs in 1963 until they disbanded in 1965. They reformed in

1968 and released a number of albums including "Thank Christ For The Bomb" in 1970.
The Buffalo Springfield formed in 1966. This seminal band had an enormous influence on the progressive rock of the

Sixties. Its line-up was Richie Furay, Neil Young, Jim Messina, Dewey Martin and Stephen Stills. Earlier members were Doug Hastings and Bruce Palmer. They disbanded, resulting in Crosby Stills Nash & Young, Poco, and Loggins and Messina.
Jance Garfat, bass player with Dr. Hook and The Medicine Show, born in California in 1944.
Don Gibson born in 1928. "Oh, Lonesome Me" was his 1958 US hit.
Dave Dudley born in 1928. "Six Days On The Road" made US No. 32 in 1963.
The Five Keys record "Red Sails In The Sunset" in New York City in 1952.
Junior Parker (Herman "Little Junior" Parker) born in West Memphis, Arkansas. One of the Beale Streeters, his first recording was in 1952. "Feelin' Good" was a big R&B hit for him in 1953 and his "Mystery Train" was covered by Elvis in 1955. He died following eye surgery in 1971.
Gary Glitter's "Rock And Roll, Parts 1 and 2" released in Britain in 1972. The record reached UK No. 1 Gary Glitter had finally made it after releasing records under

the names of Paul Raven, Paul Munday and Rubber Bucket which went nowhere. Gary and his group The Glitterband became teenie-bop idols in Britain. He "retired" in 1976.
Jean Harlow born. "Excuse me while I slip into something more comfortable".
Alexander Graham Bell, inventor of the telephone, born in 1847.
Vincent Van Gogh born in 1853.

MARCH 4

Mary Wilson, of the Supremes, born in Mississippi, in 1944. As the Primettes they played Detroit clubs as sister group to the Primes (later

The Temptations). Still at school, Motown Berry Gordy discovered them after winning a talent contest. Their first release "Your Heart Belongs To Me" was in 1962, but it was not until 1964 that "Where Did Our Love Go" began a series of million-selling No. 1s. She is the only original Supreme still in the group.

Bobby Womack born in Cleveland, Ohio, in 1944. First noted as the originator of The Rolling Stones' "It's All Over Now", he began working solo in 1965 with such numbers as "It's Gonna Rain" and "More Than I Can Stand".

Chris Squire, bass player with Yes, born in London in 1948. A group whose fans have elevated to cult status. He made a solo album in 1976.

Eric Allandale, trombone player with The Foundations born in 1936. They were launched in October 1967 and had instant success with "Baby Now That I've Found You".

Miriam Makeba born in South Africa, in 1932. "The Click Song" was based on the gluttal-stop found in African dialects.

Most expensive stuffed bird. The highest price ever paid in an auction for a stuffed bird was £9,000 at Sotheby's in 1971. The bird in question was a Great Auk, a bird which became extinct in 1844.

The Third International set up in Moscow in 1919, to organize working-class power in all five continents of the world.

MARCH 5

"The Ballad of The Green Berets" by Sgt. Barry Sadler reaches No. 1 in 1966, in the US charts, staying for thirteen weeks and hitting a new low in American taste.

Eddie Hodges born in 1947. "I'm Gonna Knock On Your Door" was a June 1961 US hit.

Eddie Grant, lead guitar with The Equals, born in

1948. "Baby Come Back" was UK No. 1 in 1968.

Tommy Tucker (Robert Higgenbotham) born in Springfield, Ohio, in 1939. "High Heel Sneakers" was recorded in 1963 but didn't become a hit until the following year.

Clodagh Rodgers born in Warrenpoint, Northern Ireland. Her "Come Back and Shake Me" was an April 1969 UK No. 3.

Mike Jeffrey, Jimi Hendrix's manager, killed in a plane crash over France in 1973.

Patsy Cline, Cowboy Copas and Hawkshaw Hawkins killed in 1963, when their single-engine plane crashed after leaving Dyersburg, Tennessee. They were returning from Kansas City to Nashville to do a benefit for the widow of DJ Cactus Jack Call who had been killed in a car crash.

Stalin (Joseph Vissarionovitch Djugashvili) dies in Moscow, in 1953, of a brain haemorrhage and a stroke.

KIKI DEE.

MARCH 6

St. Perpetua and St. Felicitas. Day devoted to Perpetual Felicity, form of Vesta, by the pagan Romans.

Kiki Dee (Pauline Matthews) born in Bradford, in 1947. In 1970 she was the first English girl to be signed to Tamla Motown. When Elton John's manager John Reid formed Rocket Records she joined them and her first album for them, "Loving and Free", entered charts in 1973, She had a UK No. 1 in 1976 with "Don't Go Breaking My Heart", recorded with Elton John.

Sylvia Vanderpool born in New York City in 1936. Her biggest hit was in 1973 with "Pillow Talk", 23 years after her first release.

Doug Dillard, of The Dillards, born in 1937. An electric Ozark Mountain Bluegrass player who finally left to form Dillard and Clark with ex-Byrd Gene Clark, in 1968.

Randy Meisner born in

1945. Bass player who played with Rick Nelson, Poco and Linda Ronstadt, before joining with other

members of Ronstadt's backing group in August 1971 to form The Eagles. Their first album "Eagles" gave them a US hit with "Take It Easy" and they have enjoyed great success from that time on.

Hugh Grundy, drummer with The Zombies, born in 1945.

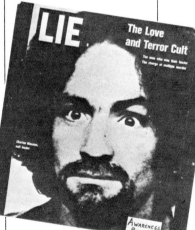

Charles Manson released LP "Lie" in 1970, to finance his defense in the Sharon Tate murder trial. The sleeve showed the cover of "Life" magazine on which he had appeared, with the "F" edited-out.

Women's Liberation has its first demonstration in London in 1971. A march from Hyde Park Corner demands equal pay, equal rights, free contraception and abortion on demand.

Michelangelo born in 1475.

MARCH 7

Chris Taylor White, bass guitar with The Zombies, born in 1943. ''She's Not There'' was a UK 1964 hit.

Matthew Fisher born in 1946. Joined Procul Harum when it first began and played organ on their original hits ''A Whiter Shade Of Pale'' and ''Homburg'' in 1967. He left after their third album, ''Salty Dog''.

First jazz record released in the US was in 1917. Called ''The Dixie Jazz Band One Step'' it was recorded by Nick LaRocca's Original Dixieland Jazz Band.

Commercial Radio. The first three home-town commercial stations in Britain, Radio Merseyside, Leicester and Sheffield, announced in the House of Commons in 1967.

Ronald Reagan, Governor of California, angry at people accepting free food from the kidnappers of Patricia Hearst in 1974, said ''It's just too bad we can't have an epidemic of botulism''.

Rolling Stones play Palace Theater, Manchester, in 1965. A girl falls off the balcony.

Alexander Graham Bell takes out US patent number 174465 for his invention of the telephone in 1876. He designed the telephone as a by-product of his job as a speech therapist teaching deaf-mutes to talk.

MARCH 8

Flora, Goddess of Flowers. Floral dance in Cornwall.
International Women's Day.

Ralph Ellis, of The Swinging Blue Jeans, born in Liverpool, in 1942. ''Hippy Hippy Shake'' was UK No. 2 in January 1964.

Pigpen (Rod McKernan), Grateful Dead organist, found dead in his apartment in Corte Madera, California, of alcoholic poisoning in 1973.

Dick Hyman born in 1927. His version of ''Moritat'' was a January 1956 US hit.

Little Peggy March born

in 1948. ''I Will Follow Him'' was US No. 1 in March 1963.

Shel Macrea (Andrew Semple), of The Fortunes, born in 1947. ''You've Got Your Troubles'' was US No. 7 in August 1965.

Mick Jagger becomes a ''Friend of Covent Garden Opera House'' in 1969.

Muhammad Ali and Joe Frazier meet in the ''Fight of the Century'' at Madison Square Garden in 1971. Ali was defeated.

Mississippi John Hurt born in 1892; bluesman.

WPAX-Hanoi goes on the air in 1971. Abbie Hoffman, John Giorno, and many others made tapes in a loft studio in the NY Bowery. The tapes were broadcast to US troops over Hanoi radio. The station opened with the Jimi Hendrix version of The Star Spangled Banner.

Paul McCartney fined £100 for growing cannabis on his farm in Campbeltown, Scotland, in 1973.

Shirley Bassey's first UK chart entry was ''The Banana Boat Song'' in 1958. She entered the charts one week after Harry Belafonte's original version. She reached No. 8. He reached No. 2. Both established their English reputation by the song.

MARCH 9

Lloyd Price born in 1933, in New Orleans. He wrote ''Lawdy Miss Clawdy'' which Elvis covered. His first US hit was ''Stagger Lee'' in 1959.

Robin Trower born in London, in 1945. Originally with Gary Brooker in the

Southend R & B group The Paramounts which had a minor hit with ''Little Biddy Pretty One'' before breaking up in 1966. Trower joined Procul Harum after their highly successful single ''A Whiter Shade Of Pale'' but in time to play on their first album, ''Procul Harum''. He left in July 1971 and formed the ill-fated Jude before forming the highly successful Robin Trower Band.

Gary Leeds, drummer of Walker Brothers fame, later with Rain, born.

Trevor Burton, of The Move, born in Acton, in 1949. A prototype heavy rock group of the late Sixties London Underground scene.

Jimmy Fadden, guitar and bass player of The Nitty Gritty Dirt Band, born in 1948. Their music contained a mixture of electric blues, jug-band, bluegrass and original songs. They made the Top Ten with ''Mr. Bojangles'' in 1970.

Billy Ford, of Billie and Lillie, born in 1925. ''La Dee Dah'' was a US hit in 1957 reaching No. 9.

Brian Jones enters hospital with respiratory problems, in 1967.

Smothers Brothers Show cancelled by CBS in 1969, after a refusal by the brothers to censor a comment made by Joan Baez on one of her songs. She wished to dedicate a song to her husband David Harris, who was just about to go to jail for objecting

to the draft. An edited version of the show was broadcast on March 30.

Allen Klein gave UNICEF a first payment cheque for $1,200,000 in 1972 towards the sales of the George Harrison album ''The Concert for Bangla Desh''. Considerable controversy ensued as people alleged that since $5 on each set

was to go to Bangla Desh, and as over two million sets had been sold, there should have been $10,000,000.

George McGovern given a fund-raising concert at the Los Angeles Forum in 1972. Among those who played were Barbra Streisand, Carole King, James Taylor and Quincy Jones. Ushers included Carly Simon, Cass Elliott, Britt Eckland, Lou Adler, Jack Nicholson, Julie Christie, Burt Lancaster and Jon Voight.

Jan and Dean

MARCH 10

Apollonius of Tyana

Dean Torrence, of Jan and Dean, born in Los Angeles, in 1940. Beginning in 1958 as Jan and Arnie they had a hit with "Jenny Lee", but their most productive period was during their close relationship with The Beach Boys, having a No. 1 in 1963 with Wilson's "Surf City" and with Jan singing lead on "Barbara Ann". "Little Old Lady From Pasadena" and "Dead Man's Curve" were among their top 10 hits. In 1966 Jan had a near-fatal car crash which terminated their career. Dean played with the Legendary Masked Surfers but then opened the Kittyhawk design studio in Hollywood.
Ted McKenna, drummer with The Sensational Alex Harvey Band, born in 1950. "Delilah" was their first big hit in 1975.
"The Explosive Freddy Cannon" entered UK album charts in 1960 to reach No. 1.
Bruce Channel reaches US No. 1 with "Hey Baby" in 1961.
Bix Beiderbecke, jazz musician, born in 1903.

James Earl Ray, assassin of Martin Luther King, born in Alton, Illinois, in 1928.
Suffragette Mary Richardson in 1914, attacks the Velasquez Venus in the National Gallery, London, with an axe.

Zelda Sayre Fitzgerald, wife of writer Scott Fitzgerald, dies in 1948 during a fire at the Highland Hospital, Asheville, North Carolina. Her body was identified by a charred slipper. Eight other patients died with her.

MARCH 11

St. Constantine, Celtic King of the Arthurian period.

Mike Hugg born in Andover, Hampshire, in 1940. He met Manfred Mann playing in a jazz quartet at a Butlin's Holiday Camp and with Paul Jones, Mike Vickers and Dave Richmond formed the Mann-Hugg Blues Brothers in which he played drums. After a name change to Manfred Mann they made their first single in July 1963. Their third, "5-4-3-2-1" saw Richmond's replacement by Tom McGuiness. The record became the theme tune for BBC-TV's "Ready Steady Go". The group split in 1969 and Hugg formed Manfred Mann Chapter Three with Mann.
Harvey Mandel born in Detroit in 1945. Learnt blues guitar in Chicago and since 1968 has made many solo albums. Has played with Canned Heat and John Mayall, and was tipped to join the Stones after Mick Taylor left. A sought-after sessionman.
Mark Stein, lead singer with Vanilla Fudge, born in Bayonne, New Jersey.

MARCH 12

James Taylor born at 5.06 am in Boston General Hospital, in 1948. In 1966 he played with Danny Kortchmar in The Flying Machine. In 1968, produced by Peter Asher at Apple, he made his first solo album, but it was "Sweet Baby James" which really launched him. Married to Carly Simon.

Marlon Jackson, of The Jackson Five born, in Gary, Indiana.
Brian O'Hara, lead guitarist with The Foremost, born in 1942. Originally The Four Jays, then The Four Mosts, Brian Epstein changed their name when he signed them. They had a UK No. 6 in 1964 with "A Little Lovin'".
Charlie Parker dies in 1955, aged 35. All over New York City the phrase "Bird Lives" began to appear.

Les Holroyd, bass player of Barclay James Harvest, born in 1948. This Manchester-based group have never achieved the fame their hard work deserved, their classically-orientated music never finding favor.

John Lennon and Harry Nilsson cause a disturbance in 1974, at Doug Weston's Troubadour Club in Los Angeles during the Smothers Brothers act. In the break, Lennon and Nilsson sang ''I Can't Stand The Rain'' and attracted photographers, one of whom got punched in the eye shortly after they had been forcibly ejected.

Jack Kerouac, author of ''On the Road'' and, so the media thought, the spokesman of the Beat Generation, born in Lowell, Massachusetts, in 1922.
Love's first album ''Love'' released in 1966.

Paul McCartney marries Linda Eastman at Marylebone Register Office in 1969.

George and Patti Harrison charged with possession of one hundred and twenty joints in 1969. The raid on their home was deliberately timed to coincide with McCartney's wedding. ''I'm a tidy man. I keep my socks in the socks drawer and my stash in my stash box. Anything else, they must have brought .''

Edward Albee, author of ''Who's Afraid of Virginia Woolf'', born in 1928.
Reptiles. Details were published in 1975, of the discovery in West Texas of the fossil of an extinct winged beast with an estimated wingspan of fifty-one feet.

MARCH 13

St. Nicephorus, Christianized form of one of the titles of Jupiter.

Neil Sedaka born in 1939. Carole King wrote ''Oh! Neil!'' in answer to his ''Oh! Carol!'' recording. He wrote hundreds of teenqueen love songs, including ''I Go Ape'' and ''Breaking Up is Hard To Do''.

The Beatles began filming the Austrian sequences of the film ''Help!'' in 1965.
The Planet Uranus discovered in 1781.

MARCH 14

Jim Pons born in Santa Monica, California. He joined The Turtles after The Leaves broke up. When the Turtles broke up he joined Kaylan and Volman in The Fluorescent Leech and Eddie. Also played bass with the Mothers Of Invention.
Loretta Lynn born in Butcher's Hollow, Van Leer, Kentucky in 1940. Her first recordings were in 1960 and she had country hits such as ''With Lovin' On Your Mind'' and ''You're Not Woman Enough (To Take My Man Away From Me)''.
Walter Parazaider, sax

and clarinet player with Chicago, born in 1945.
Les Baxter born in 1922. ''Poor People of Paris'' was a US No. 1 in 1956.

The Beatles win a gold disc for ''Yellow Submarine'' in 1969. This was their 14th gold album.
Rolling Stones play a Farewell Concert at The Roundhouse, London, before moving to France to escape English taxes, in 1971.
Michael Caine (Maurice Micklewhite) born in the East End of London, in 1933. Came to fame in the movie ''Alfie'' (1966) the title song of which was recorded by Cilla Black.

Albert Einstein born in 1879, in Ulm, Bavaria.
Karl Marx dies in 1883.

MARCH 15

Ides of March.
St. Aristobalus, Founder of the Celtic Church.

Mike Love, cousin of the other Beach Boys, born in 1941. The group got together during a Wilson family holiday to Mexico in September 1961, leaving the house free for the brothers, cousin Mike Love and friend Al Jardine to rent instruments and play.

Mike shared the lead vocals with Brian Wilson during the period Wilson played with the group and is a vital part of the group's sound. Love was heavily involved in Transcendental Meditation and its founder, the Maharishi, with whom the Beach Boys did a tour of the States.

Ry Cooder born in Los Angeles in 1947. A session man in the late Sixties and a member of Captain Beefheart's Magic Band, he became an innovator of the

bottleneck guitar and a unique devotee of the American southern folk heritage. ''Chicken Skin Music'' in 1976 showed a switch towards the music of Hawaii.

Phil Lesh (Philip Chapman Lesh), bass player with The Grateful Dead, born in 1940. ''The Grateful Dead'' album was released in March 1967 and they have remained the spirit of Haight/Ashbury ever since.

Lightnin' Hopkins, bluesman, born in Centerville, Texas in 1912.

Sly Stone (Sylvester Stewart) born in Dallas, Texas, in 1944. Formed Sly and The Family Stone in New York City in 1968. ''Dance To The Music'' was their first hit and they went on to have US No. 1s with ''Everyday People'' (1968), ''Thank You'' (1970), and ''Family Affair'' (1971).

Howard Scott, guitarist with War, born in 1946. As The Creators, The Romeos, Senor Soul and The Night Shift they made it through the Sixties until they joined up with Eric Burdon as his backing group, before finally going it alone.

Arif Mardin born in Istanbul, Turkey in 1932. A leading record producer for Atlantic, he has recorded an enormous list of top-selling albums for artists such as Steve Stills, Bette Midler, Average White Band and Aretha Franklin.

Hughie Flint born in 1942. Originally drummer with John Mayall, Flint joined McGuinness Flint as a founder member in 1969. Their ''Lo And Behold'' album in 1972 was a selection of rare Dylan numbers, some never previously recorded. The group folded after ''C'Est La Vie'' in 1974.

David Harris released from jail after twenty months for refusal to be inducted into the US armed forces. He flew to San Francisco and gave a press conference with his then wife, Joan Baez. ''They stole twenty months of mine. They stole my son's infancy from me. That's a fucking big theft, man!''

First Student Sit-In at the London School of Economics in 1967.

KHJ in Los Angeles was raided at 7 am in 1972. The police were called by the radio station's fans who thought something was amiss at the station as Robert W. Morgan played Donny Osmond's ''Puppy Love'' over and over from 6.00 pm to 7.30 am. The police left with no arrests.

Julius Caesar murdered in 44 BC. ''Beware the Ides of March''.

MARCH 16

Jerry Jeff Walker born in Oneonta, New York in 1942. A ''new Nashville'' singer, he wrote ''Mr. Bojangles'', a hit for The Nitty Gritty Dirt Band and recorded by Bob Dylan.

Betty Johnson born in Possum Walk, North Carolina, in 1932. ''I Dreamed'' was her biggest US hit in 1956.

Tammi Terrell (Tammy Montgomery), Motown singer famous for her duets with Marvin Gaye, dies in 1970 of a brain tumor in Philadelphia, aged 24.

Arthur Gunter dies at the age of 50, in 1976. He is best known for his blues record ''Baby Let's Play House''.

Ahmet Ertegun, president of Atlantic Records, takes Jade Jagger (Mick and Bianca's daughter) on her first visit to Disneyland. in 1974.

Nashville. The new $15 million Opry House held its inaugural show in 1974. Richard Nixon opened it, played three tunes on the piano, applauded himself and played the yoyo.

Louis Armstrong has a UK No. 1 with ''Wonderful World'' in 1968.

''(Sittin' On) The Dock Of The Bay'' by Otis Redding reaches No. 1 in the US in 1968.

Winifred Attwell's only UK No. 1, ''The Poor People Of Paris'' entered the charts in 1956.

Aubrey Beardsley, ''The Fra Angelico of Satanism'' dies in 1898, at Menton, France, of haemorrhages.

MARCH 17

St. Patrick's day. Blessing and distribution of shamrock.

Paul Lorin Kantner born in 1941. Guitar and vocals with The Jefferson Airplane. Got together with Grace Slick and recorded the ''Sunfighter'' album when the Airplane seemed to fragment before Jefferson Starship took off.

John Sebastian born in 1944. He grew up in Greenwich Village where he formed the Lovin' Spoonful in 1964, which produced what came to be known as ''good time music''. They had 7 successive US Top 10 singles in 1965-66, reaching No. 1 with ''Summer In The City''. The group began to deteriorate by 1967 and broke up. Sebastian made a comeback at the Woodstock Festival in 1970. In 1974 he re-formed The Spoonful after making several solo albums.

Harold Brown, drummer with War, born in 1946. Played through the Sixties under various names until,

as Eric Burdon's backing group they became known as War and finally went it alone.

Patti Harrison (née Boyd) born. She played a schoolgirl in the first scene of ''A Hard Day's Night'' and there met George. She later met Eric Clapton and inspired his ''Layla'' album when she left Harrison.

Vito Picone, lead with The Elegants, born on Staten Island, New York City, in 1940. ''Little Star'' was a US No. 1 summer 1968 hit.

Dean Mathis born in Hahira, Georgia, in 1939. Together with Mark Mathis he had a hit in 1959 with ''Tell Him No'' as Dean and Mark. Joined by Larry Henley they became The Newbeats and their first record ''Bread And Butter'' made US No. 2 in 1964.

Pat Lloyd, guitar with The Equals, born in 1948. ''Baby Come Back'' was UK No. 1 in 1968.

Clarence Collins, of Little Anthony and The Imperials, born in 1939.

Buddy Holly and The Crickets play The Gaumont, Doncaster, in 1958.

Birth Control. In 1921 Marie Stopes opens the world's first family planning clinic in London. It closed in 1976 with the advent of free contraceptives in Britain.

MARCH 18

Wilson Pickett born in 1941, in Prattville, Alabama. With over thirty US chart entries, ''Land of 1000 Dances'' (1966) and ''Funky Broadway'' (1967) made

the US top 10. In the UK he is best known for ''In The Midnight Hour'' (1965).

Kenny Lynch born in Stepney, London, in 1939. He made UK No. 10 in January 1963 with his cover version of ''Up On The Roof''.

Robert Lee Smith, of The Tams, born in 1936. Their first hit was ''Untie Me'' in 1962, three years after they started and they didn't reach the UK charts until 1971 when the reissue of ''Hey Girl, Don't Bother Me'' reached No. 1.

Rolling Stones involved in a famous public urination incident at a filling station after a show at Romford ABC in Essex, in 1965. They were fined £5 each.

Charlie and Shirley Watts' daughter Serafina born in 1968.

Barry Wilson born in Middlesex, in 1947. Originally the drummer with Gary Brooker and Robin Trower in the Southend R & B band The Paramounts, which had a minor hit with ''Little Biddy Pretty One'' breaking up in 1966. Together with Trower he joined Procul Harum after their highly successful single ''A Whiter Shade Of Pale'' but before their first album, ''Procul Harum''.

Country Joe McDonald was convicted and fined

PATTI HARRISON WITH ERIC CLAPTON IN 1974.

COUNTRY JOE McDONALD / PHOTO: MICK GOLD.

Cooking'' was released in 1970.

Derek Longmuir, drummer with The Bay City Rollers, born in Edinburgh in 1955.

Paul Atkinson, lead guitarist with The Zombies, born in 1943. Their only US chart entry was ''She's Not There'' in September 1964.

Wyatt Earp born in 1848, in Monmouth, Illinois.

William Reich's books burnt by order of the US courts in 1954. Reich had been found guilty and imprisoned for his work on the orgone theory which the Food and Drug Administration claimed was ''worthless''. Books burnt included titles written before he even developed the orgone theory.

break-up of a great musical partnership. It took me a year to realize they were in love.''—Paul McCartney.

Joe Rivers, of Johnnie and Joe born, 1937. ''Over The Mountain, Across The Sea'' was their big 1957 US hit.

T. Rex reach UK No. 1 with ''Hot Love'' in 1971.

Patty Hearst found guilty of armed robbery in 1976. A film of her holding an automatic weapon while taking part in a bank robbery

MARCH 20

David Bowie marries Mary Angela Barnetty at Bromley Register Office, in 1970.

John Lennon marries Yoko Ono in Gibraltar, in 1969. ''You can't blame John for falling in love with Yoko any more than you can blame me for falling in love with Linda. At the beginning I was annoyed with him, jealous because of Yoko, and afraid about the

Janis Joplin reaches US No. 1 with ''Me And Bobby McGhee'' in 1971.

''My Old Man's A Dustman'' reaches UK No. 1 for Lonnie Donegan in 1960.

$500 in 1970 for shouting ''Fuck'' at a concert in Worcester, Massachusetts, after he, The Fish, and the audience had spelled out the traditional Fish chorus: ''Gimme an F! Gimme a U! . . .'' The statute under which he was convicted dated back to 1783.

Andrew Loog Oldham's Immediate Records held a meeting of creditors in 1970 to pick up the financial threads of what was left of this pioneering company. Among Immediate's artists

were The Small Faces and The Nice.

The Planet Pluto discovered.

MARCH 19

Mickey Dolenz, of The Monkees, born in Los Angeles. The group was formed especially for a TV series which was a blatant plagiarism of Richard Lester's Beatle movies.

Jeff Neighbor, bass player with The Joy Of Cooking, born in 1942. ''Joy Of

---

was used in the trial.
Watergate, John Ehrlichman born in 1925. As one of "the Germans" who ran Nixon's White House, Ehrlichman was officially Chief Adviser on Domestic Affairs until forced into resigning on April 30th, 1973.

The Chicago Grand Jury in 1969, indicted eight police and eight civilians for conspiring to cause a riot during the 1968 Democratic Party convention. The Chicago Eight: Rennie Davis, Dave Dellinger, John Froines, Tom Hayden, Abbie Hoffman, Jerry Rubin, Bobby Seale and Lee Weiner were all sentenced, whereas the eight police were acquitted in one of the biggest travesties of justice ever to gain media publicity.

MARCH 21

Vernal Equinox. Sun enters Aries.
Feast of Bema.
Crucifixion of Mani.

The Beatles make their debut performance at The Cavern Club in Liverpool, in 1961. By July they had a regular Wednesday night gig and appeared there two or three times a week in addition to lunch-time sessions.

John and Yoko Ono Lennon begin their bed campaign for peace at the Amsterdam Hilton in 1969.
Rubin "Hurricane" Carter released from jail in 1976, following the publicity given to his case by Bob Dylan's song "Hurricane" and his campaigning which involved Muhammad Ali and many others.
Sharpeville Massacre in South Africa in 1960. Police fire at close range into an African demonstration, killing 70 and wounding 150.
Watergate. Maurice Stans born in 1908. Big-game hunter Stans stood trial with John Mitchell for electoral

malpractice involved with CREEP. He was acquitted.
David Bowie busted after a concert in New York City in 1976, for possession of marijuana. He was released on bail and later fined.

Johann Sebastian Bach born in 1685.
Drugs. J. Russell Reynolds, physician to Queen Victoria, writes in "The Lancet" of 1890: "In almost all painful maladies I have found Indian hemp by far the most useful of drugs".

MARCH 22

Confucius born, 571 BC.

Keith Relf born in Richmond, Surrey, in 1943. After seeing The Rolling

Stones at the Station Hotel, Richmond, in early 1963, Relf formed an art school band, The Metropolitan Blues Quartet, later to become The Yardbirds, with Eric Clapton on guitar. Despite a strong club following and a legendary album they did not make the charts until 1965. Always innovative, Relf is credited with being one of the inventors of the feedback guitar. The Yardbirds split up in 1969 and Relf formed the duo Together, with ex-Yardbird Jim McCarty, then forming Renaissance with his sister. Relf was found dead in his London home holding a live guitar in 1976.
Jeremy Clyde, of Chad and Jeremy, born in 1944. "Of Cabbages And Kings" released summer 1967 was their most respected album. They also made the ultimate summer song called "A Summer Song".
Harry Vanda (Wandan), lead guitarist and vocalist with The Easybeats, born in Holland. "Friday On My Mind" was their big 1966 hit, both in UK and US.

Randy Hobbs, bass player with Johnny Winter, born in 1948, in Winchester, Indiana.
Andrew Lloyd Webber born in London, in 1948. He wrote the music for a show called "Jesus Christ Superstar".

Carl Perkins was injured in a car crash in 1956, while driving to New York City to appear on the Perry Como and Ed Sullivan Shows to promote his new record "Blue Suede Shoes". He was unconscious for three days and broke four ribs, had three breaks in his right shoulder and was in traction for eight days. Elvis Presley covered the record and stole his hit from him. His brother Jay and his manager, who was driving, were both killed.
Electric Circus club in New York damaged by a bomb explosion in 1970. Seventeen people were hurt.
Buddy Holly and The Crickets play The Gaumont, Salisbury, in 1958.
Chico Marx (Leonard Marx), member of the Marx Brothers, born in New York City, in 1887. "Chico's friends were producers who gambled, actors who gambled, and women who screwed".—Gummo Marx.
Drugs. National Committee on Marijuana and Drug Abuse presented its case for relaxing drug laws to Richard Nixon in 1972. He ignored their recommendations.

MARCH 23

Lamentations of Isis.
John Lennon's "In His Own Write" published by Jonathan Cape in London, in 1964. His first book.

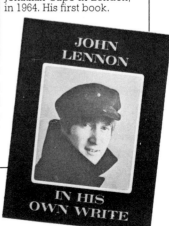

JOHN LENNON

IN HIS OWN WRITE

The Beatles "Lady Madonna" released in 1968. Went straight to UK No. 1. Their 17th record to reach Number 1 or 2 in the charts. **Rally For Decency** held in Miami Orange Bowl in 1969, in response to Jim Morrison flashing his cock at the March 2nd Doors concert. Thirty thousand people attended, about half of them adults. Nixon sent a message: "This is a very positive approach. . ." **Joan Crawford** born in 1905. Made her first film in 1925, and has worked consistently ever since. "What Ever Happened To Baby Jane" was a big success in 1962.

MARCH 24

Lao-Tse, founder of Taoism.

Mike Kellie, drummer with Spooky Tooth, born in 1947. The group had critical success as an underground band but broke up for two years in 1970. Their final album came after they reformed "The Mirror" in 1974. **Holgar Czukay**, bass guitarist with the experimental German rock band Can, born in 1938. Best known for their movie sound tracks, they reached the UK charts in the summer of 1976 with "I Want More". **Lee Oskar**, harmonica player with War, born in 1948. As Eric Burdon's backing group they made two albums with him before going it alone with "All Day Music".

Elvis Presley, after a sixty-day deferment to make the movie "King Creole" reported at 6.35 am in 1958, to his local board 86 and became US 53310761 in the US Army. **Billy Stewart** born in Washington, DC, in 1937. Played in Bo Diddley's Band as a pianist. His biggest hit was "Summertime" in 1966. He died in 1970 when his car went over a bridge on the river Neuse in North Carolina, killing Stewart and three of his band.

Lou Reed was bitten on the ass during a concert in Buffalo, New York in 1973. A crazed fan leapt out beyond the stage guards, screamed "Leather!" and bit into Reed's buttock. **Colin Peterson**, of The Bee Gees, born. He was drummer with them in the days of their early hits such as "New York Mining Disaster" in 1967.

Dave Appell, of the Appelljacks, born in 1922. His "Mexican Hat Rock" was a dance hit on the TV show "American Bandstand" from Philadelphia. **George Felton Hollis** born in 1937, in San Antonio, Texas. "Foot Stomping— Part 1" was a US hit in September 1961. **Buddy Holly and The Crickets** play the Cardiff Capitol in 1958.

Steve McQueen born in 1930. Apart from films, a fanatical car driver; his attempt to drive in the LeMans 24-hour race was foiled as no insurance company would cover him.

MARCH 25

Lady Day.
The Rejoicing of Isis, Resurrection of Osiris, the Green Man of Ancient Egypt. The Resurrection of Mithra, Tammuz, Dionysos, Bacchus, Adonis and Attis.

Aretha Franklin born in Memphis, Tennessee, in 1942. She was discovered by John Hammond (of Columbia Records) when she was 18. Her first record

was released in March 1961. From 1966 onwards she has had a string of million-selling hits beginning with "I Never Loved A Man The Way I Love You".

Elton John (Reg Dwight) born in Pinner, Middlesex, in 1947. Dwight studied at the Royal Academy of Music in London and began a career in R & B by forming Bluesology, eventually joining up with Long John Baldry. He then became a songwriter for Dick James Music, Bernie Taupin writing the lyrics. He changed his name to Elton John and, after a bad start, recorded a succession of hit albums. Success in America came suddenly in 1970, but in the next year he appeared to be suffering from over-exposure. His album "Honky Chateau" marked a come-back, and the two following albums had enormous sales. In 1973 he created his own label Rocket Records, signing Kiki Dee with whom he had a UK No. 1 in 1976 with "Don't Go Breaking My Heart". **Johnny Burnette** born in Memphis, Tennessee, in 1934. "Dreamin" and "You're Sixteen" were big US hits in 1960 and he is recognized as one of the classic rockers. **Anita Bryan** born in Tulsa, Oklahoma, in 1940. In 1959 "Till There Was You" entered the US charts,

followed in 1960 by "Paper Roses" which made US No. 5. **John Rowles** born in Kawerau, New Zealand, in 1947. "If I Only Had Time" was UK No. 3 in 1968. **The Turtles** reach US No. 1 with "Happy Together" in 1967. Turtles, Mark Volman and Howard Kaylan later joined the Mothers Of Invention, and this number was recorded by them at the end of the "Live At The Fillmore" album. They also sang on T. Rex's "Get It On, Bang A Gong". **King Faisal**, of Saudi Arabia, assassinated in 1975, by his nephew.

MARCH 26

Diana Ross, of The Supremes, born in Detroit, Michigan, in 1944. A dozen US No. 1s in the Sixties, including "Where Did Our Love Go" and "Baby Love" (both 1964), "Stop, In The Name Of Love" (1965), "The Happening" (1967) and "Love Child" (1968). From the summer of 1967 the group was known as Diana Ross and The Supremes. She quit the group in 1970 and starred in the film "Lady Sings The Blues", where she played Billie Holiday.

Fred Parris born in 1936. Lead singer with The Five Satins. "In The Still Of The Night" was in the US charts in July 1956, January 1960 and January 1961.

Harold McNair dies of lung cancer in 1971. He was flute and sax player with Ginger Baker, amongst others.

Peter Yarrow, of Peter, Paul and Mary, pleads guilty in 1970 to "taking immoral" liberties with a fourteen-year-old girl, at a Washington District Court. His group had just won the Grammy Award for the Best Children's Recording.

"Eye", the Hearst Corporation's rock and youth culture magazine folded in 1969. "Far short of profitable."

Noel Coward dies in 1973. Playwright, director, actor, author and writer of the

wittiest English songs of the century.

Robert Frost, author of "The White Goddess", Bob Dylan's favorite book of 1963, born.

MARCH 27

formed by a collection of song-writers at a private school near London. They were discovered by Jonathan King, and by the mid-Seventies their brand of melodrama on stage and on record had found much following, especially in Europe.

Tom Edwards born in 1923. "What Is A Teenage Girl", an all-American narrative record made US No. 57 in 1957.

Richard Hayman born in 1920. His "Theme from the Threepenny Opera" reached US No. 12 in January 1956.

Trial of Angela Davis starts in Berkeley, California, in 1972. Davis, a Communist college lecturer, was accused of helping Jonathan Jackson in his attempted escape from his own trial when he killed a judge and was

killed himself. Davis allegedly supplied the weapons. James Baldwin wrote "If they come for her in the morning, they will come for us in the afternoon". She was eventually freed.

Jerry Garcia busted for speeding on Interstate 295 near Philadelphia, in 1973. Police found marijuana, LSD, cocaine and prescription drugs in a suitcase.

Grapefruit, the Apple group managed by John Lennon, made their first ever stage appearance at the Royal Albert Hall, London, in 1968.

The Yardbirds "For Your Love" enters British charts in 1966 to reach No. 2.

P. J. Proby ordered off stage in 1965, at Hereford Municipal Ballroom and called "disgusting and obscene" by Mrs. June Carter, wife of a Tory alderman.

MARCH 28

Charlie McCoy born in Oak Hill, West Virginia, in 1941. A major Nashville

session man he has played on numerous important albums including many by Bob Dylan, beginning with "Highway 61 Revisited". Played with Area Code 615 on their two albums during 1969-70.
Arthur "Big Boy" Crudup dies in Virginia, in 1974, after a stroke. He was the composer of many hit records including "That's All Right Mama" which Presley recorded in 1954, eight years after Crudup's version was released. He was swindled out of almost all of his royalties and died in poverty.

John Evans, keyboard player with Jethro Tull, born in 1948. Joined the group late on in 1971, just in time for the series of concept albums which was to bring the group their critical success.
Dean Webb, mandolin player with The Dillards, born in 1937.

Rufus Thomas born in Collierville, Tennessee, in 1917. He joined The Rabbit Foot Minstrels in 1935 and it wasn't until 1953 he had his first hit with "Bear Cat". In 1963 he had a hit with "Walking The Dog" and again in 1970 with "Funky Chicken". His daughter is

Carla Thomas of "Gee Whiz (Look In His Eyes)" fame which was a hit in 1961.
"Can't Buy Me Love" by The Beatles enters UK charts to reach No. 1 in 1964.
Pirate Radio. Radio Caroline, Britain's first offshore station begins broadcasting in 1964.

MARCH 29

Lonnie Donegan (Anthony James Donegan) born in 1931, in Glasgow. Took his name from guitarist Lonnie Johnson. He had twenty-six UK chart entries between January 1956 with "Rock Island Line" and September 1962 with "Pick A Bale Of Cotton". He reached No. 1 with "Cumberland Gap", "Putting On The Style", "Gamblin' Man" and the comedy number "My Old Man's A Dustman".
Speedy Keen (John Keen) born in Ealing, London, in

1945. Wrote "Armenia, City In The Sky" for The Who and was produced by Townshend when he formed Thunderclap Newman. Had an international hit with "Something In The Air" in 1969. Has made solo albums since Thunderclap broke up.
Eden Kane born in Delhi, India, in 1942. "Well I Ask You" made UK No. 1 in June 1961.
The Southside Fuzz, four cops from Chicago who formed a rock group, performed their first gig before two thousand people in 1969. They intended to show "teens have something in common with the police".
Royal Albert Hall, London, opened by Queen Victoria in 1871.

MARCH 30
St. Aphrodisius and St. Amator. The Venus and Adonis myth.

Eric Clapton born in Ripley, Surrey, in 1945. "At school I was the one that used to get stones thrown at me because I was so thin and couldn't do physical training very well. I was always the seven-stone weakling, and pimply, and no one wanted to know you. You get into a group and you've got thousands of chicks there. And there you are with thousands of

little girls screaming their heads off. Man, it's Power! . . . Phew!"
Sonny Boy Williamson (John Lee Williamson) born in Jackson, Tennessee, in 1914. In his teens he played harp with Sleepy John Estes. He made his first records in Chicago in 1947, including the classic "Good-Morning Little Schoolgirl". He was one of the first bluesmen to use a band on record anticipating modern rock. He died in 1948, after being attacked and robbed.

Jim Dandy, vocalist with Black Oak Arkansas, born in 1948. "High On The Hog" was their first gold album in 1974. Jim Dandy is the visual focal point of the group's stage act as he prances round the stage.

Graeme Edge, drummer with The Moody Blues, born in Rochester, Staffordshire, in 1942. After a series of six gold albums they were able to start their own Threshold label. In 1975 the Moodies began to try out solo projects.
Frankie Laine (Frank Lo Vecchio) born in Chicago. Had a UK No. 1 with "Woman In Love" in 1956 and a string of US hits including "Cool Water" in 1955.
Dave Ball born in 1950. Replaced Robin Trower on guitar with Procul Harum in July 1971 but was in turn replaced by Mick Grabham.

The Crystals reach US No. 1 with "He's So Fine" in 1963. A Phil Spector production.

MARCH 31

Thijs Van Leer born in 1948. Organ, flute and vocals of Focus, the Dutch band that formed for the

Amsterdam version of "Hair". His scat-singing is a feature of this classical-jazz-rock group, who have had a couple of UK Top Twenty hits. He has also made a solo album.
Al Goodman, of The Moments, born in 1947. Their All Platinum Sound soul has brought them a number of million-sellers including "Sexy Mama" in 1973.
Richard Hughes, drummer with Johnny Winter, born in Trenton, New Jersey, in 1950.
Richard Chamberlain born in Los Angeles, California, in 1935. He naturally had a hit with "Theme From Dr. Kildare" in 1962.
John D. Loudermilk born in Durham, North Carolina, in 1934. Very big as a Country and Western artist, he entered the US pop charts with "Language Of Love" in 1961.

Muhammad Ali has his jaw broken by Ken Norton in 1973, during their World Heavyweight Title fight in San Diego. Ali survived the twelve rounds to win.
Herb Alpert born in Los Angeles, California, in 1935. He and Jerry Moss formed A & M Records in 1962. He had chart entries with his instrumentals all through the Sixties. Tunes such as "A Taste Of Honey" (1965) and "Spanish Flea" (1966) reaching the US Top 40.

APRIL 1

All Fools.
Day of Noah. The custom of sending people on fruitless errands on this day (hence, All Fools Day) is derived from a ceremony commemorating the sending of the dove out of the Ark.
One of the days of Venus (her symbol was the dove).

Ronnie "Plonk" Lane born in the East End of London, in 1946. Bass player with The Small Faces. Hits with "Itchycoo Park" (1967) and "Lazy Sunday" (1968) typified the Mod Scene of the Sixties. Their "Ogden's Nut Gone Flake" album in 1968 was a classic. Married Kate McKinnerney and formed new band, Ronnie Lane's Slim Chance.
Rudolph Isley, of The Isley Brothers, born in 1939. "Twist And Shout" was a big US hit in 1962, covered in the UK by The Beatles. Their first UK chart entry was in 1968 with "This Old Heart Of Mine".

Simon Crowe, of Lindisfarne, born in 1948. The all-Newcastle band had the top-selling album in Britain of 1971-72, "Fog On The Tyne". But they were never accepted in America, and split up in 1975.

Arthur Conley born in Atlanta, Georgia, in 1946. In 1967 "Sweet Soul Music" made the US Top 5.
Frank Gari born in 1942. "Utopia" was a 1960 hit in the US.

Rolling Stones tour of Britain in 1976, draws over one million ticket applications and they are moved by security men to specially guarded vaults. The tickets were chosen by ballot. The Post Office made over £30,000 out of the postage.
David Bowie's first solo single released. "Anything You Say"/"Good Morning Girl" in 1966.
Drugs. At the Conference on Alcoholism and Drug Dependence held at Liverpool, in 1973, the delegates managed to drink the students' union bar out of Newcastle Brown Ale for the first time in living memory.
Beach Boys sue Capitol Records for $2,041,446.64 in 1969.
First automatic-change gramophone introduced by HMV, in 1928, price £125.

Scott Joplin, famous rag-time composer and player, died impoverished in New York City, in 1917.

APRIL 2

Marvin Gaye born in Washington, DC, in 1939. "Stubborn Kind Of Fellow" was his first record and his first hit, in 1962. "I Heard It Through The Grapevine" was his greatest hit, reaching US No. 1 in 1969. He did a number of duet records with Mary Wells, Kim Weston and Tammi Terrell.

Leon Russell born in Lawron, Oklahoma, in 1941. The archetypal super

Larry Coryell born in Galveston, Texas, in 1943. A jazz guitarist who has had considerable impact on rock and jazz-rock circles. Known mainly for his early work with the Gary Burton Quartet and his early Vanguard albums.

Kerry Minnear born in 1948. Graduated from the Royal Academy of Music and straightway joined Gentle Giant which the Shulman brothers were getting together. Part of the new wave "intellectual" bands from England, who are being approached with caution in the States. It

sessionman. He has worked with Jerry Lee Lewis, Phil Spector, Byrds, Herb Alpert, Rolling Stones, Joe Cocker, Delaney and Bonnie, and George Harrison. Formed Shelter records with English Denny Cordell and recorded his first solo album in London in 1969. The next year he put together the Mad Dogs and Englishman tour with Joe Cocker, which resulted in an album and a film. Following this he released a varied selection of solo albums, usually featuring superstar line-ups.

Serge Gainsbourg born in Paris, in 1928. Together with Jane Birkin he had numbers 1 and 2 in the UK charts in October 1969, with the censored and the uncensored versions of "Je T'Aime Moi Non Plus".

Bud Deckelman born in Harrisburg, Arkansas, in 1927. He had a hit in 1954 with "Daydreamin'" while he was with The Daydreamers.

Open City, the L.A. underground newspaper, folded in 1969.

APRIL 3

Jimmu Tenno, mythical Founder of Shintoism born.

Richard Manuel, pianist with The Band, born in 1943. Formed in the late Fifties as backing group to Toronto Rock 'n' Roller Ronnie Hawkins. They played with John Hammond, Jr., in New

York and through him met Bob Dylan whom they backed when he moved into electric rock, first as The Hawks and later as The Band. Their first solo album "Music From Big Pink" was highly praised for its simplicity.

in 1958. Good friends of the Beach Boys they had a number 1 with Brian Wilson's "Surf City" in 1963 and Jan sang lead on the Beach Boys' "Barbara Ann". Jan was almost killed in a car crash in 1966, which terminated their career.

Jimmy McGriff born in Philadelphia, Pennsylvania, in 1936. Originally a policeman, he became a jazz player at college and in 1962 had a US Top 20 hit with an instrumental version of "I've Got A Woman".

Dee Murray born in 1946. Bass player with Spencer Davis, he formed the backing band, with Davis' drummer Nigel Olsson, to Elton John. They caused a sensation when they opened in 1970, and John shot to instant stardom.

Mel Schacher, bass player with Grand Funk Railroad, born in 1951. Grand Funk got underway with a row of ten million–selling albums before turning to producers such as Todd Rundgren and Frank Zappa to improve their critical reception.

Tony Orlando, of Dawn, born in New York in 1944. "Tie A Yellow Ribbon Round The Old Oak Tree" was the group's biggest hit in 1973.

Jeff Barry, of the writing team Barry and Greenwich, born in 1939. They wrote many hits for Phil Spector including the classic "Do Doo Ron Ron". "Leader Of The Pack" is also theirs.

Marlon Brando born in 1924. First film was "The Men" in 1950. Best known for "On The Waterfront" (1954), "One Eyed Jacks" (1960) and "Last Tango In Paris" (1973).

Barry Pritchard, of The Fortunes, born in Birmingham, in 1944.

Jim Morrison turns himself over to the FBI in Los Angeles. He was charged with interstate flight to avoid

Jan Berry, of Jan and Dean, born in Los Angeles, in 1941. Their first record was a hit, "Jenny Lee" which they recorded as Jan and Arnie

prosecution on six charges of lewd behavior and public exposure at a concert in Miami on March 2nd, 1969. He was later released on $5,000 bail.

Brinsley Schwarz launched in 1970, by a $120,000 hype that involved flying a planeful of London journalists to the New York Fillmore East for one performance and back again. The management company, Famepushers, later folded with enormous debts, but the group survived.

Jesse James shot dead in 1882.

Billy Preston signs with Apple Records in 1969, with George Harrison as his producer, after having played organ on "Get Back".

Bob Dylan enters the UK charts for the first time with "The Times They Are A-Changin' " which reached No. 7.

Lois Ann Wilkinson born in 1944. The Caravelles, all from Barnet, Hertfordshire, reached UK No. 6 with "You Don't Have To Be A Baby To Cry" in August 1963.

Joe Vann (Canzana), of The Duprees, born in 1943. He was replaced in 1964 by Mike Kelly. In 1962 they had a US hit with "You Belong To Me".

APRIL 4

Muddy Waters (McKinley Morganfield) born in

Rolling Fork, Mississippi, in 1915. The Rolling stones took their name from his song. He first recorded in 1941 and had a string of Rhythm and Blues hits in the US through the Fifties. In 1955 it was Muddy that took Chuck Berry to Chess Records.

Berry Oakley, bass player with The Allman Brothers Band, born in Jacksonville, Florida, in 1948. Played on all their best early albums including "Idlewild South" and "Eat A Peach" which was completed after the death of leader Duane·Allman. He died in a motorcycle accident in Atlanta, Georgia in October 1971 and Berry Oakley died in a similar accident in almost the same place a year later on November 11th, 1972.

Christophe Franke born in 1942. Originally the drummer with Tangerine Dream until they all changed to purely electronic instruments. Now plays synthesizer Began working on solo projects in early 1976.

Major Lance born in Chicago, in 1941. Curtis Mayfield songs gave him a line of hits in the pop and R & B charts between 1963-67 including "Um Um Um Um Um Um".

Kris Jensen born in 1942. "Torture" was his US Top 20 hit in 1962.

The Beatles "Can't Buy Me Love" reaches US No. 1, replacing "She Loves You" which in turn replaced "I Want To Hold Your Hand" at No. 1 in 1963.

Kurt Weill dies in 1950. His compositions have been used extensively in the pop world with many instrumentals based on themes from "The Threepenny Opera" or "Mahogany". Artists from Louis Armstrong to Jim Morrison have had hits with his material. He worked mainly with playwright Bertolt Brecht.

Dave Hill, lead guitarist with Slade, born in Fleetcastle, Devon, in 1952. "Get Down And Get With It" was UK No. 16. Their following singles all made the UK charts.

APRIL 5

Day of Avalokiteshvara, the Great God of Mercy in Tibetan Buddhism. Bodhisattva protector of Tibet.

Dave Swarbrick, folk music fiddle player, born in 1941. He joined the Fairport Convention in time for their "Liege And Lief" album in 1969 which was so important to their career.

Billy Bland born in Wilmington, North Carolina. in 1932. "Let The Little Girl Dance" reached US No. 7 in February 1960.

Tony Williams born in 1928. Lead with The Platters. "Only You" was US No. 5 in 1955, but "The Great Pretender", released two months later, made No. 1. They followed these with a row of hits including three more US No. 1 hits: "My Prayer" (June 1956), "Twilight Time" (March 1958) and "Smoke Gets In Your Eyes" (November 1958).

Jane Asher born in 1946. Actress, famous for roles in "The Masque Of The Red Death" (1964) and "Alfie" (1966). Once engaged to Paul McCartney, now married to satirical cartoonist, Gerald Scarfe.

Paul McCartney flies to America for Jane Asher's 21st birthday party in Denver, Colorado, in 1967, carrying a large diamond, which she later lost.

Crispian St. Peters born in Swanley, Kent, in 1944. "You Were On My Mind" was UK No. 2 in 1966.

Spencer Tracy born in 1900. Star of numerous films from 1930 until his death in 1967.

Bette Davis (Ruth Elizabeth Davis) born in 1908. Her debut was in "Bad Sister" in 1931. Made a film comeback in the late Sixties.

APRIL 6

Asoka, Emperor, c. 250 BC who made Buddhism state religion of India.
Julie Rogers born. "The Wedding" reached US No. 10 in December 1964.

Merle Haggard born in Bakersfield, California in 1937. A country music superstar, he started recording in 1963 after leaving his job in the oil fields. By 1965 he had three country hits and a Top Twenty hit. He challenged Buck Owens as top Nashville-West star, and married his ex-wife.
Gerry and The Pacemakers reach UK No. 1 with "How Do You Do It".
Syd Barrett officially leaves the Pink Floyd in 1968. After this he made two solo albums before retiring completely from public life and becoming the subject of much rumor and conjecture.
Harry Houdini (Ehrich Weiss) born in Appleton, Wisconsin, in 1874. Houdini baffled and delighted the world with his death-defying escapology. Nonetheless, he was first and foremost a magician.
Handel makes his last public performance, conducting the "Messiah" in 1759. He died eight days later.
Watergate. Alexander Butterfield born in 1926. He destroyed the last opportunity left to Richard Nixon in his struggle against resignation, when he revealed the existence of the notorious "White House Tapes" on July 16, 1973.
Howard Hughes, million-aire recluse, dies in 1976. He left $2,000 million behind him. In the Thirties he was famous for his affair with Jane Russell, and as a pilot. He died in a plane while being flown to hospital.

APRIL 7

Day of Adam.
Billie Holiday (Elenora Holiday) born in Baltimore, Maryland, in 1915. Classic, blues singer known as "Lady Day". Some greats include "Strange Fruit", "God Bless The Child" and "Lady Sings The Blues". She died in June 1959. Lester Young, Charlie Shavers and Benny Carter played on her small group recordings between 1935 and 1943.

Janis Ian born in 1951. "Society's Child" made US No. 14 in May 1967. She made a comeback in late 1975.
Mick Abrahams, born in 1943. Guitarist with Jethro Tull in their early days before leaving in 1969 to form Blodwyn Pig.
Percy Faith born in 1918. "Summer Place" in 1960

was a typical instrumental hit for him.
Bobby Bare born in Irontown, Ohio, in 1935. "500 Miles Away From Home" made US No. 10 in October 1963.

Spencer Dryden, drummer with Jefferson Airplane, born in 1938. Formerly a jazz drummer, he joined the Airplane in 1967, forming an exemplary rhythm section with bassist Jack Casady. He left in 1970, after being featured on the group's best albums.
Charley Thomas, tenor and lead with The Drifters from 1959 to 1966, born in 1937.
Steve Ellis, of Love Affair, born. Five UK hits in 1968-1969 of which "Everlasting Love" was a UK No. 1.
Freddie Hubbard, trumpet player, born in Indianapolis in 1938.
The First Aldermaston March, from London to the Aldermaston Atomic Weapons research station, was organized by the Campaign for Nuclear

Disarmament (CND) in 1958. 10,000 marched.
Joseph "Crazy Joe" Gallo shot in 1972, in front of his family and friends. He died at 5.23 am in Little Italy, New York City, outside Umberto's Clam Bar, the victim of a Mafia hit, and was later immortalized by Bob Dylan in his song "Joey".

LSD Synthesized in 1943 by Albert Hofman at Sandoz Laboratories, Basel, Switzerland. Experimenting with ergot derivatives, Hofman took a minute sample of d-lysergic acid diethylamide 25, thus taking the first ever acid trip. He fell off his bicycle on his way home.

APRIL 8

Japanese Flower Festival.
Buddha's birthday observed in Japan. Birthday of Rama in India.
Steve Howe born in 1947. Originally guitarist with Tomorrow, the only British underground group not to achieve rightful recognition, he joined Yes and became one of this

cult band's brightest stars. In 1976 he recorded a solo album for Atlantic

Roger Chapman, vocalist with Family, born in Leicester in 1942. An important London underground group immortalized in Jenny Fabian's book, "Groupie".

Julian Lennon, son of John and Cynthia, born at Sefton General Hospital, Liverpool, in 1963. Played drums on the last track of his father's "Walls And Bridges" album in 1974.
Charley Chinn, of Cat Mother and The All Night Newsboys, born in New York City. The group was discovered and produced by Jimi Hendrix.
Neil Young's film, "Journey Through The Past" premiered at the US Film Festival in Dallas, in 1973.
Pablo Picasso dies in 1973.

APRIL 9

Gene Parsons born in 1944. Drummer with The Byrds from "Dr. Byrds And Mr. Hyde" onwards until McGuinn disbanded the group in 1972.

Carl Perkins born in Tipton County, Tennessee, in 1932. He wrote "Blue Suede Shoes" which Elvis covered. His own version was a hit in January 1956. " 'Blue Suede Shoes' was the easiest song I ever wrote. Got up at 3.00 am when me and my wife Valda were living in a government project in Jackson, Tennessee. Had the idea in my head, seeing kids by the bandstand so proud of their new city shoes—you gotta be real poor to care about new shoes like I did— and that morning I went downstairs and wrote out the words on a potato sack —we didn't have any reason to have writing paper around."
Terry Knight born in Flint, Michigan, in 1943. Made a fortune when his old backing group changed their name from Terry Knight and The Pack to Grand Funk Railroad and made 10 platinum albums. Complex lawsuits between him and Grand Funk, whom he managed, resulted in him quitting the record business in 1973.
Emil Stucchio, lead vocalist with The Classics, born in Brooklyn, in 1944. He is now a transport policeman in Long Island.
Charles Baudelaire, French poet, born in 1821. Influenced Bob Dylan.
Mary Pickford (Gladys Smith) born in 1893. Comedian actress "The World's Sweetheart" of silent pictures.

APRIL 10

Day of Ezekiel, the prophet.

Glen Campbell born in Delight, Arkansas, in 1936. "By The Time I Get To Phoenix" in October 1967 was his first big hit.
Nathaniel Nelson, lead vocalist of The Flamingos, born in Chicago, in 1932. "Golden Teardrops" was their first hit in the US in 1953.

Bobby Hatfield, of the Righteous Brothers, born in Beaver Dam, Wisconsin, in 1940. Phil Spector signed and produced them, and "You've Lost That Lovin' Feelin' " was an international No. 1 in 1964. In 1968 they split up. Bobby took on Jimmy Walker as a new partner but it didn't work. In 1974 he and Medley reunited and entered the US Top 10 with "Rock 'n' Roll Heaven" and "Give It To The People".
Ricky Valence born in Ynsddu, South Wales, in 1940. He did the UK version of the Ray Peterson hit "Tell Laura I Love Her" which was banned by the BBC.
Martin Denny born in 1921. His instrumental "Quiet Village" was a US hit in the summer of 1969, reaching No. 2.

Stu Sutcliffe dies of a brain haemorrhage in 1962. Almost a Beatle.

Chuck Willis dies after an operation in Atlanta, Georgia, in 1958. His last hit, recorded two months earlier, was "What Am I Living For ?"/ "Hang Up My Rock And Roll Shoes".
Nat King Cole badly beaten up on stage before a white audience in 1956, in Birmingham, Alabama. He was attacked by six anti-Rhythm & Blues vigilantes.
The Who begin a six-day season at Brian Epstein's Saville Theater in 1967. Also on the bill is The Jimi

Hendrix Experience. **Freddie and The Dreamers** reach US No. 1 in 1965 with "I'm Telling You Now".

Jim Morrison at a 1970 Boston concert, the power having been switched off by the management, asks audience if "anyone would like to see my genitals".

Omar Sharif born in 1933. Best known for "Dr. Zhivago" (1966) and "Funny Girl" (1968) as well as "Lawrence Of Arabia" in 1962 which first established him as an international actor.

Vladimir Ilyich Ulyanov-Lenin born in Simbirsk, in 1870.

The Titanic leaves Southampton on her first and last voyage in 1912.

APRIL 11

The Beatles "From Me To You" single and their album "Please Please Me" released in 1963. The LP was to stay at No. 1 in the album charts for six months. In 1965, they play at the "New Musical Express"

Poll Winners Concert, Empire Pool, Wembley, with the Rolling Stones, and on the same night, The Beatles appear on the Eamonn Andrews TV Show on ABC-TV.

Tony Victor, of The Classics, born in 1943. "Till Then" was a 1963 US hit.

BOB DYLAN'S FIRST N.Y. APPEARANCE: FOLK CITY 4-11-61

Bob Dylan played his first "professional" gig in 1961 at Gerde's Folk City. He was on the same bill as John Lee Hooker. He sang Dave Van Ronk's arrangement of "House Of The Rising Sun" and his own "Song To Woody" supported by friends such as Joan Baez who were in the audience.

Millie Small enters UK charts in 1964 with "My Boy Lollipop".

Rudi Dutschke, left-wing leader of German SDS student revolutionaries was wounded by a shot in the head in 1968. "Red" Rudi, with Danny "the Red" Cohn-Bendit from France was seen by the Right as the architects of bloody anarchy in Europe.

The American Civil War began in 1861.

APRIL 12

Mahavira, founder of Jainism's birthday:

John Kaye, leader of Steppenwolf, born in Prussia in 1944. He formed the group in 1967. Broke up in 1972, and John Kaye recorded two solo albums. The group later reformed. Major group of the late Sixties heavy rock scene.

Herbert Jeffrey Hancock (Herbie Hancock) born in the South Side of Chicago, in 1940.

Bill Haley and The Comets cut "Rock Around The Clock" in 1954, at Pythian Temple on the West Side of New York City. The song was first released as a Rhythm & Blues number by Sonny Dae but flopped. Haley's version did badly at first but became a hit by being featured in the film "Blackboard Jungle". It has sold over seventeen million copies.

David Cassidy born in New York City, in 1950. His best year as a teenybopper idol was 1972, with such songs as "How Can I Be Sure".

Carol Lindsay, of The Kaye Sisters, born in Oldham, Lancashire, in 1930. Their last UK hit was "Paper Roses" in 1960.

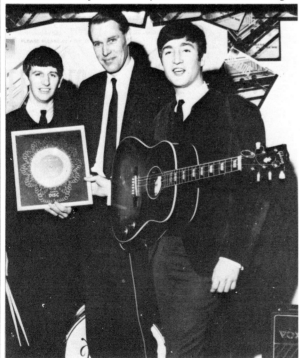

Ronan O'Rahilly, founder of Radio Caroline states, in 1965, that the pirates' case is "based on the Declaration of Human Rights . . . which acknowledges the right of anyone to broadcast, providing he does not interfere with established frequencies".

Lonnie Donegan reached UK No. 1 with "Cumberland Gap" in 1957 and The Skiffle craze was born.

Tiny Tim born. He sometimes claims to have been born on February 29th

as well. He is from Brooklyn and sings, in a high-pitched voice, songs such as "Tiptoe Through The Tulips".
"Spies For Peace" released in 1963, the details of UK Regional Seats of Government. The announcement of this official secret was part of the Committee of 100's campaign against the bomb.

Yuri Gagarin becomes, in 1961, the first man in space.

APRIL 13

John William "Jack" Casady, bass player of Jefferson Airplane, born in 1944. He and Kaukonen formed the spin-off group Hot Tuna in 1970. "Hot Tuna", "First Pull Up The Pull Down" and "Burgers" got more critical acclaim than their later albums.

Al Green born in Forest City, Arkansas, in 1946. "Let's Stay Together" was US No. 1 in December, 1971.
Lester Chambers, of The Chambers Brothers, born in Flora, Mississippi, in 1940. The nearest soul came to the psychedelic-rock of the late Sixties.

Roy Loney, of the Flaming Groovies, born in San Francisco, in 1946. Their first album became a collector's item of pure punk rock.
Tim Field, of The Springfields, born in Surrey, in 1936. Had hits with "Say I Won't Be There" and "Island Of Dreams" in the UK in 1963.
Eve Graham, of The New Seekers, born in Perth, Scotland, in 1943. Among their hits was the Coca-Cola jingle "I'd Like To Teach The World To Sing" in 1972. They disbanded in 1974.
Horace Kay, of The Tams, born in 1934. Their first hit was "Untie Me" in 1962 but they didn't reach the UK charts until 1971 when a reissue of "Hey Girl Don't Bother Me" made No. 1.

Roger Daltrey's first solo album, "Daltrey" released in 1973. It was produced by late-Fifties UK teen-idol Adam Faith.
Handel's "Messiah" first performed in Dublin, in 1742. It raised £400 in aid of charity.

APRIL 14

Day of Hanuman, birthday of this Monkey Demigod of the Hindus.

Ritchie Blackmore, lead guitarist of Deep Purple, born in Weston-Super-Mare. Their first album, "Shades

Of Deep Purple" was released in 1968. Heavy rock group that became heavier as they progressed. They disbanded in July, 1976.

Buddy Knox born in Happy, Texas in 1933. In 1957 "Party Doll" reached No. 2 in the US.
Patrick Fairley, of Marmalade, born in 1946. Their cover of Beatles "Ob-la-di Ob-la-da" reached No. 1 in the UK in 1968.
Dan Dare born in 1967. Futuristic comic strip hero of the British "Eagle". The date given as his birth in the first episode.
Pirate Radio. National Opinion Poll reveals in 1966 that more than one-third of the population of the United Kingdom listens to pirate radio stations.

Stephen Stills breaks his wrist in a car smash in 1970 resulting in the cancellation of a cross-country US tour by Crosby Stills Nash & Young. He drove into a parked car while surveying a police patrol car in his rear-view mirror.
G. F. Handel dies in 1759.

APRIL 15

St. Basilissa and St. Anastasia. The names respectively Queen and Resurrection and are attributes of Cres who had a festival at this time.
Muhammad's birthday.

Bessie Smith born in Knoxville, Tennessee, in 1898. The greatest woman

blues singer ever. Her songs have influenced all, from Billie Holiday to Janis Joplin. She died in a car crash in 1937, leaving behind her such classic recordings as "St. Louis Blues" and "Gimme A Pig-foot And A Bottle Of Beer".

Allan Clarke, of The Hollies, born in 1942. His distinctive vocal style helped create the immense run of hits which the group had through the Sixties, beginning with "Searchin' " in 1963. "I'm Alive" made UK No. 1. It wasn't until "Bus Stop" in 1966 that they broke through in

the US. Clarke left in 1971 to go solo, but after three unsuccessful solo albums he rejoined the band in 1973, which enabled them to continue with even more single hits.

Marty Wilde (Reg Smith) born in Greenwich, London, in 1939. His first chart success was "Endless Sleep" in 1958. He was well known to British TV viewers for his regular appearances on BBC's "6.5 Special" and "Oh Boy" programs. He married one of the Vernon Girls, Joyce Baker.

Wooley Wolstenholme, keyboards and vocals with Barclay James Harvest, born in 1947. The group have remained a cult band since their formation in 1967, despite their hard work and the opulent presentation of their music, though their second album "Once Again" won them large critical acclaim.

Frank Frost born in Auvergne, Arkansas, in 1936. He is a guitar, harp and blues traditionalist.

George Goldner dies in 1970. Together with Leiber and Stoller he formed the Red Bird label in 1964 and recorded the Shangri-las, The Dixie-Cups, and The Tradewinds.

Patricia Hearst photographed robbing the Hibernia Bank, San Francisco, in 1974. Nineteen-year-old Hearst was caught by the security cameras holding a rifle, together with members of the Symbionese Liberation Army.

Titanic sinks on her maiden voyage in 1912.

Henry James, novelist, born in 1843.

APRIL 16
Patanjali, founder of Yoga school, born.

Dusty Springfield born in West Hampstead, London, in 1939. She first played with her brother Tom and Tim Field in The Springfields. Their first record "Dear John" was released in April 1961. In 1963 she went solo, reaching No. 1 in the UK in April 1966 with "You Don't

Have To Say You Love Me". Famous for her heavy black eye make-up which was rumored to take hours to apply.

Jimmy Osmond, the youngest of The Osmonds, born in 1963. This tennybopper group spread their message of the Mormon faith and All-American puritanism 'til late 1975 when they finally began to decline in popularity.

Stefan Grossman born in New York City in 1945. An ex-Fug member, he became a disciple of ragtime and blues guitar, learning it direct from Rev. Gary Davis. A leader of the country blues revival in 1968 in Europe, he now lives in Rome. He was hotly tipped to join Paul Simon after the departure of Garfunkel, but in the end only played on one album track with him.

Hayley Mills born in 1946. Daughter of John Mills, while a child actress she had a hit in the UK with

"Let's Get Together" in 1961, and later with "Jeepers Creepers".

Bobby Vinton born in 1935. "Blue Velvet" was his big US hit in July 1963.

Roy Hamilton born in 1929. A string of hits through the Fifties included "You'll Never Walk Alone" in 1954 and "Unchained Melody" in 1955.

Henry Mancini born in Cleveland, Ohio, in 1924. wrote "Moon River" with Johnny Mercer which was from his score for "Breakfast At Tiffany's". He has won more Oscars and Grammys than any other artist.

Temperance Seven reach UK No. 1 with "You're Driving Me Crazy" in 1961.

Elektra Records kick out the MC5 in 1969, after they placed an ad in a local newspaper reading "Fuck Hudsons", a record store that refused to stock their albums.

Spencer Davis's "Somebody Help Me" reaches UK No. 1 in 1966 with Stevie Winwood on guitar.

Lenin arrives at the Finland Station, St. Petersburg, in 1917. Smuggled back through neutral Switzerland in a sealed train, Lenin's return to Russia after the February start to the revolution set off the movement towards its Bolshevik control.

Wilbur Wright, with his brother, the first man to fly, born in 1867.

APRIL 17

Bill Sommers (William Kreutzmann) born in 1946. Guitarist with The Warlocks, who changed their name to The Grateful Dead after collectively taking acid. They moved to 710 Ashbury, San Francisco, and became the representative band of the communal, drug-oriented hippie culture. The commune included designers, sound engineers and LSD manufacturer Stanley Owsley who designed their extraordinary sound system. Their first album "Grateful

Dead'' was released in March 1967, but the essence of their music has always remained live performances.

Billy Fury (Ronald Wycherley) born in Liverpool, in 1941. His row of nineteen hits in the UK began with ''Maybe Tomorrow'' in April 1959. In 1961 he had three No. 4 hits with ''Halfway To Paradise'', ''Jealousy'' and ''I'll Never Find Another You''. He played Stormy Tempest in the film ''That'll Be The Day'', which also starred Ringo Starr and David Essex.

Eddie Cochran dies in 1960. During an English tour Cochran's car blew a tire at Chippenham, Wiltshire, while returning to London in the early hours of the morning from Bristol, where he had just done a week at the Hippodrome. Cochran died of severe head injuries in Bath Hospital shortly after the crash. Also in the car were songwriter Sharon Sheeley and rock and roller Gene Vincent who both survived.

Roy Ralph Estrada, bass player, born in 1943. He was a member of The Mothers Of Invention in their early days.

Chris Barber, trombone player and jazz-band leader of the Trad era, born in Welwyn Garden City, in 1930. His club was a center for the London scene for many years. Paul McCartney produced one of his later records.

Bobby Curtola born in 1944. ''Fortune Teller'' was a US hit in 1962.

James Last, of easy-listening fame, born in Bremen, Germany, in 1929.

Vinnie Taylor of Sha-Na-Na dies in 1974, allegedly of a heroin overdose.

Johnny Cash appears before Richard Nixon in the East Room of the White House, in 1970. Nixon wanted to hear ''Okie From Muskogee'', ''A Boy Named Sue'' and ''Welfare Cadillac''.

Nikolai Khrushchev born at Kalinovka, Kursk Province, USSR, in 1894.

Rolling Stones first album ''Rolling Stones'' released in UK in 1964.

Charlie Chaplin born in East London, in 1889. He went to the US in 1910. Accused of anti-American activities, he moved to Switzerland.

Bernadette Devlin becomes the youngest member of the British House of Commons when she is elected in mid-Ulster in 1969.

APRIL 18

Mike Vickers, alto and clarinet player with Manfred Mann, born in 1941. The group began as the Mann-Hugg Blues Brothers in 1962 and had a hit with ''5-4-3-2-1'' in January 1964, after changing the group name to Manfred Mann. The group became known for its masterful interpretations of Bob Dylan numbers, ''Mighty Quinn'' and ''Just Like A Woman'' which Dylan was very pleased with.

APRIL 19

Alexis Korner born in Paris, in 1928. Founded Blues Incorporated in 1962. A galaxy of names have been in his various line-ups: Jack Bruce, Charlie Watts, Dick Heckstall-Smith, Mick Jagger, Robert Plant, Eric Burdon, Paul Jones, Long John Baldry, Marsha Hunt . . . In 1967 he formed Free At Last, and in 1969 New Church. Sings vocals for CCS, whose single ''Whole Lotta Love'' is the signature tune of BBC TV's ''Top of the Pops'' show.

Alan Price born in Newcastle, in 1942. The Alan Price Combo had an enormous following in home town Newcastle and in 1964 moved to London, changing their name to The Animals. Alan Price's original organ sound, together with Eric Burdon's unique voice, formed the core of their many hits ''House Of The Rising Sun'' becoming a classic. Price left in May 1965 and had a string of solo hits in the UK

with ''Simon Smith And His Amazing Dancing Bear'' and ''Hi-Lili-Hi-Lo''. He toured with Bob Dylan in the 1965 British tour, appearing in the movie ''Don't Look Back''. Wrote the score to Lindsay Anderson's ''O Lucky Man''.

Paul Krassner born in Brooklyn, New York, in 1932. Founder and editor of ''The Realist'' newspaper and satirical commentator on politics and culture.

Mark Volman, ex-leader of The Turtles, born, in 1944. Has played with Mark Bolan, Frank Zappa and as a duo with Howard Kaylan as The Fluorescent Leech and Eddie.

Albert Einstein dies in 1955.'' If only I had known, I should have become a watch-maker''.

ALEXIS KORNER RECORDING WITH B. B. KING & STEVE MARRIOTT.

APRIL 20

Sun enters Taurus, ruled by Venus, who was worshipped about this date. The Vinalia at which she received offerings of roses, myrtle and incense.

Johnny Tillotson born in 1939, in Jacksonville, Florida. "Poetry In Motion" was a US No. 2 in 1960, and his only UK hit.

Bob Braun (Robert Earl Brown) born in Ludlow, Kentucky, in 1929. "Till Death Do Us Part" was US No. 26 in August, 1962.

Rolling Stones play Montreux, Switzerland, at the International TV Festival in 1964.

Free Festival in the Venice section of Los Angeles, erupts in violence in 1969, with many injured and one hundred and seventeen people arrested.

JOHN HEARTFIELD.

Adolf Hitler, house painter and chancellor of Germany, born in 1889.

APRIL 21

Alan Warner, guitarist with The Foundations, born in 1947. "Baby, Now That I've Found You" was their first hit in 1967 followed by another million-seller "Build Me Up Buttercup" the next year.

PANARIVER presents

JANIS JOPLIN

21· 17·   6 5·

Janis Joplin plays the Royal Albert Hall, London, in 1969. One of her greatest ever performances and attended by a glittering array of British rock performers.

The Beatles go to the Crawdaddy Club in Richmond, in 1963, to see The Rolling Stones. They recommend them to their ex-publicist Andrew Loog Oldham.

Earl Hooker, Chicago blues guitarist, dies of tuberculosis in 1970.

Don Drummond, sax player, dies in 1971.

Harold Smith of Forgan, Oklahoma, successfully defended his title as Cow Chip Throwing Champion of the World by throwing a six-inch diameter of dried cow manure 166 feet 11 inches in Beaver, Oklahoma in 1973.

Queen Elizabeth II of England, born in 1926.

APRIL 22

Peter Frampton born in Beckenham, Kent, in 1950. He was with The Herd, then in 1969 with Humble Pie. Formed Frampton's Camel next which disbanded in 1974. He has a series of solo and group albums to his name. A track off his 1976 live album made US No. 1.

Charles Mingus, the bass player, born in 1922. His groups are very much a feature of modern jazz in the post Charlie Parker era. Dissatisfaction with the record business led him to release his own albums in the mid-Sixties.

Mel Carter born in Cincinnati, in 1943. "Hold Me, Thrill Me, Kiss Me" was a US Top 10 hit in 1965 and led on to ''All Of A Sudden My Heart Sings'' and ''Band Of Gold'', all chart entries.

Timothy Leary released from jail in San Diego, California, in 1976. He had served half of a ten-year sentence for marijuana possession.

The Last American Covertible comes off the production line in 1976. In 1965 half a million were bought in the US but due to pollution, sales dropped to nil. The last was a Cadillac Eldorado built in Detroit.

Pink Floyd enter the UK charts in 1967, with their first single ''Arnold Layne'' despite a BBC ban on airplay.

APRIL 23

Saint George's Day in England.

Roy Orbison born in Vernon, Texas, in 1936. ''Oh, Pretty Woman'' was his US No. 1 in 1964. He had many Top 40 hits with numbers such as ''Only The Lonely'' (1960), ''Crying'' (1961) and ''In Dreams'' (1963). His first US No. 1 was ''Running Scared'' in 1961. He was discovered by Norman Petty, Buddy Holly's manager, after moving to record on the Sun label.

Ray Peterson born in Denton, Texas, in 1939. ''Tell Laura I Love Her'' was his biggest hit, banned on British radio.

The Ash Grove in Los Angeles, burned down in 1969. Famous folk and blues club. Canned Heat, Taj Mahal, The Chambers Brothers all got their start there.

Bernadette Devlin born in 1948. Youngest ever member of the British House of Commons.

Timothy Leary given a six month to five year sentence in 1973, for his 1970 jail escape which was organised by the Weather Underground.

Ban The Bomb biggest ever demonstration as 150,000 gather in Hyde Park, London, in 1962.

William Shakespeare dies in 1616.

Egg-Shelling. In 1971 Harold Witcomb and Gerald Harding, two blind kitchen workers, set the world record by shelling 1,050 dozen eggs in 72 hours.

APRIL 24

Buddaghosa. Translator of Buddhist Scriptures in Sri Lanka (Ceylon).

Glen Cornick, bass guitar with Jethro Tull, born in 1947. Soon after the band's early success he left to form Wild Turkey.

Robert Knight born in Franklin, Tennessee in 1945. Produced frothy, danceable hits in the late Sixties, including ''Everlasting Love'', covered in UK by Love Affair. Made a comeback in 1974, after continuing his career in chemistry.

''Cathy's Clown'' reaches UK No. 1 for the Everly Brothers, in 1960.

''Game Of Love'' by Wayne Fontana and The Mindbenders reaches US No. 1, in 1965.

Muddy Waters records ''Fathers And Sons'' album live in Chicago with Paul Butterfield, Mike Bloomfield and many others in 1969.

''Easter Rising'' in Dublin against the British in 1916.

APRIL 25

Roman Rubigalia, or feast of blasts and mildews. Sacrifice to avoid pestilences as Middle of Spring.

Albert King born in 1924. First recorded the blues for the Pad label in Chicago in the early Fifties. Eventually signed to Stax, benefiting from the new-found white rock audiences. No relation to fellow blue guitarists BB or Freddie King.

Earl Bostic born in 1920. Great alto player and bandleader. One of those in his many line-ups was John Coltrane.

Otis Spann, blues singer, dies in 1970.

Elvis Presley reaches US No. 1 for the first time with ''Heartbreak Hotel'' in 1956.

Ella Fitzgerald, great blues and jazz singer, famed for her scat-singing, born in 1918.

Pam Morrison, Jim Morrison's widow, dies of an overdose in 1974.

Marvin Rainwater makes UK No. 1 in 1958 with ''Whole Lotta Woman''.

Peter and Gordon reach UK No. 1 with ''World Without Love'' by Paul McCartney, in 1964.

The 1974 Coup in Portugal sparked off by the playing of the outlawed popular song ''Grandola Villa Moreno'' over the armed forces radio. The coup ended nearly fifty years of fascism in Portugal.

Frank Clearwater dies as a result of wounds sustained in the Wounded Knee shoot-out, between the American Indian Nation and US Marshals in 1973. He was the first fatality.

Guglielmo Marconi born in 1874. The inventor of radio.

APRIL 26

Duane Eddy born in Corning, New York, in 1938. ''Rebel Rouser'' made US No. 6 in 1958 and ''Because They're Young'' was a US No. 4 in 1960. It reached No. 2 in the UK and stayed in the charts thirteen weeks.

Pete Ham, of Badfinger, born in Swansea in 1947. A Liverpool group who played The Cavern when they were known as The Iveys. The Beatles signed them to Apple and they had UK Top 20 hits with ''Day After Day'' and ''Come And Get It''. He committed suicide in 1975.

Gary Wright, of Spooky Tooth and later of solo fame, born in Englewood, New

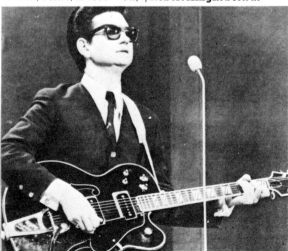

Jersey, in 1945. An integral part of underground rock, Spooky Tooth finally disbanded in 1974.

The Beatles enter the UK charts with "Get Back" in 1969. It was recorded "live" on the roof of the Apple building in Savile Row, London.

Rolling Stones play the "New Musical Express" Poll Winners Concert at Wembley in 1964.

Claudine Clark born in Macon, Georgia in 1941. "Party Lights" made US No. 5 in June, 1962.

Ludwig Wittgenstein born in 1899. "I would rather read 'thrillers' than Wittgenstein" said Jean Paul Sartre.

Guernica bombed by Nazi Luftwaffe bombers in 1937. In a three-hour saturation raid, 1,654 of the townspeople were massacred. Picasso commemorated the first modern air-raid in his most famous painting.

William Shakespeare born in Stratford-on-Avon, in 1564.

APRIL 27

Ann Peebles born in 1947, in East Saint Louis. "Part Time Love" and "I Pity The Fool" made the US charts in the early Seventies.

Phil King, of Blue Oyster Cult, the heavy metal rock group, murdered in 1972 during a gambling fight in New York. He was shot three times in the head with a .38 magnum.

Maxine Brown, of The Browns, born in 1932.

The Beatles "From Me To You" enters the UK charts in 1963. This was to be their first No. 1 record.

Drugs. Marijuana Tax Act heard before the Committee on Ways and Means of the House of Representatives in 1937.

David Bowie, delayed for several hours when his special train is stopped on the Russian-Polish border in 1976. Customs confiscate Nazi books and mementoes.

He states Britain would benefit from a fascist leader and says he would eventually like the job of Prime Minister for himself. "I don't intend to jump straight from pop to politics".

Mary Wollestonecraft born in 1759. Later the wife of Percy Shelley, she is best known for writing the horror classic "Frankenstein" and her advocacy of women's rights.

APRIL 28

Andrew Loog Oldham sees the Rolling Stones at the Crawdaddy Club in Richmond for the first time in 1963.

Hair opens in New York City, in 1968.

Abortion. The first recorded advertisement for an Abortion Clinic appeared in the pages of the "Morning Post" in London, in 1780.

Benito Mussolini executed by Italian partisans in 1945, whilst trying to flee the country.

The Mutiny On The Bounty starts in 1789.

APRIL 29

Carl Gardner, lead vocalist with The Coasters, born in 1928. "Yakety Yak" made US No. 1 in May 1958 and entered the UK charts

in August. "Charlie Brown" was a January 1959 hit in the US and "Poison Ivy" a summer hit in 1959.

Hugh Hopper, bass with Soft Machine, before going solo and then joining Isotope, born in Canterbury, in 1945. He was one of the original Canterbury "Wilde Flowers" with Robert Wyatt, Mike Ratledge and Kevin Ayers.

Michael Karoli, guitarist with the experimental German group Can, born in 1948.

Tommy James, leader of Tommy James and The Shondells, born in Dayton, Ohio.

J. B. Lenoir dies when hit by a car in Detroit in 1967. A great bluesman and a big influence on John Mayall, who recorded a memorial track to him on his album "Crusade".

LeRoy Carr, blues pianist and singer, dies in 1935. He drank himself to death.

Andrew Loog Oldham signs the Rolling Stones to management in 1963.

International Times 14 Hour Technicolor Dream All Night Rave at Alexander Palace, London, in 1967. Among the forty-one groups playing, often two at once— one at each end of the huge hall—were the Pink Floyd who premiered their second single "See Emily Play". The first event of the "Summer of Love".

First television interview takes place in 1936. Actress Peggy O'Neal was interviewed at the Ideal Home Exhibition, London.

APRIL 30

St. Donat (Aidoneus). Dragon-slaying saint, connected with Hades or Pluto, Greek God of the Underworld, corresponding with the Earthly sign Taurus, which rises when Scorpio, the dragon, sets.
Japanese Spring Festival begins today and lasts three days. Swedish Coming of Spring celebration starts today and lasts two days.

Frankie Lymon, of The Teenagers, dies in 1968 of a heroin overdose. He was fourteen when he recorded "Why Do Fools Fall In Love".

Bobby Vee (Robert Thomas Velline) born in Fargo, in 1943. "Devil Or Angel" was his first US Top 40 record which reached No. 6 in 1960. "Take Good Care Of My Baby" was his US No. 1 in 1961. Bob Dylan used to claim that he was Bobby Vee and even auditioned to be his pianist.

Merrill Osmond born in 1953. This Mormon group's massive teenybopper appeal finally began to decline in 1975.

Mike Deacon, keyboard player with John Entwhistle's Ox, born in Guildford, Surrey, in 1945.

Johnny Horton born in Rusk, Texas, in 1927. "Battle Of New Orleans" was US No. 1 in 1959.

Richard Farina dies in a motorcycle crash, in 1966, after the party given to launch his only book "Been Down So Long It Looks Like Up To Me". He was married to and recorded with Joan Baez's younger sister, Mimi.

Allman Brothers Band road manager, Twiggs Lyndon, arrested for murder in 1970. He stabbed a club manager for breach of contract in a crowded bar.

MAY 1

May Day.
Day of Bona Dea, The Mother Goddess.
Maypole ceremonies.
Morris dancing begins.
Central American Tree Ceremony.

Judy Collins born in Seattle, Washington, in 1939. Brought-up in Denver, Colorado, where her father was a well-known radio figure. She wrote "My Father" about him. After a formal musical education, she gravitated towards folk music, singing the political songs of Paxton, Dylan and Phil Ochs. Her album "Who Knows Where The Time Goes" featured Stephen Stills on guitar. She had a brief affair with him, which resulted in his composition "Suite : Judy Blue Eyes". She was instrumental in the discovery of Randy Newman, Joni Mitchell and Leonard Cohen.

Little Walter (Marion Walter Jacobs) born in Alexandria, Louisiana, in 1930. Unsurpassed blues harmonica technique. Hired by Chess in 1951 to back Muddy Waters and later Jimmy Rogers. His first solo session produced "Juke" in 1952, a huge R & B hit. Heavy influence on The Rolling Stones, he wrote "Confessin' The Blues". He died in 1968, as a result of injuries received in a fight.

Rita Coolidge born in Nashville, Tennessee, in 1944. Sister of Priscilla Coolidge, worked with Joe Cocker's Mad Dogs and Englishmen and also Delaney and Bonnie, before beginning a series of solo albums in 1971. In 1973 married Kris Kristofferson and recorded with him. Her work is mainly in the country rock area such as "This Lady's Not For Sale" and "Fall Into Spring".

Bob Dylan and Johnny Cash TV special taped for ABC TV at The Grand Ole Opry in Nashville, Tennessee, in 1969.

The Beatles and The Rolling Stones play at the "New Musical Express" Poll Winners Concert at the Empire Pool, Wembley, in 1966.

Bob Dylan opens his 1965 UK tour in Sheffield.

CARO (The Cannabis Action and Reform Organisation) launched jointly by Release and NCCL in London in 1973.

Watergate. John Dean resigns, and Haldeman and Ehrlichman quit under duress in 1973.

Adolf Hitler commits suicide in 1945.

Mimi Farina (née Baez) born in 1945. She made three albums with her husband Richard Farina, the anniversary of whose death is yesterday. She continued her career, working with her sister, Joan Baez and making further records.

Elvis Presley marries Priscilla Beaulieu in Las Vegas, in 1967.

"Citizen Kane" Premiere at Radio City Music Hall, New York, in 1941. Orson Welles' masterpiece, written by Herman Mankiewicz and performed by members of Welles' Mercury Theater epitomized the "newspaper movie" genre with its barely disguised story of media baron Charles Foster Kane, in real life William Randolph Hearst.
J. Edgar Hoover dies in 1972. "The job is never done".
Ink Newspaper published in London in 1971. An attempt at an alternative newspaper, headed by the editors of "Oz" magazine.
The Great Exhibition opened in Hyde Park, London, in 1851.

AND THUS IS BORN THIS WEIRD FIGURE OF THE DARK.. THIS AVENGER OF EVIL. 'THE BATMAN'

"Batman Detective Comics" launched in America, in 1939.

MAY 2

Nativity of Gautama Buddha. Maya, Mother of Buddha.
Link Wray born in 1935. "Rumble" was a big US hit in April 1958. He made a comeback in the Seventies.

His work was a big influence on British guitarists, such as Pete Townshend and John Lennon.
John Verity, vocals and guitarist with Argent, born in 1944. Joined the group with John Grimaldi as a replacement for Russ Ballard who left in 1974 to go Verity plays on "Circus" and "Counterpoints".

Randy Cain born in Philadelphia in 1945. A member of the Four Guys he left to study, only returning to replace Ritchie Daniels when he was drafted in 1967, and the group changed its name to The Delfonics.
Goldy McJohn, organist with Steppenwolf, born in 1945. A major heavy rock group of the late Sixties.
Bing Crosby (Harry Lillis Crosby) born in Tacoma, Washington, in 1904.

John Leon (Bunk) Gardner, sax and drums with The Mothers Of Invention, born in 1933.
Lesley Gore born in 1946. "It's My Party" was US No. 1 in 1963.

Hilton Valentine, guitarist with The Animals original line-up, born in 1943.
Elias and His Zig Zag Jive Flutes enter the UK charts in 1958 to reach No. 2.
Drugs. First annual Ann Arbor Hash Festival held in 1972.
Joseph McCarthy, architect of McCarthyism, the anti-Communist scare campaign, dies in 1957. Discredited after his attempt to prosecute the US army for "red" leanings, McCarthy was a broken man. He turned to drink and fell apart.
Caryl Chessman executed in 1960. A convicted murderer, Chessman

became world famous for the eleven years he spent trying to have his death sentence commuted. Despite many appeals he was finally sent to the electric chair in San Quentin.

Dr. Benjamin Spock born in New Haven, Connecticut, in 1903.

MAY 3

Chunti, Chinese form of Druga.

James Brown born near Augusta, Georgia, in 1928. Discovered in Macon leading The Famous Flames vocal group. They recorded "Please, Please, Please" in 1956, which was a regional hit. Entered national charts in 1958 with "Try Me". A great soul showman, his act ranged from complicated dance routines to slow histrionic sermons. He broke box office records in every US Black venue. His 1962 album "Live At The Apollo" sold over a million, unprecedented for an R & B record. The "hardest working man in show business" broke into the white market with Top 20 hit "Out Of Sight" in 1964.

Frankie Valli (Frank Castelluccio), lead with The Four Seasons, born in 1937.

Mary Hopkin born in Ystradgynlais, Wales, in 1950. First seen by Twiggy on the TV talent show "Opportunity Knocks". Twiggy called Paul McCartney, who signed her to Apple and produced her first record "Those Were The Days" which was a smash hit.

Peter Staples, bass player with The Troggs, born in Andover, in 1944. "Wild Thing" was a world-wide hit in 1968.

John Richardson, of The Rubettes, the Seventies teeny-bopper group, born in Dagenham, in 1948.

Joe Ames, of the Ames Brothers, born in 1924.

PETE SEEGER / PHOTO: CAMERA PRESS.

Pete Seeger born in New York, in 1919. Father figure to the early Sixties folk scene in the US. A veteran of the US radical movement and great folk music scholar and collector, performing and teaching others. He has made over fifty albums.

Les Harvey, of Stone The Crows, electrocuted on stage at the Top Rank Ballroom, Swansea, before an audience of twelve thousand students in 1972.

Jimi Hendrix busted at Toronto International Airport in 1969, for "illegally possessing narcotics". He was released on $10,000 bail.

"Dreams Do Come True" by Heinz released in the UK in 1963.

The Grand Funk Railroad "consented to talk with the US press" for the first time in 1971. Of the one hundred and fifty reporters invited only six turned up. Terry Knight, their manager, called it "the grossest case of non-recognition in the history of the business".

Rock concert at Madison, Wisconsin broken-up by two hundred mace spraying police in 1969.

Henry Cooper born in 1934. Fighting Cassius Clay in 1963, he was the first pro to knock him down, but still lost the fight. Today he runs a fruit and vegetable shop.

Niccolo Machiavelli born 1469.

The General Strike began in Britain, in 1926.

JAMES BROWN / PHOTO: MICK GOLD.

MAY 4

Tammy Wynette (Wynette Pugh) born in Itawambe County, Mississippi, in 1942. Began working on the Country Boy Eddie Show in 1965 and then began a

series of country hits with "Apartment Number 9". She continued with "D-I-V-O-R-C-E" and "Stand By Your Man" which as a re-release in the UK made No.1 in 1975.

Ed Cassidy, drummer of Spirit, born in Chicago. The stepfather of the group's guitarist, Randy California. They produced a quartet of exceptional albums between 1967 and 1970, when they broke up. They reformed in 1975.
Zal Cleminson, guitarist with The Sensational Alex Harvey Band, born in 1949. In 1975 the group suddenly hit big with "Delilah".
Peggy Santiglia, of The Angels, born in 1944. She replaced the former lead Linda Jansen in 1962. They had a US No. 1 summer hit in 1963 with "My Boyfriend's Back".
Ronnie Bond, drummer with The Troggs, born in 1944.
Jackie Jackson, of The Jackson Five, born in Gary, Indiana, in 1951.
Mary Hopkin appears on "Opportunity Knocks" TV Talent show in 1968, the day after her birthday.
Gene Vincent and The Bluecaps, record

KENT STATE UNIVERSITY, 1970 / PHOTO: POPPERFOTO.

"Be-Bop-A-Lula" (and "Woman In Love") in Nashville in 1957. An attempt by Capitol Records to tread in RCA's Presley

footsteps, it launched Vincent's traumatic career.
Audrey Hepburn born in 1929. Her many films include "The Lavender Hill Mob" (1951), "War And Peace" (1956), "Breakfast At Tiffany's" (1961) and "My Fair Lady" (1964).

Alice Liddell (the original Alice In Wonderland) born in 1852.
Emily Davison, a suffragette, died when she threw herself under King

George V's horse at the Derby in 1913. As part of the

militant women's rights campaign of the time, Davison's sacrifice shocked the public, but the First World War probably hastened female emancipation more urgently.
Kent State University Massacre, as US National Guardsmen shoot into unarmed students in 1970.

MAY 5

Ananda, Chief disciple of Gautama Buddha.
Bill Ward born in 1948. The drummer of the ultimate heavy metal death and destruction band, Black Sabbath.
Jim King born in Kettering, Northants. Played flute and saxophone with the first line-up of Family.
Scott McKenzie "San Francisco (Be Sure To Wear Flowers In Your Hair)" enters US charts in 1967, to reach No. 4. In UK it was No. 1 for four weeks.
Jonnie Taylor born in Crawfordsville, Arkansas, in 1938. "Who's Making Love?" was a 1968, million selling, Top Ten entry for him.

Captain Crunch, John Thomas Draper, was arrested by the FBI in 1972, in Los Gatos, California. Named after Captain Crunch cereal which used to give away toy whistles that had a perfect 2,600 cycle tone, the tone needed to enter the "tandems", long distance telephone circuits between cities. He was the friend of "Phone Phreaks" everywhere, famous for his free telephone conversations which sometimes reached his friends via every continent on Earth.

The Rev. Gary Davis dies of a heart attack in New Jersey, in 1972. He was seventy-six. He sang on street corners for twenty-five years. "Sampson And Delilah" was also recorded by Peter, Paul and Mary.
Bartolomeo Vanzetti and Nicola Sacco arrested in 1920, for possession of anarchist literature in New York City. They were then charged with a $16,000

payroll heist, and the murder of two guards. Scapegoats for the Twenties "red scare", they were sentenced to death and despite a public outcry, were executed in 1927.

Karl Heinrich Marx born in Trier, Germany, in 1818. "The rich will do everything for the poor but get off their backs."

MAY 6

Peggy Lee (Norma Dolores Eastrom) born in Jamestown, North Dakota, in 1920. Middle of the road singer who later worked with Paul McCartney.

Herbie Cox, leader of The Cleftones, born in 1939. "Heart And Soul" made the US Top 40 in May 1961.

Orson Welles born in 1915. "Citizen Kane" in 1941 established him as a new force in the cinema. Also acted in "The Long Hot Summer" (1958), "A Man For All Seasons" (1966), "Catch 22" (1970) and many other films. Recently taken to TV commercials.

Jeff Beck enters UK charts in 1969, with "Hi-Ho, Silver Lining" which re-entered again in November 1972.

Sigmund Freud born in Freiberg, Moravia, Austria, in 1865. "I do not think our successes can compete with those of Lourdes. There are so many more people who believe in the miracles of the Blessed Virgin than in the existence of the unconscious."

MAY 7

Jimmy Ruffin born in Carlinsville, Mississippi, in 1939. First appeared in the charts with "What Becomes Of The Broken Hearted" in 1966.

Mitch Jayne, bass player with The Dillards, born in 1930.

Pete Wingfield born in 1948. Made two albums with Jellybread, "First Slice" in 1969 and "Sixty Five, Parkway" in 1970, while still at Sussex University. His solo single "Eighteen With A Bullet" in 1975 shot him into the British and US charts.

Teresa Brewer (Theresa Breuer) born in Toledo, Ohio. She had many US chart entries between 1955 and 1961, "A Tear Fell" in 1956 being the biggest.

Jim Lowe born in Springfield, Missouri. "The Green Door" was a US No. 1 hit in 1956. Frankie Vaughan covered it in the UK and reached No. 2.

Johnny Maestro (Mastrangelo), lead of The Crests, born in Brooklyn, in 1939. "16 Candles" made US No. 2 in November, 1968.

Dan Peak, of the group, America, falls through a window and receives stitches, in 1971. Their single "Horse With No Name" had been riding high in the UK charts until the end of February.

The Mamas and The Papas reach US No. 1 with "Monday, Monday" in 1966.

Derek Taylor born in 1952. Presented The Beatles image to the world as their press officer, now a top Warner-Elektra-Atlantic executive.

The Lusitania torpedoed by a German U-Boat in 1915.

President Tito (Josip Broz), of Yugoslavia, born in 1891.

Piotr Ilyitch Tchaikovsky born in 1840.

World War II ends in 1945.

Dien Bien Phu falls to the Viet Minh in 1954, ending the French attempt to hang onto Vietnam. Their role was quickly taken up by the US.

MAY 8

Rick Nelson (Eric Hilliard Nelson) born in 1940, in New Jersey. "Poor Little Fool" was his first hit in the US in June, 1958. He was picked for his good looks then taught to sing.

Gary Glitter (Paul Gadd) born in Banbury, Oxfordshire, in 1944. "Rock And Roll Parts 1 & 2" made UK No. 2 and US No. 7 in July 1972. His UK No. 1 hits are "I'm The Leader Of The Gang" and "I Love, You Love, Me Love" in 1973. He "retired" from rockbizz in February 1976.

Graham Bond, power-organist, leader of the Graham Bond Organisation, jumps before a London underground train at Finsbury Park Station in 1974. Bond's bands featured Ginger Baker, Jack Bruce, Jon Hiseman, John McLaughlin, Dick Hecktall-Smith and many other super-stars of later days.

MARC BOLAN / PHOTO: BARRY PLUMMER.

Marc Bolan (Mark Feld) born in Barking, Essex. He first got his name when Decca released "Wizard"/ "Beyond The Rising Sun" in November 1965 and called him Mark Bowland. In October 1970 he released "Ride A White Swan" which became his first UK No. 1, the first of a string of hits which for some reason he could never transfer to the States.

Euclid James "Motor-head" Sherwood, of The Mothers Of Invention, born in 1942. He was featured in Zappa's film "200 Motels".

Paul Samwell-Smith, bass player with The Yardbirds, born in 1943. Originally The Metropolitan Blues Quartet, The Yardbirds were formed in 1963. He left in 1966 to be replaced by Jimmy Page.

Radio London's first London disc show held at the Marquee Club in Wardour Street, London, in 1965. Compered by Pete Brady, guest artistes included the Walker Brothers and Elkie Brooks.
Johnny Bragg, lead with The Prisonaires entered Tennessee State Penitentiary in 1943, where the group was formed. He later sang solo and with The Marigolds when he got out.
John Fred born in Baton Rouge, Louisiana, in 1941. He had a Louisiana style transatlantic hit in 1967 with "Judy In Disguise (With Glasses)", a take-off on The Beatles "Lucy In The Sky".
"Look Back In Anger" premiere in 1956, at the Royal Court Theater, London. John Osborne's play epitomized the attitudes and agonies of the "Angry Young Men" of the Fifties in Britain. Its "Kitchen sink" style of social realism also revolutionised the staid British theater.
Coca-Cola invented in 1886, by John S. Pemberton, who first mixed up the ingredients (including a form of cocaine) that were

used in the basic Coca-Cola syrup, at Jacob's Pharmacy, Atlanta, Georgia. By September 1919, the Coca-Cola company was sold for $25,000,000.

MAY 9

Remus. First day of the Remuria; continued for three nights in honor of the dead.

Richie Furay, of Poco, born in Yellow Springs, Ohio, in 1944. He organized Poco after the breakup of Buffalo Springfield.

Steve Katz, guitar, harmonica and vocals with Blood Sweat and Tears, born in Brooklyn, New York. Began with Al Kooper in the Blues Project.

Dave Prater born in Ocilla, Georgia, in 1937. Joined with Sam Moore in 1958 to form Sam and Dave. Success was a long time coming but finally in 1966 "You Don't Know Like I Know" and "Hold On I'm Coming" were big chart entries and in 1969 they had a US No. 2 with "Soul Of Man" which sold over a million.

Pete Birrell, bass player with Freddie and The Dreamers, born in 1941. "I'm Telling You Now" was US No. 1 in 1963. Freddie and Birrell remained together after the group split up and starred in the children's television show "Little Big Time" on British TV.
Don Dannemann, of The Cyrkle, born in 1944. Originally The Rondells, a New York vocal group, they were renamed by Brian Epstein. They had a US No. 1 with "Red Rubber Ball" in 1966.
Mike Millward, rhythm guitarist with The Fourmost, born in 1942. Originally The Four Jays then The Four Mosts before their manager Brian Epstein changed their name. They made UK No. 6 in 1964 with "A Little Lovin' ".
Radio Atlanta begins broadcasting in 1946 off Great Britain. It later becomes known as Radio Caroline South.
The Beatles sign recording contract with EMI's Parlophone label in 1962.
Paul McCartney first meets Jane Asher after a concert appearance at the Royal Albert Hall, London, in 1963.

MAY 10

The day of Job.

Danny Rapp, lead of Danny and The Juniors, born in 1941. "At The Hop" was their only real hit reaching US No. 1 in November 1957 and UK No. 3 in January 1958.
Larry Williams born in New Orleans, in 1935. He wrote and recorded "Short Fat Fanny" in June 1957. His "Bony Maronie" made the charts in 1957.
Dave Mason born in 1945, in Worcester. Has played with Traffic, Jimi Hendrix, Eric Clapton, Delaney and Bonnie and Friends, and also solo. As well as being a respected guitarist, he

DAVE MASON.

wrote "Hole In My Shoe" (for Traffic 1967) and produced "Music In A Doll's House" album for Family in 1967. His solo album successes include "Alone Together" and "Headkeeper".

Donovan (Leitch) born in Glasgow, in 1946. Dylan: "Who is this Donovan? Let's put him right out on the sidewalk." Alan Price: ". . . He's a very good guitar player. He's better than you." Dylan: "Right away I hate him."

Rolling Stones begin recording at Olympic Studios in 1963. Their first recording session. Tapes later issued as a bootleg "Bright Lights, Big City".

Jackie Lomax born in Wallasay, Cheshire, in 1944. Soloist produced by George Harrison. Was involved in Heavy Jelly, a fictitious group invented first by "Time Out" Magazine and then, after the publicity had died, was created in reality.
Mick Jagger and Keith Richard prosecuted on drug charges at Chichester in 1967 and sent to trial at the West Sussex Quarter Sessions.
Brian Jones (meanwhile) was charged with possession of marijuana, also in 1967.

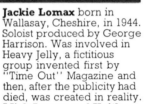

Night of the Barricades in Paris, in 1968. Thousands occupy the Latin Quarter, The police invade with CS gas.
The Who do four concerts at Madison Square Gardens in New York in 1974. They sell out all 80,000 seats within eight hours.
Jay Ferguson, lead singer with Spirit, born in Los Angeles, in 1947. Wrote many of the group's songs.
Bert Weedon, guitarist, born in East Ham, London, in 1921. Originally a session man with Tommy Steele, Marty Wilde and Cliff

Richard, his first solo record was in April 1953 "April In Paris".

Bob Dylan played the Royal Albert Hall, London in 1965. It was the climax to his British tour and in 1966 played the Colston Hall, Bristol.
The Turtles and The Temptations played and allegedly snorted coke at the White House 1969, for Tricia Nixon's Masque Ball. Said Mark Volman, "Lots of Congressmen were there and, boy, were they wrecked!"
Fred Astaire (Frederick Austerlitz) born in Omaha. Nebraska, in 1899.

BRIAN JONES / PHOTO: GERED MANKOWITZ.

MAY 11

St. Illuminatus.
Parsi Fire Ceremony.

Les Chadwick, bass guitarist with Gerry and The Pacemakers, born in 1943, in Liverpool. Among their big hits was "Ferry 'Cross The Mersey" in 1965.

Carla Bley born in Oakland, California, in 1938. She married jazz pianist Paul Bley. In 1974 she and Michael Mantler formed the Jazz Composers Orchestra. Her major work is "Escalator Over The Hill", a three-volume "opera" with Jack Bruce and Linda Ronstadt, John McLaughlin, Don Preston, Don Cherry and many others. Was in the short lived Jack Bruce Band in 1975.
Brian Jones remanded on £250 bail on drugs charges in 1967.
Salvador Dali born in 1904. Originally a member of the Surrealist Group but expelled for his support of the fascist regime in Spain.

Asked to do cover of Johnny Winter album, but charged £3,000. Did a hologram of the head of Alice Cooper.
Irving Berlin born in 1888.

Elvis Presley first enters the UK charts, in 1956, with "Heartbreak Hotel" and reaches No. 2.
First scheduled TV service began in 1928, by the GEC station, WEY in New York. In an announcement of the time a spokesman was quoted, "Only the faces of men talking, laughing or smoking will be broadcast, no elaborate effects are planned at this time."

MAY 12

St. Nereus, probably pagan sea-god Nereus.
St. Achilleus, probably hero-son of sea nymph Achilles.

Steve Winwood born in Great Barr, Birmingham, in 1948. First played in local groups with his brother Muff. Hailed as child genius in 1964 as singer, guitarist and keyboard player in The Spencer Davis Group.

Traffic was formed in 1967 and built up a great following in summer of Flower-Power. In 1968 Traffic split up and Winwood joined the first supergroup, Blind Faith. After its collapse, Traffic eventually came back together for a series of varying albums and a traumatic number of personnel changes. In 1976 Winwood teamed up with Japanese percussionist Stomu Yamashta to record an album, "Go", and give concerts in London and Paris.

Ian McLagan born in 1945. Keyboard player with The Small Faces, when Steve .

Marriott left in 1968, he formed The Faces with drummer Kenny Jones and bassist "Plonk" Lane, bringing in Rod Stewart and Ronnie Wood from the Jeff Beck Band.

Mick Jagger marries Bianca Perez Morena de Macias, in St. Tropez Town Hall, 1971. Afterwards, a star-studded reception.
Jayotis Washington, of The Persuasions, born in Detroit in 1941. The group first formed in 1968.
Bob Rigg, of the psychedelic rock group Frost, born in Alpene, Washington, in 1945.

SALVADOR DALI WITH EDGAR FROESE OF TANGERINE DREAM.

James Purify born in Pensacola, Florida, in 1944. Together with cousin Bobby Purify, had a US Top 10 hit with "I'm Your Puppet" in 1966.

GAMES FOR MAY THE PINK FLOYD

On Friday 12th May, 1967 at 7.45 p.m. in the Queen Elizabeth Hall, South Bank, S.E.1. Christopher Hunt and Blackhill Enterprises present Games for May - space-age relaxation for the climax of Spring. Electronic compositions, colour and image projections, girls, and the Pink Floyd. Tickets 20/-, 15/-, 10/- from the box office, Royal Festival Hall, S.E.1. WAT 3191 and adverts.

QUEEN ELIZABETH HALL MAY 12

Pink Floyd "Games For May" was presented at the Queen Elizabeth Hall, London, in 1967. The first use of quadrophonic sound in concert.

LITTLE STEVIE WONDER

pacifica

Pacifica Radio, the non-commercial radical network, had its Houston Texas station KPFT-FM fire-bombed by the extreme right wing (probably Cuban exiles), in 1970.

Rolling Stones play at "The New Musical Express" Poll Winners Concert at Wembley in 1968.
Sun Records run a trade paper ad in 1956, announcing a disc "by one of the truly great talent finds" Johnny Cash. The record was "I Walk The Line" which he also wrote. His first publicity.
The Day They Drove Old Dixie Down. Richmond, Virginia fell in 1865.
The General Strike of 1926 in Britain, ended when union leaders under J. H. Thomas accepted government terms, against the continued opposition of the miners, whose claims had initiated the whole stoppage. "We've been twisted" said a trade council.

MAY 13

Ritchie Valens (Ritchie Valenzuela) born in 1941. His big hit "Donna" was written for his high school sweetheart Donna Ludwig. The record was a hit in November 1958 in the US and March 1959 in the UK.
Stevie Wonder (Steveland Morris Hardaway) born in Saginaw, Michigan, in 1950. He opened up in the US with a No. 1 in 1963 with "Fingertips Part 2", maintaining a string of hits and having another No. 1 with "Superstition" in 1972.
Mary Wells born in Detroit in 1943. "My Guy" was a US hit in March 1964. It reached UK charts in June.

Danny Kirwan, guitarist with Fleetwood Mac, born in 1950. He joined the band after their initial success but just in time to cut the million selling single "Albatross".

Peter Gabriel, founder-member of Genesis, born in 1950. After the group was signed to Decca in 1969 by Jonathan King, they developed a melodramatic style, using long song-cycles. They became very popular in Europe, but in 1975 Gabriel left, leaving the group to look for a new vocalist. It was Gabriel who had masterminded their elaborately theatrical stage shows.

Pete "Overend" Watts born in 1947. Bassist of Mott The Hoople, who after losing most of their line-up in many changes, and having a hit with David Bowie's "All The Young Dudes", became the simpler Mott.

Joe Brown born in Swarby, Lincolnshire, in 1941. "Picture Of You" was a 1962 British hit.
BeeGees first enter UK charts in 1967, with "New York Mining Disaster 1941".
The Beach Boys enter UK charts with "Then I Kissed Her" in 1967.
Test Flight. First airplane to be fitted with a lavatory was the giant passenger plane, designed by Sikorsky, test flown in 1931.
Viet Nam. Britain recognized the Communist Provisional Government of South Viet Nam in 1975.

MAY 14

Gautama Buddha. The Wesak Festival.

Bobby Darin (Walden Robert Cassotto) born in the Bronx, in 1936. "Splish Splash" was a US hit in May 1968, Charlie Drake's UK cover version prevented it from reaching higher than No. 20 in the UK. He died in 1975.

Eddy Arnold born in Tennessee, in 1918. Managed for eight years by Colonel Tom Parker (Elvis Presley's manager), in the late Forties, when he made such Country and Western hits as "Cattle Call" and "Anytime".

Trini Lopez born in Dallas, Texas, in 1937. "If I Had A Hammer" was a hit in 1963.

Tich of Dave, Dee, Dozy, Beaky, Mick and Tich born. "Hold Tight" was their first British hit in 1966.

Jack Bruce born in Glasgow, in 1943. First with The Graham Bond Organisation, then John Mayall's Bluesbreakers, Manfred Mann, Cream and when they broke up in 1969 did some solo albums. Then comes West Bruce and Laing, and the Jack Bruce Band with Carla Bley and Mick Taylor which broke up in 1975. One of Britain's top vocalist/bass players.

Art Grant, bass player with the Edgar Broughton Band, born in 1950.

Al Ciner, guitarist with The American Breed, born in 1947. They were first called Gary and The Nite Lights. After the name change they had a US No. 24 with their first single "Step Out Of Your Mind" in 1968.

Mike Preston born in Hackney, London, in 1934. "A House, A Car And A Wedding Ring" made US and UK charts in August 1958, showing the appeal of bourgeois values.

MAY 15

St. Daphne, Christianized form of Aurora, Goddess of the Dawn. Japanese Festival of the Hollyhock. San Isidro Day in Mexico.

Brian Eno born in 1948. Joined Roxy Music soon after it began and virtually co-starred with Brian Ferry on their first two albums. Since this was not to Ferry's .liking, he left the group and produced a series of solo albums "Here Come The Warm Jets", "Taking Tiger Mountain By

Strategy" and "Another Green World". In 1975 he began his own Obscure Records label to release experimental material.

The Battle of People's Park, 1969. It began at 4.15 am when three hundred police cleared this small park off Telegraph Avenue in Berkeley, California, which the University authorities claimed as theirs. In the attempt five days later by the street people to regain the park, over two hundred and fifty were arrested and

James Rector was shot dead by the police while sitting on the roof of a nearby building. He was unarmed. Ronald Reagan called out 2,000 National Guardsmen who, with bayonets fixed, finally cleared the park. Schoolchildren in a nearby school were tear-gassed by police helicopters and gas seeped into the Cowell Hospital, upsetting operations and gassing patients.

Radio Northsea International bombed by commando frogmen, hired

by a director of the rival station, Radio Veronica, in 1970.

MAY 16

Barbara Lee, of The Chiffons, born in 1947. "He's So Fine" was a 1963 UK and and US hit.

Marty Balin, vocalist of Jefferson Airplane, busted for possession of marijuana at the Thunderbird Motel, Bloomington, Minnesota, in 1970. He got $5,000 bail.

Jack Casady, bassist of Jefferson Airplane, busted at the Royal Orleans Hotel in New Orleans, in 1969. He received a two and a half

BRIAN ENO

year suspended sentence. He and Jorma Kaukonen formed Hot Tuna shortly afterwards.

Pete Townshend spends a night in jail in New York City, in 1969, after being charged with assault. A supermarket next to the Fillmore East was on fire and a plain-clothes policeman leapt onto the stage yelling "Give me the mike!" Townshend, thinking he was just a member of the audience, kicked him off stage. He was bailed out by Bill Graham, owner of the Fillmore.

Liberace born in 1919. The King of Piano-Kitsch.
Henry Fonda born in 1915. Apart from his own film fame, he sired Peter ("Easy Rider") and Jane (reformed sex symbol).

Michael Abdul Malik (Michael X) was hanged in 1975 in Port of Spain, after being convicted of killing Joseph Skerrit in 1971.

MAY 17

Plato (approximate date of birth).

Taj Mahal born in New York City, in 1942. His first album as a solo blues artist was released in 1967. From traditional black roots, one of the few bluesmen to appeal to white audiences by heading the West Coast blues revival of the late Sixties.

Jesse Winchester born in Shreveport, Louisiana in 1944. A teenage rock'n'roll guitarist, he draft-dodged in Canada. The Band's Robbie Robertson produced his first album with Todd Rundgren in 1970. His second album "Third Down, 110 To Go" was met with enormous acclaim. His music ranges from full-tilt rockabilly to a mellow, but humorous country ballad style.
Bill Bruford born in 1950. Originally played drums with Yes but left to pursue a "free lance" career, touring with Genesis but playing full time with the more experimental National Health.
Keith (James Barry Keefer) known for his US hit "98.6", born.
Guy Mitchell reaches UK No. 1 in 1957 with "Rock-A-Billy".
Bob Dylan appears at The Royal Festival Hall in 1964, his first major London concert. On the same day in 1967 "Don't Look Back", the documentary by D. A. Pennebaker on Bob Dylan's UK tour of 1965, is premiered at the Presidio Theater in San Francisco.
First color photograph exhibited at the Royal Institution. Taken in 1861. It showed a tartan ribbon bow on a black velvet background.
Mafeking relieved in 1900.

MAY 18

Rick Wakeman born in Perivale in West London, in 1949. He left The Royal

College of Music and did session work. He was with The Strawbs and Yes for a time. In 1973 the first of his solo concept albums was released with "The Six Wives Of Henry The VIII" which began his career as performer and master of light orchestral music.
Joe Turner born in Kansas City, in 1911. His biggest hit, "Corrina Corrina" was in the US charts in April 1956. "The Father of Rock".

Albert Hammond born in Gibraltar. A singer/songwriter of "It Never Rains In Southern California" fame.
Rodney Dillard born in 1942. Began as a high powered electric Ozark Mountains Bluegrass group called The Dillards (with brother Doug). After Doug left in 1968 they became more electric orientated particularly on "Roots And Branches" and "Tribute To The American Duck".
Perry Como born in Canonsburg, Pennsylvania. The barber who sang to his customers and became an Easy Listening best seller.
George Alexander, of the punk rock group Flamin' Groovies, born in San Mateo, California.

Bertrand Russell born in Ravenscroft, Monmouthshire, in 1872. "Few people can be happy unless they hate some other person, nation or creed."

MAY 19

Peter Dennis Blandford Townshend born in Chiswick, London, in 1945. He claims he learnt the guitar to gain respect from his peers. After meeting Daltrey and Entwistle in a coffee bar the Detours were formed. Keith Moon joined and they became the High Numbers. Townshend re-wrote Slim Harpo's "Got Love If You Want It" as the Mod song "I'm The Face", released in 1964. From the time they were discovered and became The Who, Townshend has always been the motivating creative force, moving from Pop Art to Meher Baba.

Eric Burdon born in Newcastle, in 1941. When the Newcastle-based Alan Price Combo was joined by Burdon in 1963 they began to have some success and moved to London, changing their name to The Animals. Burdon's "black" voice featured on their classic hit "House Of The Rising Sun" which was UK No. 1 in 1964. Burdon broke up the group in 1966 but reformed it during "Flower Power" only to go solo in 1969. In 1970 backed by War he cut two solo albums and later one with Jimmy Witherspoon in 1971.

Alma Cogan born in Golders Green, in 1932. Many hits through the Fifties in UK with Tin Pan Alley material such as "Sugartime". Died of throat cancer.

PETE TOWNSHEND IN 1966 / PHOTO: COLIN JONES.

Jerry Hyman, trombone and recorder player with Blood Sweat and Tears, born in Brooklyn.

Coleman Hawkins dies of pneumonia in 1969, in New York City. He was sixty-nine and had been playing tenor sax for forty years.

Bobby Darin releases "Splish Splash" in 1958. It was the first recording made on an eight-track recorder at Atlantic Records.

B. Bumble and The Stingers. "Nut Rocker" reaches UK No. 1 in 1962. It was his real name.

Ho Chi Minh born in 1890. Father of the communist movement in Viet Nam, he died before he could witness final victory.

but it was The Beatles' "A Little Help From My Friends" which gave him his No. 1 in 1968. He had a big US hit with "The Letter" in 1970.

Cher (Cherryl La Piere, half French according to one source; Cherilyn Sakisian, half Indian according to another source) born in El Centro, California, in 1945. First came to fame with her husband Sonny Bono as Sonny and Cher in the mid-Sixties. Sang backing on "Da Doo Ron Ron" by the Ronettes when Darlene Love failed to show at the Phil Spector session. Now the top female act in US, as well as being Mrs. Greg Allman.

Malcolm X born in Omaha, Nebraska, in 1925. From hustling, drug addiction and imprisonment, Malcolm Little became Malcolm X, fervent Black Muslim, and prophet of black revolution. He was murdered in 1966 after his breakaway from the parent Muslim group.

MAY 20

Manjushri, Bodhisattva of Wisdom and Learning.
Patron of Astrology.

Joe Cocker born in Sheffield, in 1944. His first record was made under the name of Vance and The Avengers, "I'll Cry Instead" and released in 1963. His career under his own name began in 1967 with "Marjorine",

Vic Ames, of the Ames Brothers, born in 1926.

"Little" Jimmie Henderson, lead guitarist with Black Oak Arkansas, born in Jackson, Mississippi, in 1954. Southern boogie band with a dynamic stage act.

Alex Broughton, drummer with his brother's Edgar Broughton Band, born in 1950.

James Rector shot dead by police in "People's Park", Berkeley, when two thousand National Guardsmen with helicopters occupy a waste lot near Telegraph Avenue that street people had taken over, in 1969.

Pete Cetera, bass player and vocalist of Chicago, has four teeth knocked out and is hospitalized, requiring five hours of surgery, when three men beat him up because of the length of his hair at a Dodger-Chicago Cubs baseball game, in 1971.

T. Rex reach UK No. 1 with "Metal Guru" in 1972.

John Stuart Mill born in 1806. British economist, philosopher and early advocate of Women's Rights.

Columbus dies in 1506.

MAY 21

Sun enters Gemini, ruled by Mercury, but associated with Apollo by the Romans.

Burt Bacharach born in Kansas City, Missouri, in 1929. Studied music at university but became an accompanist. Started

working with Hal David in 1958. They were immediately successful, writing for such as Perry Como. They discovered Dionne Warwick and through her had many hits such as "Walk On By" and "Anyone Who Had A Heart". They wrote Gene Pitney's "24 Hours From Tulsa".

Ronald Isley, of The Isley Brothers, born in 1941. Their first US hit was "Shout" in 1959.

Vincent Crane (Vincent Rodney Cheesman), multi-instrumentalist with The Crazy World Of Arthur Brown, born in Reading, in 1943.

Marcie Blane born in 1944. "Bobby's Girl" was a US hit in October 1962.

Pete Townshend and Karen Astley marry at Didcot register office in 1968. Karen was a dress designer and was responsible for some of Townshend's more amazing outfits during 1966-7.

The Who release "Anyway, Anyhow, Anywhere" in 1965. Became the signature tune of the ABC-TV rock 'n' roll program "Ready Steady Go".

Brian Jones arrested for possession of marijuana in 1968. He was given £2,000 bail.

Baader–Meinhof Gang trial begins in Stuttgart in 1975. The security arrangements, including a special courthouse, cost over £2,000,000.

Charles "Plucky" Lindbergh arrives at Le Bourget, Paris, in his transatlantic flight from New York City, in 1927. It took thirty-three and a half hours.

MAY 22

Bernie Taupin born in Lincoln, England in 1950. He met Elton John through a talent competition in 1967. His lyrics range from old American West imagery to superb romantic balladry, from superficial profundity to a fascination with Hollywood. In 1971 he released a solo album "Taupin" and in 1972 produced a David Ackles album. The bitter "Captain Fantastic And The Brown Dirt Cowboy" is drawn from his early experiences with Elton John.

Ian Robertson Underwood, keyboards with Frank Zappa and The Mothers Of Invention, born. The most consistent player with Zappa, he survived the break-up of the Mothers to be in the "Hot Rats" group.

Kenny Ball born in 1937. He formed his Jazzmen in December 1958 and was "discovered" by Lonnie Donegan. Had a string of Trad Jazz hits in the UK during the early Sixties.

Al Brown, of Al Brown's Tunetoppers, born in 1934. He invented "The Madison".

"Tarzan", John Clayton, Lord Greystoke, born in 1888. As Lord of the Jungle, Tarzan pledged himself as the scourge of evil. His adventures have been charted by Edgar Rice Burroughs in a long line of books.

Bob Dylan's Bar Mitzvah in 1954.

Sir Arthur Conan Doyle born in 1859. The creator of Sherlock Holmes.

People's Park, Berkeley, 1969. Police arrest four hundred and eighty-two people including some innocent shoppers, during a peaceful march down Shattuck Avenue, to complain about methods used by the police to defend the new metal fence they had erected to keep people out of the park.

MAY 23

Robert A. Moog born in 1934. His music sythesizers were the first to be used extensively in rock music.
Rosemary Clooney born in Maysville, Kentucky. Her first US No. 1 was ''Come On-A My House'' in 1951.

Clive Davis, president of Columbia Records, was fired in 1973 by boss Arthur Taylor. He returned to his office from Taylor's fortieth floor suite to find it empty and all of his personal effects already waiting for him in reception. CBS hit him with a civil suit for $100,000 including $20,000 for his son's bar mitzvah. Davis bounced back by forming the aggressively commercial Arista Record Company.
Mungo Jerry play before 25,000 people at the Hollywood Festival in England and their single ''In The Summertime'' reaches No. 3 in the US and No. 1 in the UK, in 1970. They preceded The Grateful Dead who played for four hours at this, their first English appearance.

MAY 24

Hermes Trismegistus, 'Thrice Greatest Hermes'. Patron of Alchemy. Incarnation of Mercury.
Bob Dylan (Robert Allen Zimmerman) born in Duluth, Minnesota. From there he moved to Hibbing where he grew up and formed his group The Golden Chords. Moved to New York City to see his hero Woody Guthrie. Released his first record ''Bob Dylan'' in 1962, having become well-known in the Greenwich Village folk scene. A year later ''Blowin' In The Wind'' was a world-wide hit. ''I didn't change my name in honor of Dylan Thomas. That's just a story. I've done more for Dylan Thomas than he's ever done for me. Look how many kids are probably reading his poetry now because they heard that story.''

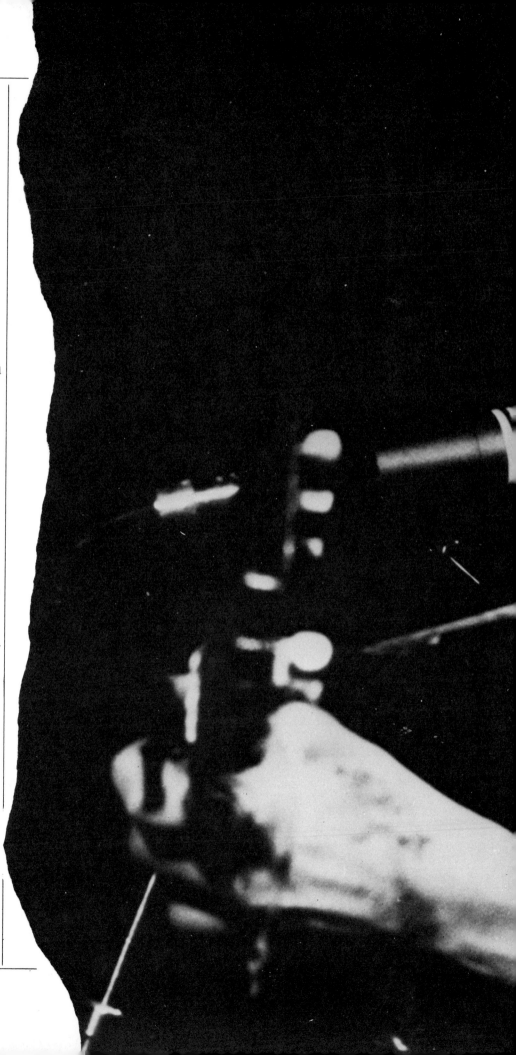

Leo Sayer born in Shoreham, Sussex, in 1948. Originally in Patches he left to team up with Dave Courtney as a songwriter. Wrote Roger Daltrey's "Giving It All Away" then made own top ten single "The Show Must Go On". In 1973 "Silverbird" and in 1974 "Just A Boy" were both chart successes.

Elmore James dies in 1963. Legendary blues singer-guitarist, and creator of the most distinctive riff in blues and rock, as used by Eric Clapton, George Harrison, and many other white rock guitarists.

Derek Quinn, lead guitarist with Freddie and The Dreamers, born in 1942. The biggest of their seven hits was "I'm Telling You Now" which was a US No. 1 in 1963.

Sarah Dash born in 1942. Originally with the Del Capris she joined schoolmate Patti Labelle to form The Blue Belles in 1962, and had a hit with "I Sold My Heart To The Junkman". In 1972 they became Labelle and had a million seller with "Lady Marmalade".

Steve Upton, drummer with Wishbone Ash, born in 1946. The group began in winter 1969 and by 1972 their third album "Argus" was No.3 in the UK album charts.

Mick Jagger and Marianne Faithfull charged with possession of marijuana in their Cheyne Walk, London home in 1968, and given £50 bail. Mick called his publicist, Les Perrin, "Les, the police are coming in through the windows!"
Queen Victoria born in 1819.

MAY 25

St. Urgan, Patron of Vineyards.

Miles Davis born in Alton, Illinois in 1926. Over the quarter of a century since his debut in 1945 he has brought about a number of radical changes in jazz, and since "Miles In The Sky" in 1967 has developed an interest in rock forms.

Duke Ellington dies in 1974. One of the greatest big band leaders, famous for his compositions, his band and his own work at the piano. Ella Fitzgerald sang on many of his recordings.

Brian Davison, drummer with The Nice, born in 1942. The group was formed as a backing group for P. P. Arnold, often upstaging her, and managed by Andrew Loog Oldham. Most of their albums reached the Top 10 in the UK and they broke up in 1970. Davison formed Refuge with bassist Lee Jackson.

Tom T. Hall born in Olive Hill, Kentucky in 1936. Apart from writing redneck war songs during Vietnam, he has produced a line of good country songs. Best known for "I Wash My Face In The Morning Dew".

Poli Palmer, who joined Family after Rick Grech had left for Blind Faith, born in 1943. The band was folded in a blaze of glory with a memorable farewell tour in 1973.

John Grimaldi born in 1955. Replaced Russ Ballard in Argent in 1974 and appears on the "Circus" and "Counterpoints" albums.

Kitty Kallen born in 1926. "Little Things Mean A Lot" was US No. 1 in 1954.

Sonny Boy Williamson II, blues singer and harmonica

player, dies in Helena, Arkansas, in 1965. His last record, "Don't Send Me No Flowers" was made in London with Brian Auger and Jimmy Page, just before he died.

Julie Driscoll and Brian Auger Trinity enter UK charts for the only time with "This Wheel's On Fire", one of the numbers on the famous Bob Dylan demo tapes which were later issued in 1975 as "The Basement Tapes".

Carole King's "Sunset Concert" in Central Park, New York City, in 1973 drew the largest crowd ever to gather there to hear music, variously estimated as being between 65,000 to 120,000 people. The MC was Mayor John Lindsay.

Provos appear in Amsterdam in 1965. Left-wing anarchist revolutionaries, they were dedicated to hard-line action for change. In turn, they created the "Kabouters".

MAY 26

Enlightenment of Buddha under the Bodhi Tree.

Verden "Phally" Allen born in 1944. With Mott The Hoople since their days as

Silence in the mid-Sixties, he left in early 1973, having played on their hit "All The Young Dudes".

Jackie Liebesit, drummer with the Experimental German rock group Can, born in 1938. They are best known for their movie soundtracks and avant garde albums though did reach the UK Top 20 in 1976 with "I Want More".

Little Willie John dies of pneumonia in 1968, in Walla Walla jail, Washington State Penitentiary, after serving three years of a sentence for manslaughter, for stabbing a man to death during a brawl in a Seattle.

Frankie Laine (Frank LoVecchio), and his partner Ruth Smith, set the all-time marathon dance record, lasting 3,501 hours (145 consecutive days) until October 18, 1932, in Atlantic City, New Jersey. They made $500 each. He later had 13 million-selling records, after being discovered by Hoagy Carmichael.

Ray Ennis, guitar and vocals for the Swinging Blue Jeans, born in 1942. "Hippy Hippy Shake" made UK No. 2 in 1964.

John and Yoko Lennon begin their "bed-in for peace" on the nineteenth floor of the Queen Elizabeth Hotel in Montreal, in 1969. They record "Give Peace a Chance" in their bedroom.

The Beatles play the Empire, Liverpool, in 1963.
John "The Duke" Wayne (Marion Morrison) born in 1908.
The Venerable Bede dies in 735.

MAY 27

Cilla Black (Priscilla Maria Veronica White) born in Liverpool, in 1943. One of Brian Epstein's stable, she soon had a hit with "Anyone Who Had A Heart" which made UK No. 1 in February, 1964. She followed it with "You're My World" three months later, which also reached No. 1. Moved to showbiz where she hosts her own TV shows.

Ramsey Lewis born in Chicago, in 1935. He began with his own jazz trio in 1956 and played on albums with Sonny Stitt and Max Roach. In 1965 his "The In Crowd" made US No. 5 and he followed it with "Hang On Sloopy" in 1965 and "Wade In The Water" in 1966, before the trio broke up.

The Crickets released their first record in 1957, with Buddy Holly as lead singer.

Alain Geismar, one of the leaders of the May 1968 revolution in Paris, found guilty of inciting a riot. His trial had been celebrated by guerilla raids including the burning of seventeen new cars at a Citroen factory and smearing the Ministry of Justice with paint. Jean Paul Sartre refused to testify. Geismar was given 18 months in jail.

Marty Kristian, of the New Seekers, born in Leipzig, Germany, in 1947. Of their many MOR hits the biggest was the Coca-Cola jingle "I Want To Teach The World To Sing" in 1972. They disbanded in 1974.

Isadora Duncan born in 1878. Free dance pioneer, movement "springing from the soul". She had many lovers, included sewing machine millionaire Paris Singer, but she died poor when her scarf caught in the wheel of a car in Nice. Her influence increases.

Henry Kissinger born in Germany, in 1923. "Fat Little Heinzi" may have cheated at school, but now he's trying to run the world single-handed. See Stanley Kubrick's film "Dr. Strangelove" for one version of the story.

Dashiell Hammett, originator of the hard-boiled detective story, born in 1894.
Arnold Bennett born in 1867. Gave his name to haddock quiche.

MAY 28

St. Augustine of Canterbury. First primate of England.
Public holiday in Jamaica.

Gladys Knight born in Atlanta, Georgia, in 1944. Together with The Pips she had her first US hit with "Every Beat Of My Heart". Another big one was her version of "I Heard It Through The Grapevine" in October 1967. Her only UK chart entries were "Take Me In Your Arms And Love Me" in 1967 and

"Help Me Make It Through The Night" in December 1972.

John Fogerty born in Berkeley, California in 1945. The main man behind Creedence Clearwater Revival until their break-up in 1972. He recorded solo

material at Fantasy's studios and as The Blue Ridge Rangers had a Top 20 single with "Jambalaya" in 1972. He has recorded solo ever since then.

Prince Buster born in Kingston, Jamaica, in 1939. He began his career as a boxer and DJ before "Wash Wash" and "I Feel The Spirit" brought him fame in 1962. "Al Capone" reached No. 18 in the UK charts in 1967. After over 200 singles he finally concentrated on production.

Ray Laidlaw, of Lindisfarne, born in 1948. They produced the best-selling British album in 1971-72, "Fog On The Tyne", produced by Nashville and Bob Dylan producer Bob Johnston. They never found acceptance in the USA and after a bad tour broke-up in 1975.

Carroll Baker born in 1932. Began as a night club dancer, then played child-wife in "Baby Doll" in 1956. Had a role in the infamous "happening" at the Edinburgh Festival in 1963, when a nude woman appeared in the audience at a concert hall.

MAY 29

Gary Brooker born in Hackney, London, in 1945. Originally with the Southend R & B group, The Paramounts, they had a minor hit with "Little Bitty Pretty One" before the group broke up in 1966. Brooker got together with lyricist Keith Reid and formed Procul Harum. Their first single (and only one with the original line-up) "A Whiter Shade Of Pale" was a world wide hit, reaching No. 1 in June 1967.

Irmin Schmidt, pianist with Can, born in 1937. This German rock group first entered the UK charts with "I Want More" in the summer of 1976, but are best known for their experimental sound tracks.

Mike Rossi, of Status Quo, born. "Pictures of Matchstick Men" was a 1968 hit.

Roger McGuinn gives his first solo performance after the breakup of the Byrds in 1973 at the New York Academy of Music.

Roy Crewsdon, guitarist with Freddie and The Dreamers, born in 1941. Among their seven big hits was "I'm Telling You Now" which made US No. 1 in 1963.

"Cathy's Clown" by The Everly Brothers reaches US No. 1 in 1960.

MAY 30

St. Joan of Arc burnt at Rouen in 1431.

Lenny Davidson, guitar with The Dave Clark Five, born in 1942. "Glad All Over" knocks The Beatles, "I Want To Hold Your Hand" from the UK No. 1 position (where it had been for five weeks), on January 18, 1964.

MAY 31

John Bonham, drummer with Led Zeppelin, born in Worcestershire, in 1948. Originally from the Birmingham group Band Of Joy. Led Zeppelin, known for their very long concerts of sometimes three or four hours, often include extended drum solos by Bonham.

Charles Miller, saxophone flute with War, born in 1939. In the Sixties they played as The Creators, Senor Soul, The Romeos and finally as The Night Shift before joining Eric Burdon as his backing group. They became War and then made it alone.

Peter Yarrow, of Peter Paul and Mary, born in New York City in 1938. Their first hit was "Lemon Tree" in April 1962, but under Al Grossman's management, they had world-wide success with Bob Dylan's "Blowin' In The Wind" in 1963 and went on to become the most popular of the early Sixties folk groups.

Augie Mayer born in 1940. Joined The Sir Douglas Quintet in San Antone, Texas, in 1964 and his

JOHN BONHAM/PHOTO: DICK BARNATT, SWANSONG

organ-playing is heavily featured on their first hit ''She's About A Mover'' which reached the Top 20 in 1965. The band folded in 1971.

Mick Ralphs, of Mott The Hoople, born in 1944. As Silence in the mid-Sixties in the West of England, they sent tapes to Island Records who signed them up and Ian Hunter joined. They disbanded, and re-formed in 1972 under David Bowie's direction, and Ralphs left in 1973 to join Bad Company.
Junior Campbell, lead guitar with Marmalade, born in 1947.
Sheb Wooley has US No. 1 hit in 1958 with ''Purple People Eater''.
The Doors play The Mexico City Bullring in 1969.
Walt Whitman, American poet, author of ''Leaves of Grass'', born in 1819. One of the first American bohemians, a big influence on the Beat Generation.

JUNE 1

Nirvana of the Buddhists. Buddha dies in 543 BC.

Marilyn Monroe (Norma Jean Baker) born in Los Angeles, in 1926. Great actress, star of ''Bus Stop'', ''Some Like It Hot'', ''The Misfits'' and supposed friend of both John and Robert Kennedy.
Ron Wood born in Hillingdon, Middlesex, in 1947. His two elder brothers

were musicians, and he learnt the clarinet and drums. He joined the English group The Birds, who made one album. In 1966 he went to the Jeff Beck group, and in 1969 to the remaining Small Faces to form The Faces with Rod Stewart. In April 1974 he recorded a solo album ''I've Got My Own Album To Do'' which featured Keith Richard. He stood in on the 1975 Rolling Stones' tour of America, and in December left The Faces, causing them to split. By 1976 he was a full member of The Stones.
Johnny Bond born in Enville, Oklahoma, in 1915. His hit, ''Hot Rod Lincoln'' of August 1960 was later recorded by Commander Cody and The Lost Planet Airmen in 1970.
Sonny Boy Williamson (John Lee Williamson) dies as a result of a brutal attack and robbery in Chicago in 1948. He was the

author of ''Good-Morning Little School Girl'' and cut his first records in Chicago in 1937, on the Blue Bird label.

Pat Boone (Charles Eugene Pat Boone) born in 1934. ''Ain't That A Shame'' was the first of many hits in June 1955.

Nelson Riddle born in 1921. The man behind the music behind Frank Sinatra.

''Sgt. Peppers Lonely Hearts Club Band'' released in the UK in 1967. It entered the charts the same day and stayed for forty-three weeks. The first concept album and the anthem of the ''hippie'' movement.
Robert Wyatt breaks his spine falling from a window during a party in 1973 and never walks again. Ex-member of The Soft

CHARLIE WATTS 1965 PASSPORT PHOTO / GERED MANKOWITZ

Michael Clarke, born in New York City, in 1944. He was the final person needed to complete the line-up of the original Byrds. Dave Crosby brought him in and he played drums with the group until he was replaced by Kevin Kelley at the time they added Gram Parsons and went honky in 1968.

Suzie Quatro born in Detroit, Michigan, in 1950. Her father was a band leader and her sister Patti is in the rock group Fanny. She came to England in the early Seventies and hit success under Mickie Most's management and production.

Machine, he has moved away from drumming to a greater use of his vocal ability. He released a single of the old Monkee's number ''I'm A Believer'', produced by Pink Floyd's Nick Mason, and a number of solo albums.
Simon and Garfunkel reach US No. 1 with ''Mrs. Robinson'', from the film ''The Graduate'', in 1967.

''Superman'' launched by Action Comics in 1938.
Rolling Stones, Tour of The Americas in 1975 starts with a concert in Baton Rouge.

JUNE 2

St. Elmo Erasmus, Patron of Sailors.

Charlie Watts born in Islington, London, in 1941. Jazz and Rhythm and Blues drummer with Alexis Korner's Blues Unlimited, he joined the Rolling Stones when Korner's band looked like becoming successful and making travel unavoidable.
Donatien Alphonse Francois Marquis de Sade born in 1740. Author of ''Justine'', ''Juliette'', ''120 Days of Sodom'', as well as a political radical.
Jimmy Jones born in 1937. ''Handy Man'' was his first US hit in 1960 but in the UK it was ''Good T1min' '' that made No. 1 in 1960.
William Guest, Pip of Gladys Knight and The Pips, born in 1941. ''I Heard It Through The Grapevine'' sold two million copies.
Sir Edward Elgar, English composer, born in 1857.

JUNE 3

Ian Hunter born in 1946. Joined Mott The Hoople after they were signed to Island Records and became center-point of the group with his blatant Dylan

stylings. In 1974 he and Mick Ronson both left the group to pursue solo careers. His ''Diary Of A Rock Star'' is an autobiographical account of their 1972 US tour. His solo album ''All-American Boy'' was well received.

Rolling Stones begin their first American tour in 1964. It continues until June 20

Bob Dylan graduates from Hibbing High School, Minnesota, in 1959.
Lord Kitchener drowned in 1916.

JUNE 6

Gary U S Bonds (Gary Anderson, changed to Gary Ulysses Samuel Bonds) born in 1939. He hit the US charts with "New Orleans" in October 1960. "Quarter To Three" was a May 1961 hit.

Allen Ginsberg, author of "Howl" and leading member of the Beat Generation, born in Paterson, New Jersey, in 1926.

John G. Peatman begins publishing his "Weekly Survey" in 1942, which lists records classified according to their radio airplay demand. The first charts.

Diana Ross loses her two pet dogs, when they are poisoned by rat bait left in her dressing room at the Latin Casino Nite-Club in Philadelphia in 1969. She was "emotionally upset".

Anita Harris born. "Just Loving You" was a 1967 UK hit.

Ed White is the first man to "walk" in space, during the Gemini 4 flight, in 1965.

JUNE 4

Gordon Waller, of Peter and Gordon, born in 1945. "World Without Love" and "Woman" were the biggest hits in the mid-Sixties. Has been the less active of the two since they split up.

Cliff Bennett born in 1940. He formed The Rebel Rousers in 1961. His early hits included cover-versions of "One Way Love" in 1964 and "Got To Get You Into My Life" in 1966. When "underground" rock came along he formed a progressive group called Toe Fat.

Murray Wilson, father of three of the Beach Boys, dies of heart attack in 1973.

He had a great deal to say about their careers and even took a hand in producing some records, although he knew little about music.

"Don't Bring Me Down" by The Animals, produced by Mickie Most, enters UK charts in 1966.

The Beatles play the Town Hall, Birmingham, in 1963 and leave for three days of concerts in Denmark in 1964.

JUNE 5

Bill Hayes born in 1926. In 1955 he sold a million copies of his No. 1 hit "The Ballad Of Davy Crockett", sparking off a craze for Davy Crockett hats.

Rolling Stones are first group to receive record royalties from the USSR when copyright laws are changed in 1975. Previously Russia had made no payment to any artist for work released or used in the country.

Edgar Froese born in West Berlin in 1944. Formed Tangerine Dream originally as a German Rolling Stones, but soon became the premier electronic rock band, finally making a number of albums in which all three members of the group played nothing but synthesizers. He began making solo albums in 1974 with "Aqua".

Peter Albin, bass and vocals with Big Brother and The Holding Company, born in 1944.

Bill Haley's "Rock Around The Clock" reaches US No. 1 and stays for eight weeks, in 1955.

ALLEN GINSBERG / PHOTO: PEARCE MARCHBANK.

Larry "The Mole" Taylor, of Canned Heat, born in Brooklyn, New York, in 1942. He played bass with Jerry Lee Lewis before joining Canned Heat's early line-up.

Beatles begin their first recordings for EMI, at Abbey Road studios in 1962.

Tony Williams left The Platters to go solo in 1960.

Alex Saunders, English hereditary witch, born in 1926. With his wife Maxine he recorded an album of an actual initiation ceremony in 1970, in one take of fifty minutes. The couple, influencing groups such as Black Sabbath, were given much media exposure in the early Seventies.

D Day, 1944, allied invasion of Normandy beaches.

JUNE 7

The Prophet Mohammed, founder of Islam.

Clarence White, guitarist and vocalist with The Byrds, born in Lewiston, Maine, in 1944. Died after being hit by a car in Lancaster, California in 1973.

Tom Jones born in 1940, in Pontypridd. "It's Not Unusual" was UK No. 1 in 1965. Quickly left any rock content behind for the bright lights of Las Vegas.

THE BEATLES START RECORDING AT ABBEY ROAD / PHOTO: CAMERA PRESS.

Roy Orbison's first wife, Claudette, killed when her motorcycle was in a head-on collision in 1966, which he witnessed.

Gordy Garris, of Frost, psychedelic rock group, born in Detroit, Michigan, in 1949.

Teddy Reddell (Reidel) born in Quitman, Arkansas, in 1937. His biggest hit, "Judy" was covered by Elvis Presley in 1960.

Blind Faith give free concert in Hyde Park, London, to 150,000, including Mick Jagger, Donovan and Richie Havens, in 1969.

The Who perform "Tommy" at the Metropolitan Opera House, Lincoln Center, New York City in 1970. Billed as the opera's last performance, but not so.

Bob Dylan/Johnny Cash TV special, shown on ABC network in US, in 1969.

Rolling Stones make their first TV appearance on "Thank Your Lucky Stars" in 1963.

The Beatles single, "Ballad Of John And Yoko" enters UK charts in 1969. This was their seventeenth UK No. 1.

NATHAN M. WEISS & NEW ACTION LTD.
IN ASSOCIATION WITH
BILL GRAHAM
AND THE
FILLMORE EAST ORGANIZATION
PRESENT

THE
WHO
IN THE FINAL PERFORMANCE
OF THEIR ROCK-OPERA

"TOMMY"

METROPOLITAN OPERA HOUSE
LINCOLN CENTER

SUNDAY, JUNE 7, 1970

BLIND FAITH FREE CONCERT, LONDON 1969.

JUNE 8

St. Callipoa. Identified with Calliope, Muse of Epic.
Mohammed died in 632.

Boz Scaggs born in 1944. His first album was ''Boz'' in 1966 then joined the Steve Miller Band during their best period, appearing on ''Children Of The

Future'' and ''Sailor'' in 1968..Duane Allman played on his solo album ''Boz Scaggs'' in 1968.

Julie Driscoll (''Jools'') born in 1947, in London. She was producer Giorgio Gomelsky's secretary, also the secretary of The Yardbirds fanclub. Gomelsky recorded her on his label Marmalade and she, with the Brian Auger Trinity had a hit with the Bob Dylan song ''Wheels

On Fire'' in 1968. In 1970 married Keith Tippett and now records as Julie Tippett.

Nancy Sinatra born in Jersey City, New Jersey, in 1940. In 1966 Lee Hazelwood produced her biggest hit ''Boots'', a Country and Western classic.

Chuck Negron, vocalist of Three Dog Night, born in Brooklyn, New York. First album was named after the band and released in 1968.

Laverne Andrews, of The Andrews Sisters, dies of cancer in 1967. The remaining sisters made a comeback in the early Seventies following the revival of their style by Bette Midler and others.

BRIAN JONES / PHOTO: GERED MANKOWITZ

Brian Jones leaves the Rolling Stones in 1969. He is replaced by Mick Taylor who stays five years with the band. Mick Jagger stated that Jones was leaving on grounds of ''musical incompatibility''.

Oz ''School Kids Issue'' published in London in 1969. This issue of the full-color underground magazine resulted in the three editors being tried at the Old Bailey for attempting to deprave and corrupt.

JUNE 9

Mick Box, guitarist with Uriah Heep, born in London in 1947. Originally in The Stalkers, joined and made his first album with Heep in 1970 ''Very 'eavy, Very 'umble''. It was a success in in Germany. The US. Top group in France.

Jimmy Rushing dies after a short illness in 1972. Vocalist with many of the big bands, including Count Basie. He was sixty-eight.

Bob Dylan recorded an hour long show for the BBC in London, in 1965. It was broadcast in two half-hour shows on June 12th and 24th.

Les Paul (Lester Polfus) born in 1923. Together with Mary Ford he had a hit with ''How High The Moon'' in March 1951. He is best known for developing the electric guitar (The Gibson Les Paul) and for his pioneer work in overdubbing techniques with his prototype Ampex recorder.

JULIE TIPPETT (JULIE DRISCOLL) / PHOTO: G. STEWART

Mitch Mitchell (John Mitchell) born in Ealing, London, in 1947. Drummer with The Jimi Hendrix Experience, later mainly session work. Worked with The Jack Bruce Band and with Ramatan.

Jackie Wilson born in 1934. His first big hit was with his fourth US chart entry "Lonely Teardrops" in 1958. Over forty chart entries to the present.

Johnny Ace (Johnny Marshall Alexander Jr.) born in Memphis Tennessee, in 1929. "Pledging My Love" was released in January 1955.
Billy Hatton, bass player with The Fourmost, born in 1941. Originally called The Four Jays, then The Four Mosts until Brian Epstein changed their name. "A Little Lovin'" made UK No. 6 in 1964.
Elvis Presley did his first New York City show in 1972. Interviews were offered at $120,000 but there were no takers.

Bob Dylan given honorary degree at Princeton University, in 1970. He was reported to be "very nervous and hesitant, and seemed appropriately out of place".
The Beatles have "Welcome Home" night at the Cavern Club in Liverpool, after returning from the Star Club, Hamburg in 1962. And in 1963 end their second British tour at the King George Hall in Blackburn, Lancashire.
The San Francisco Free Clinic set up in 1967 by Dr. David Smith. Dealing with drug problems the Clinic immediately faced its first crisis : the new trip STP.
Drug Smuggling, In 1971 police arraigned a West German couple on charges of attempting to smuggle cocaine with a street value of $1.4 million, through Kennedy Airport in the crib of their three-year-old baby.
Ossie Clark and Alice Pollock, dress-makers to Swinging London, both born in 1942.

"The Rise And Fall Of Ziggy Stardust" album by David Bowie released in the UK in 1972. This marked the crest of Bowie's first wave of success.

JUNE 10

Howlin' Wolf (Chester Burnett) born near Aberdeen, Mississippi, in 1910. Basically a farmer, he moved to Memphis in 1948 and formed a band which gained a regular radio spot. He was introduced to Sun Records by Ike Turner in 1951 and made a number of classic, loose Blues records featuring his powerful vocal and harmonica work. In 1952 he moved on to Chicago and took up the electric guitar. He is responsible for writing many Blues classics and was one of the heroes of the Blues Revival of the Sixties. In 1972 he recorded an album in London with Eric Clapton, Steve Winwood and members of the Rolling Stones. He died in 1976.

Shirley Alston (Owens), lead vocalist of The Shirelles, born in 1941. Their big hit was with Carole King's "Will You Love Me Tomorrow" in January 1961.
Rick Price, bass player with The Move, born in Birmingham, in 1944.
Jethro Tull and audience tear-gassed by Denver police at a concert in 1971. Twenty-eight people were hospitalized.
Procul Harum reached UK No. 1 with "A Whiter Shade Of Pale" and stayed six weeks in 1967. They had appeared in public three times.

"Rain" by The Beatles released in 1966 (flip side of "Paperback Writer"). First record to use reverse tapes. "I just happened to have the tape on the wrong way 'round, it just came out backwards, it just blew my mind. The voice sounds like an old Indian."—John Lennon.
CIA. The report on President Ford's commission on the Central Intelligence Agency was published in 1975. It referred to some of the agency's activities as "plainly unlawful".

JUNE 11

Joey Dee (Joe Dinicola), lead with Joey Dee and The Starlighters, born in 1940. A major "Twist" group in 1961-2 with "Peppermint Twist" and "Shout".

"Space Oddity" by David Bowie, released in the UK in 1969. Re-released in 1975 and made No. 1.

Roger Daltrey announced as dead by Dutch, French and German radio stations in 1966. Somehow they had mixed up a news story of Pete Townshend's car crash on the M1 motorway on May 30th.

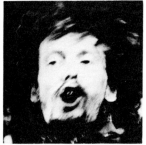

Ginger Baker's Airforce tour of the US in 1970, canceled because of the "political situation in America" eight days before first concert. Only three thousand tickets had been sold.

Brian Jones committed for trial at the Inner London Sessions, on a drugs charge in 1968.

Richard Strauss, whose compositions include "Also Sprach Zarathustra," used in Stanley Kubrick's "2001", born.

Bartolomeo Vanzetti born in 1888. "I am suffering because I am a radical".

JUNE 12

St. Onuphrius Hemphrey. Egyptian Saint identified with Onuphis. "The Good Being", Chief Title of Osiris.

Archie Bleyer born in 1949. He started the Cadence Label and had hits with his own records "Hernando's Hideaway" and "The Naughty Lady Of Shady, Lane" both in 1954.

Reg Presley, of The Troggs, born in Andover, in 1943. Originally despised by trendy London for being bumpkins, they achieved great status when Jimi Hendrix recorded their "Wild Thing".

Charlie Feathers (Charles Arthur Feathers) born in Hollow Springs, Mississippi in 1932. He recorded under the names of Jess Hooper and Charles Morgan, as well as his own.

Len Barry, lead with The Dovells, born in Philadelphia, in 1942. "Bristol Stomp" made US No. 2 in September 1961. When he went solo in 1963 he had a hit with "1-2-3-".

Medgar Evers murdered in 1963 by white Tennessee segregationists. Bob Dylan immortalized the event in his early ballad "Only A Pawn In Their Game". Ironically his brother, Charles Evers became the first black mayor of a southern city, Memphis.

The Beatles awarded the MBE (Member of the Order of the British Empire) in 1965. John later sends his back. "My only regret about it was in ever taking it. It was a sell-out. We would never have got it anyway if the Palace had read what I thought about royalty. Lots of people who complained about us receiving the MBE received

theirs for heroism in the war —for killing people. We received ours for entertaining other people. I'd say we deserve ours more. Wouldn't you?"— John Lennon.

Roy Harper born in 1941. Underground freaky-folk singer. Made first album "The Sophisticated Beggar" in 1966.

Jimmy Dorsey, bandleader with his brother Tommy, dies in 1957.

JUNE 13

Dennis Locorriere, vocalist and guitarist with Dr. Hook and The Medicine Show, born in New Jersey in 1949.

Bobby Freeman born in 1940. "Do You Want To Dance" was a US hit in April 1958.

Esther Ofarim born. With husband Abi, she had a hit with "Cinderella Rockafella" in the UK, reaching No. 1 in 1968.

Clyde McPhatter, ex of The Drifters, dies of a heart attack in Teaneck, New Jersey, in 1972. He also sang with Billie Ward and The Dominoes on songs such as "Have Mercy Baby".

Frank Zappa graduates from Antelope Valley High School, Lancaster, California, in 1958. One of his school chums was Don Van Vliet, whom Zappa later named ''Captain Beefheart''.

The Beatles ''Long And Winding Road'' reaches US No. 1. McCartney disassociated himself from it as Spector, at Allen Klein's request, added a background chorus of women's voices. ''I would never use a women's choir on a Beatles record'' said McCartney. Spector also added the strings.
Rolling Stones play a concert in San Diego in 1972. Sixty people arrested and fifteen injured in riots.
Grape catching. In 1971, Dr. Bruce Dobbs establishes the world record distance of one hundred and sixty-five feet for catching a thrown grape in the mouth.
William Butler Yeats, Irish poet, dramatist and magician, born in 1865.

JUNE 14
Amaterasu, Japanese Sun Goddess. Rice Festival.
Ernesto ''Che'' Guevara de la Serna born in Rosario, Argentina, in 1928. After playing a major role in the Cuban Revolution, was shot by the CIA in Bolivia.

Muff Winwood (Mervyn Winwood), brother of Stevie, born in Birmingham, in 1943. He was in the Spencer Davis Group, and went on to produce Patto and Kevin Ayres.

Julie Felix born. American folk singer who arrived in the UK in time to be the resident Joan Baez. Did a lot of TV work, had big selling albums and cut some weird underground records such as ''Get Ahead Get A Hole'' and ''Brain Blood Volume'', after being around the followers of self-trepanned Bart Hughes.
Burl Ives (Burl Icle Ivanhoe Ives) born in 1909. ''Little Bitty Tear'' was his biggest chart success in 1961, though ''Ugly Bug Ball'' has always been a big UK favorite.

Rodney Argent born in 1945. Originally one of The Zombies, he formed Argent in 1970. ''Hold Your Head Up'' was released as a single in 1972 in the UK.

Jim Lea, bass guitar and song writer with Slade, born in a public house in Wolverhampton, in 1952. Managed by Chas Chandler, Slade survived their teenybopper days of the early Seventies.
Gary Glitter, under the name of Paul Munday, releases ''Musical Man'' in 1968. In 1960 he had entered the music business as Paul Raven. His real name is Paul Gadd.
Biggest Soul Music Festival ever, held in the Houston Astrodome, Texas, in 1969.
Rolling Stones announce formation of their own record company in 1969. Proposed name is ''Pear'' say ''Rolling Stone'' Magazine. And play Tucson, Arizona, in 1972, when police use tear-gas to disperse would-be gate crashers.

JUNE 15
St. Vitus, Patron of Dancers.
Waylon Jennings born in Littlefield, Texas in 1947. A member of the loose ''Nashville underground'', he toured with the Grateful Dead and made many fine country albums.
Harry Nilsson born in Brooklyn, in 1941. He has never appeared in public. The Ronettes did one of his songs, but was first ''discovered'' after his clever collage of Beatles' songs ''You Can't Do That'' on his first album, which caused John Lennon to

Leopold Bloom and Stephen Dedalus on this one day in 1904, in Dublin. It was on this day in Joyce's own life that he first expounded his theory that Shakespeare was Hamlet's father.

Apollo II takes off at 9.32 am in 1969. One hundred and two hours later Neil Armstrong was walking on the moon.

JUNE 17

Orpheus, Demi-God, founder of classical culture.
King Solomon according to the Ethiopian Calendar, Patron of Magic.

sponsor him and, later, produce one of his albums, "Pussy Cats". "Everybody's Talking" was a 1969 hit. Derek Taylor produced his album "A Little Schmilsson In The Night", a montage of pre-War ballads.

Noddy Holder (Neville John Holder), vocals and guitarist with Slade, born in Walsall, Staffs., in 1950. Originally Ambrose Slade, then presenting a skinhead front, Slade became big business in 1973 with a series of UK No. 1 hits.

John Lennon meets Paul McCartney at a church fete in Woolton, Liverpool, in 1955. They were introduced by Ivan Vaughan, who later became known for his "psychedelic" posters and who was at school with Paul. John's group The Quarrymen were playing at the fete and Paul sat in with them on stage. "I was a fat schoolboy and, as he leaned an arm on my shoulder, I realized that he was drunk. We were twelve then, but, in spite of his sideboards, we went on to become teenage pals."— Paul McCartney.

Allen Ginsberg, Laurence Ferlinghetti, Gregory Corso and Andrei Voznesensky gave a joint poetry reading at the Architectural Association in London in 1965. The reading was recorded and released as a limited edition album.

JUNE 16

Lamont Dozier born in Detroit in 1941. Raised by musical parents and a member of his church choir. First recorded at 15, but success came only with the growth of the Motown

Corporation, as a songwriter. He met Brian Holland in 1961 and formed the famous songwriting team, later joined by Brian's brother Eddie. They wrote and produced a profusion of hits for Tamla, recorded by Marvin Gaye, Supremes, Temptations, Four Tops and many, many others. In 1968 Brian and Lamont left Tamla Motown to form their own company, and later returned to singing themselves.

John Rostill, bass player with The Shadows, born in 1942. Apart from being Cliff Richard's backing group, they had a series of early Sixties instrumental hits, such as "Apache" and "FBI". The group was an early influence on Neil Young.

Lonnie Johnson found dead in his Toronto apartment in 1970, aged eighty-one. He played with everyone from The Louis Armstrong Hot Five ("I'm Not Rough" was recorded on December 10th, 1927), to the "Three Kings And The Queen" sessions for Spivey Records, New York City, in September, 1961, when Bob Dylan played with Victoria Spivey. The blues-singer Johnson was one of the "Kings" on these two albums.

Rolling Stones fly back in the middle of their 1964 American tour to play at Magdalen College, Oxford, a gig arranged for £100. Their airfares cost them £1,500 alone. They played The Usher Hall, Edinburgh in 1965 on this date.

Suzie Quatro's "Can The Can" reaches UK No. 1 in 1973. A Chinn and Chapman product for Mickie Most.

"Bloomsday" "Ulysses", James Joyce's masterpiece concerns the activities of

Chris Spedding born in Sheffield, England in 1944. The all-round British session guitarist, he played on an endless list of albums. His own group Sharks was formed in 1972, but was always in trouble. In 1975 he toured with John Cale and began releasing singles. He had a small hit with "Motorbiking" the same year.

M. C. Escher born in 1898. His extraordinary drawings have been used as album covers and in rock publicity. First noticed in the music world by Graham Nash who, when in Amsterdam on a Hollies tour, looked him up in the telephone book and went to see him.

Norman Kuhlke, drummer with The Swinging Blue Jeans, born in Liverpool, in 1942. "Hippy Hippy Shake" was their first big hit.

Dickey Doo born in 1939. "Click-Clack" was the first big hit for Dickey Doo (real name) and The Don'ts, in January, 1958.

"Paper Sun" by Traffic takes them into UK charts for the first time, in 1967.

The Watergate Break-in occurred in 1972. The Democratic Party Election Headquarters were broken into by James McCord and others, which led to the downfall of the President and all his men.

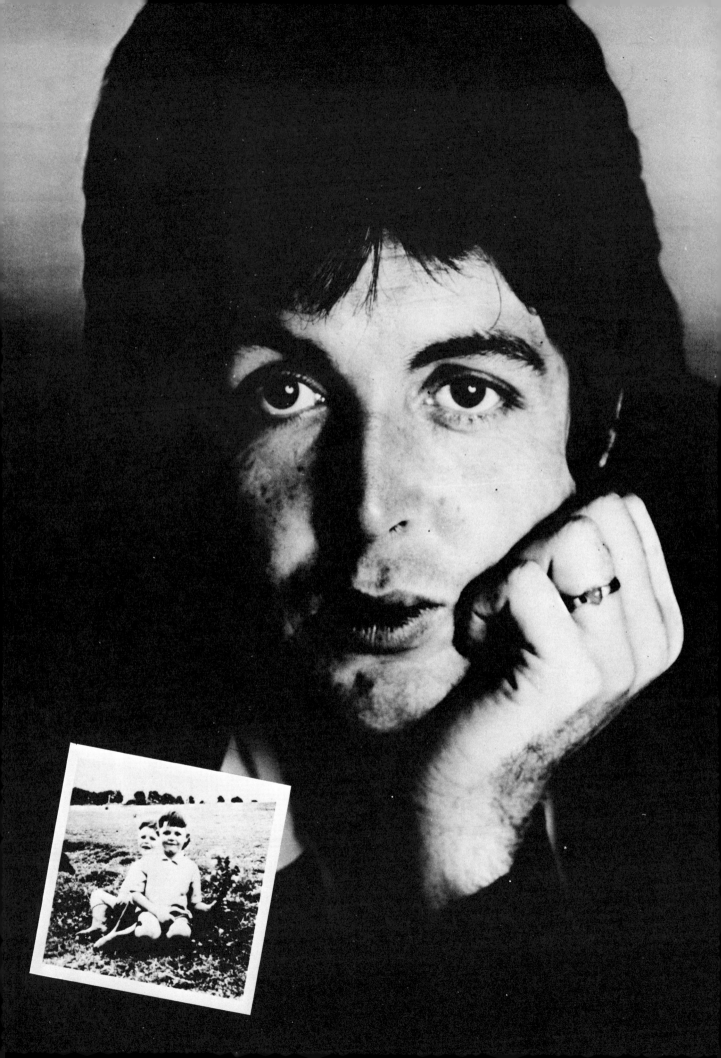

JUNE 18

James Paul McCartney born in Allerton, Liverpool, in 1942. "From a very early age I was interested in singing tunes. I like a nice tune. You know, "White Christmas", "Over The Rainbow", the old stuff . . . my Dad gave me a trumpet for my birthday. But my mouth used to get too sore. I suddenly realized that I

wouldn't be able to sing if I played trumpet so I figured guitar would be better."
"River Deep And Mountain High" by Ike and Tina Turner, enters the UK charts 1966 to reach No. 3. Phil Spector "retires" from the US record business in protest at its flopping in States.
The Beatles "Paperback Writer" enters the UK charts to reach No. 1 in 1966.
TV. Nature "magazine" published a remarkable letter in 1908, outlining the basis of the cathode ray tube and of television itself.
The Battle of Waterloo takes place near Brussels in 1815.

JUNE 19

St. Gervase and St. Protase. Giants.
Tommy de Vito, of The Four Seasons, born in 1935. First entered US charts in 1962 with "Sherry" which made No. 1, the first of many.
Charlie Drake born in London, in 1925. His cover version of Bobby Darin's original "Splish Splash" entered the UK charts in August 1958. He went onto other similar comedy records, and later appeared as a TV star.
Al Wilson born in Meridian, Mississippi, in 1939. Joined The Jewels in 1958, who later became The Rollers and had a hit with "Continental Walk".
Carole King reached US No. 1 with "It's Too Late" in 1971.
Mutiny On The Battleship Potemkin in 1905. Eisenstein's film was based on the event.

Monterey Pop Festival in 1967, stars Jimi Hendrix Experience, Janis Joplin, The Who, Moby Grape, Otis Redding, Mamas And The Papas and The Grateful Dead. Brian Jones was among the crowd.

JUNE 20

Brian Wilson born in Hawthorne, California, in 1942. Carl Wilson: "Brian was always more into music as a vibration, right? More than lyrics or anything words could ever say. It's really true—music, a really heavy vibration, says a lot more than a million words could in eternity say. As far as really holy sounds go."
Anne Murray born in Spring Hill, Nova Scotia, Canada, in 1946. One of the few Canadian singers to remain in Canada, she has had considerable success with country hits such as "Talk It Over In The Morning", "He Thinks I Still Care" and "Danny's Song".
Alan Longmuir, bass player with The Bay City Rollers, born in Edinburgh in 1953.
Jerry Keller born in 1937, in Fort Smith, Arkansas. He wrote and recorded "Here Comes Summer" in 1959 with great success.
Billy Guy, first tenor with The Coasters, born in 1936. "Searchin'" in 1957 was their second US chart entry, their first Top 20 hit.
Nigel Morris, of the experimental rock group Isotope, born in Dalston, London, in 1948.
Newport Festival at Devonshire Downs in 1969, in the north San Fernando Valley, featured Jimi Hendrix Experience, Joe Cocker, Albert King, The Edwin Hawkins Singers, Ike and Tina Turner, Spirit and Taj Mahal.
The Beatles begin their 1965 European tour in Paris.
Errol Flynn born in 1949. Maintained a world-wide film following for twenty years, but hard living got the better of him.
Neil Armstrong and Buzz Aldrin walk on the moon during the Apollo II mission in 1969. Nixon phones them up.

RAY DAVIES (LEFT) & THE KINKS

Nazz between 1968 and 1970. He then became engineer and producer for Albert Grossman's Bearsville label. He worked on many albums including those by The Band, Jesse Winchester and Paul Butterfield. He formed the trio Runt, making two albums and a Top Twenty single. Going solo he made a number of albums including the well reviewed ''Todd'' in 1974

JUNE 21

The Summer Solstice. Sun enters Cancer, ruled by the Moon, but associated with Mercury by the Romans.
Greek New Year's Day.
Druidic Festival of the Golden Dawn.
Midnight sun festival in Alaska.

Ray Davies born in London, in 1944. The Kinks were formed in 1964. First reaching No. 1 in the UK with ''You Really Got Me'' in August 1964. Ray Davies writes all their material as well as being lead vocalist. The group has become more serious, in that they have done a number of thematic and concept albums on the rock business and around the theme of English life.
Chris Britton, of The Troggs, born in Watford, in 1945. The group is generally thought of as coming from the depths of the country. Britton is obviously an exception.
Jon Hiseman born in Blackheath, London in 1944. Formed jazz-rock group Colosseum in 1968 with Dick Heckstall-Smith. They made three studio albums and one live before breaking up in 1971. A year later he formed Colosseum II.
O. C. Smith born in Mansfield, Louisiana, in 1936. In 1961 was vocalist with The Count Basie Band. In 1968 his solo single ''Son Of Hickory Holler's Tramp'' was a transatlantic hit.
Brenda Holloway born in Atascadero, California, in 1946. Her ''Every Little Bit Hurts'' reached No. 13 in

the US in 1964, becoming Motown's first West Coast-produced hit.
Terry Dene entered UK charts in 1957 with ''White Sports Coat''. He finally left show business, after throwing a ''keep left'' sign through a window while wandering down a Gloucester street in the middle of the night, in his underpants. After his following breakdown he found Jesus and devotes himself to religious work.
Humble Harve Miller, the Los Angeles DJ, who more or less invented the high-speed AM radio delivery style, charged with murdering his wife in 1971.
Newport Festival at Devonshire Downs, in 1969, featured Creedence Clearwater Revival, Steppenwolf, Buffy St. Marie, Albert Collins, Love, Eric Burdon, Jethro Tull, Sweetwater and Lee Michaels.

Jean Paul Sartre born 1915, in Paris. Famous existential philosopher, radical and author, and life-long

companion of Simone de Beauvoir.
Mary McCarthy born in 1912. ''The Group'' is her most famous book, well-known for her opposition to the Viet Nam war.
The Charlatans play their first gig at the Red Dog Saloon, Virginia City, Nevada, in 1965.

JUNE 22

St. Alban, first English martyr. Patron of the Church of England.
Todd Rundgren born in Pennsylvania in 1948. His first recordings were with

Kris Kristofferson born in Brownsville, Texas, in 1936. Wrote ''Me And Bobby McGhee''. First album ''The Silver Tongued Devil And I'' released in 1971. Married Rita Coolridge in 1973, starred with her in the ''Pat Garrett And Billy The Kid'' movie which also featured Bob Dylan. Now a movie star.

KRIS KRISTOFFERSON / PHOTO: S.K.R.

PAUL McCARTNEY & PETER ASHER IN 1965

recording sessions with Pete Drake and Charley McCoy, the top Nashville session men (who played on Bob Dylan's "John Wesley Harding" and "Nashville Skyline").

Ray Charles' "I Can't Stop Loving You" enters UK charts in 1962.

10cc single "Rubber Bullets" reaches UK No. 1 in 1973.

John Entwistle marries Alison Wise in 1967. He told the London "Daily Express", "I always suspected we would marry one day. I was already playing in an amateur group and on our first date Alison carried my amplifier".

JUNE 24

Jeff Beck born in Surrey, in 1944. Replaced Eric Clapton as lead guitarist with The Yardbirds for two years. In 1967 formed The Jeff Beck group with Rod Stewart as vocalist. In 1969 formed Beck, Bogert and Appice, but after a car crash was out of action for eighteen months. Their album was released in 1973. They disbanded in 1973 and Beck made a solo album produced by George Martin.

Peter Asher born in London, in 1944. Originally one-half of Peter and Gordon, he had such hits as "World Without Love" (1964) and "True Love Ways" (1965), the former of which was written specially for them by Paul McCartney, who was living in the Asher household at the time. (Sister Jane still lived at home as well). Peter went on to become A & R man at Apple, and to produce and manage James Taylor. With his own management company in Los Angeles, he produced best-selling Linda Ronstadt albums in 1975, "Heart Like A Wheel" and "Prisoner In Disguise".

Howard Kaylan born in New York City, in 1945. One time leader of The Turtles, he and Mark Volman became The Fluorescent Leech and Eddie playing with The Mothers Of Invention and also making solo albums. They also appear on Marc Bolan's "Bang A Gong".

Alan Osmond born in 1949. One of the six brothers and one sister Mormon teenybopper act, whose popularity finally began to decline in 1975.

Gerry and The Pacemakers' "I Like It" reaches UK No. 1 in 1963.
Judy Garland dies in 1969.

JUNE 23

Adam Faith (Terence Nelhams) born in Acton, London, in 1940. "What Do You Want" and "Poor Me" opened his career with a pair of UK No. 1 hits in November 1959 and January 1960. Went on to become a TV actor, manage Leo Sayer and record Roger Daltrey.

June Carter born in 1929. A country singer of great renown in her own right, she teamed up with Johnny Cash and married him. A member of the famous Carter family of country singers.

Ringo Starr arrives in Nashville in 1970, to start

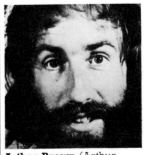

Arthur Brown (Arthur Wilton Brown) born in Whitby, Yorkshire, in 1944. His group, The Crazy World Of Arthur Brown, typified the underground scene in

London in the late Sixties. "Fire" was a 1967 hit, but he was unable to follow it up.

Colin Blunstone born in 1945. Originally with The Zombies as vocalist, he went solo when the band broke up. He made some singles and formed a group with his own name in the Seventies. He had a hit in 1972 with "Say You Don't Mind", written by Denny Laine of Wings.
Charlie Whitney, guitarist with Family, born in Skipton, Yorkshire, in 1944. Family formed in Leicester in 1966, when Roaring Sixties and The Farinas merged. Jenny Fabian wrote "Groupie" largely featuring their lifestyle. Broke up in October 1973.

Chris Wood, of Traffic, born in 1944. Played saxophones and flute. He has survived the various traumas associated with the band which remains one of the standard touring bands of Britain for good rock music.

John Lennon's second book "A Spaniard In The Works" published in 1965.

CARLY SIMON / PHOTO: NORMAN SEEFF.

JUNE 25

St. Pontius Pilate. Coptic Christians regard Pilate as a Christian martyr, as do the Ethiopian Christians.

Carly Simon born in 1945. Daughter of Richard L. Simon of Simon Schuster, the New York publishers. Originally a Greenwich Village folkie, "You're So Vain", which she sang with Mick Jagger, placed her in the pop star bracket. Now married to James Taylor. Live appearances are rare, but albums featuring superstar sessionmen are not.
Eddy Floyd born in Montgomery, Alabama, in 1935. "Knock On Wood" was a 1967 hit. Originally with the Falcons.
Clint Warwick, bass player with The Moody Blues, born in Birmingham, England, in 1949. Ever since their UK No.1 "Go Now" the group enjoyed success. A series of six gold albums enabled them to start their own label, Threshold.
The Beatles in 1967 play "All You Need Is Love" on the "Our World" International "live" television link-up. The recording was mixed and released as a live recording on July 7th. Present in the studio for the TV show were many friends of The Beatles, the backing orchestra and members of the Rolling Stones, The Who and other groups. A good time was had by all.
Drugola. US Senator James Buckley asks for an inquiry in 1973, into organized crime in the music business. Following allegations of payola and "drugola" and the firing of Columbia Records president Clive Davis, in May of that year.
George Orwell (Eric Blair) born in Motihari, Bengal, India, in 1903. Author.
The Battle of Little Big Horn in 1876.

JUNE 26

African Freedom Day.

Georgie Fame (Clive Powell) born in Leigh, Lancashire, in 1943. "Yeh Yeh" was a UK No. 1 in January 1965. He still fills clubs with his jazz/rock sound.
Richard McCracken born in 1948. Bass player of

Rory Gallagher's Taste, formed in 1968.

Sonny and Cher Bono's divorce finalized at the Santa Monica Superior Court, in 1975. She married Greg Allman, of the Allman Brothers, four days later.

Byrds reach US No. 1 with ''Mr. Tambourine Man'' in 1965, taking Dylan's lyrics into the realm of rock.

Johnny Kidd and The Pirates ''Shakin' All Over'' enters UK charts in 1960.

Rolling Stones' ''It's All Over Now'' by Bobby Womack, released in 1964.

First cinema opened in 1896, in New Orleans, by William T. Rock. Called the Vitascope Hall, it had seating for 400 people.

JUNE 27

Bruce Johnson, of The Beach Boys, born in Chicago, in 1944. When Brian Wilson stopped touring with the group his place was taken by Johnson, another relative of the Wilson brothers, who had overdubbed some vocal tracks on earlier Beach Boys numbers. He left the group in 1970.

Peter and Gordon's ''World Without Love'' reaches US No. 1 in 1964. Written by Paul McCartney on the back of a shirt packet and listed on the record under a false name, to see if a McCartney tune would make the charts even if no one knew it was his.

Denver Pop Festival, 1969, at the Mile High Stadium, featured Jimi Hendrix, Johnny Winter, Creedence Clearwater, Crosby Stills and Nash, Joe Cocker and others.

International Workers of the World, ''The Wobblies'' founded in 1917 in America. A left-wing unionizing alliance, The Wobblies fought many bitter, murderous battles with the Bosses and their hirelings.

Joe Hill, the most famous Wobbly, was executed on trumped-up charges.

BILL GRAHAM AT THE FILLMORE EAST

Fillmore East and **Fillmore West** closed down in 1971.

JUNE 28

Bobby Harrison, drummer with Procul Harum, born in East Ham, London, in 1943 and . . .

Dave Knights, bass player with Procul Harum, born in Islington, London, in 1945. ''White Shade Of Pale'' became a classic after its 1967 success, premiered at London's UFO club. He left before the first album.

Richard Nader's British Re-Invasion Show at Madison Square Gardens, in 1973, featured Herman's Hermits, Gerry and The Pacemakers, Billy J. Kramer, Wayne Fontana and The Mindbenders and The Searchers to a packed house, and later toured eighteen US cities.

''Break Away'' by The Beach Boys, enters UK charts in 1969 to reach No. 6.

Henry VIII born in 1491.

JUNE 29

Little Eva (Eva Narcissus Boyd) born in Belhaven, North Carolina, in 1945. Originally Carole King and Gerry Goffin's baby sitter, she had a US No. 1 in July 1962 (and a UK No. 2) with ''Locomotion'' which they wrote, produced, arranged, conducted the orchestra .

Ian Paice, drummer with Deep Purple, born in Nottingham. Formed in February 1968, they played a mixture of classical and rock music. Their first album was ''Shades Of Deep Purple'' in 1968.

Tim Buckley dies in Santa Monica, California, in 1975. Officially of a heroin overdose. The folk singer was negotiating for the title role in the film about Woody Guthrie, ''Bound For Glory'' at the time of his death.

Shorty Long drowns when his boat capsizes in Sandwich Island, Ontario, in 1969. His first US chart entry was ''Function At The Junction'' which reached No. 97, but in June 1968 ''Here Comes The Judge'' reached No. 8.

Jayne Mansfield decapitated in car crash, in 1967. Her first film was the Rock and Roll classic ''Girl Can't Help It''.

Mick Jagger and Keith Richard both found guilty at West Sussex Quarter Sessions on drugs charges in 1967. Mick sentenced to three months in jail and sent to Brixton Prison; Keith sentenced to one year in jail and sent to Wormwood Scrubs. Shocked fans demonstrate in front of the ''News Of The World'' newspaper offices which they thought had set up the Stones bust.

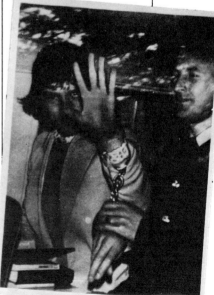

Johnny Richardson, of Johnny and Joe, born in 1945. "Over The Mountains Across The Sea" was a 1957 hit in the US.

Dervin Gordon and Lincoln Gordon, vocals and guitar respectively, with The Equals, born twins in 1948. "Baby Come Back" was No. 1 in the UK in 1968.

Gay Liberation Front founded in 1969, when police raiding the Stonewall, a notorious gay bar in Sheridan Square, Greenwich Village, met with physical opposition from the patrons.

Longest Sausage. Constructed in 1966 by a team of butchers from Humberside, England. The monstrous frankfurter was 3,124 feet long.

First musical recording in Great Britain, made in 1888 at the Crystal Palace, on the occasion of the Handel Festival, using Edison equipment.

JUNE 30

Guru Padma-Sambhava, founder of Tantric Buddhism in Tibet. Sariputra, a Disciple of Buddha. St. Lucina. Identified with the Classical Goddess of Childbirth, Lukina.

Billy Brown, of The Moments, born in 1946. Their sweet soul has been dubbed the All Platinum Sound. Their first million-seller was in 1970 with "Love On A Two-Way Street".

Brian Epstein signs The Fourmost in 1963. The Mersey Sound was taking off in Britain and anyone from Liverpool was signed as fast as possible. Similar to the scramble in San Francisco when record company executives arrived carrying checkbooks.

Larry Hall born in 1941. His only chart entry was "Sandy" reaching No. 15 in the US charts in 1959.

Larry Henley, of The Newbeats, born in Arp, Texas, in 1941. Their first release, "Bread And Butter" made US No. 2 in August 1964.

Mick Jagger and Keith Richard each given £7,000 bail in the High Court after spending the night in jail in 1967.

Cher and Greg Allman marry in 1975, but she petitions for divorce only nine days later.

David Bowie plays Earls Court Stadium in London, in 1973.

US Congress fails to extend the draft law in 1971.

JULY 1

Conception of Gautama Buddha. Canada Day.

Delaney Bramlett born in Pontotoc, Mississippi in 1939. He was a member of

The Shindigs, house band for the TV show. He married Bonnie Lynn and they made their first album together in 1968. They toured with Blind Faith in 1969 and made "Accept No Substitute". Eric Clapton joined them for a tour and a live album. Their band deserted them for Joe Cocker and in 1972 they divorced. Both have had solo albums released.

Marc Benno born in Dallas, Texas, in 1947. Together with Leon Russell he constituted The Asylem Choir, releasing their first album in 1968 and using an ad involving a naked girl, which got the Los Angeles underground newspaper "Open City" busted. Made three solo albums before returning to session work.

Eddie Bond born in Memphis, Tennessee, in 1933. He led the hillbilly Rockabilly band The Stompers. They made "Rockin' Daddy", "Boppin' Bonnie" and many other similar records in the Fifties.

Caroline TV, the proposed pirate TV station in the UK, launches in 1970. It was to have been broadcast from shifts of Constellation aircraft, circling over the North Sea. The project never materialized. It was headed by Ronan O'Rahilly, who started pirate radio in the UK in 1964, with the ship Radio Caroline.

June Monteiro, of The Toys, born in New York City, in 1946. "Lovers Concerto", their 1965 million seller, was a rearranged Bach melody.

Rolling Stones defended by a "Times" editorial entitled "Butterfly On A Wheel", which criticized the sentencing and

MR & MRS GREGG ALLMAN / PHOTO: LONDON FEATURES INTERNATIONAL

THE TIMES

PRINTING HOUSE SQUARE, LONDON, E.C.4. TELEPHONE: 01-236 2000

HO BREAKS A BUTTERFLY ON A WHEEL?

R. JAGGER has been sentenced to imprisonment for three months. He is raling against conviction and sentence, and has been granted bail until the ring of the appeal later in the year. In the meantime, the sentence of arisonment is bound to be widely scussed by the public. And the circumstances are sufficiently unusual to arrant such discussion in the public terest.

MR. JAGGER was charged with being in possession of four tablets containing mphetamine sulphate and methyl mphetamine hydrochloride; these ablets had been bought, perfectly egally, in Italy, and brought back to this country. They are not a highly dangerous drug, or in proper dosage a dangerous drug at all. They are of the benzedrine type and the Italian manufacturers recommend them both as a stimulant and as a remedy for travel sickness.

In Britain it is an offence to possess without a doctor's prescription doctor says that h

They were separate cases, and no evidence was produced to suggest that he knew that MR. FRASER had heroin tablets or that the vanishing MR. SNEIDERMANN had cannabis resin. It is indeed no offence to be in the same building or the same company as people possessing or even using drugs, nor could it reasonably be made an offence. The drugs which MR. JAGGER had in his possession must therefore be treated on their own, as a separate issue from the other drugs that other people may have had in their possession at the same time. It may be difficult for lay opinion to make this distinction clearly, but obviously justice cannot be done if one man is to be punished for a purely contingent association with someone else's offence.

We have, therefore, a conviction against MR. JAGGER purely on the ground that he possessed four Italian pep pills, quite legally bought but not legally imported without a prescription. Four is not a large number. This is not the quantity which a pusher of drugs woul nor even the o

that JUDGE BLOCK should have decided to sentence MR. JAGGER to imprisonment, and particularly surprising as MR. JAGGER'S is about as mild a drug case as can ever have been brought before the Courts.

It would be wrong to speculate on the JUDGE's reasons, which we do not know. It is, however, possible to consider the public reaction. There are many people who take a primitive view of the matter, who might call a pre-legal view of the matter. They consider that MR. JAGGER has "got what was coming to him". They resent the anarchic quality of the Rolling Stones' performances, dislike their songs, dislike their influence on teenagers and broadly suspect them of decadence, a word used by Miss MONICA FURLONG in the Daily Mail.

As a sociological concern this may be reasonable enough, and at an emotional level it is very understandable, but it has nothing at all to do with the case. One -ferent question: has MR.

LONDON "TIMES" EDITORIAL

imprisonment of Mick Jagger and Keith Richard in 1967, on drug charges.
The Beatles in 1966 play Budo Kan Hall, Tokyo. A famous bootleg album, "Three Nights In Tokyo" was made of this concert series.

Slade reach UK No. 1 with "Take Me Back 'Ome" in 1972.
Ralph Nader in 1969, states that rock'n'roll is producing a nation with impaired hearing.
Drugs. UK Misuse of Drugs Act came into force in 1971.
"Little Red Schoolbook" Trial opens in London in 1972. Originally written and published in Denmark, it was a radical guide for school-children, including open, and therefore contentious, sex counseling for teenagers. This, plus directives against the traditional role of teacher as God, meant the inevitable guilty verdict. An appeal was made to the International Court at The Hague.
First film nude scene played by Australian Annette Kellerman, in a movie called "Daughter Of The Gods" in 1915.
A-Bomb exploded at Bikini Atoll in 1946, giving rise to swim-wear of the same name.

JULY 2

Mountain formed in 1969, almost accidentally, when Felix Pappalardi (who produced Cream with great success) entered the studios with Leslie West to record the album "Mountain Climbing". They added Corky Laing and Steve Knight and had a group.
Tom Springfield, of The Springfields, born in West Hampstead, London, in 1936. They did well, but sister Dusty did better when she went solo after the group disbanded.
"Quarter To Three" by Gary US Bonds, reaches US No. 1 in 1961.
Robert and Maria Watson of Newton, Massachusetts start a six-day bed-in in support of John and Yoko, in 1969.
Herman Hesse born in Calw, Wuttenberg, West Germany, in 1877.
Franz Kafka born in Prague, in 1883.
Patrice Lumumba, African nationalist, born in 1925. Assassinated by the CIA.

JULY 3

Hippocrates, Father of Medicine.
Buddy Holly Memorial Day in Lubbock, Texas.

Jim Morrison dies of heart failure in Paris in 1971. Suspicions that his death was connected with drugs and that he, in fact, died in a Paris nightclub and was taken home in secret, still circulate in Paris underground Rock circles. He was buried in a Paris cemetery under the epitaph "James Morrison, Poet".
Brian Jones drowns in the swimming pool of his home, Cotchford Farm, near Hartfield, in 1969.

Mississippi Fred McDowell dies of cancer, at Baptist Hospital in Memphis, in 1972. One of Alan Lomax's discoveries, he toured and sang in coffee houses on the blues circuit. The Rolling Stones recorded his number "You Gotta Move". His best known album "I Do Not Play No Rock and Roll" was nominated for two Grammys in 1970.
Matthew Fisher, of Procul Harum, born in Croydon, in 1946. Organist with the group, he produced their third album "Salty Dog" in 1969, before leaving that year to go solo and produce records.
Victor Unitt, guitarist with the Edgar Broughton Band born in 1946.

Fontella Bass born in St. Louis, Missouri, in 1940. Recorded for Ike Turner in 1963, but her first hit was not until she duetted with Bobby McClure on "Don't Mess Up A Good Thing" in 1965. The Motown-style follow-up "Rescue Me" was an even bigger hit.
Maureen Kennedy, of The Vernons Girls, born in 1940. Originally a publicity group for the football pools company, Vernons, they achieved pop success with "Lover Please" in 1962.

David Bowie, in a surprise announcement at the Hammersmith Odeon in 1973, claims he's retiring from live performances. At a party at London's Cafe Royal afterwards were Barbra Streisand, Sonny Bono, the Jaggers, Ringo,

Paul McCartney, Keith Moon, Dr. John, Lou Reed and Tony Curtis. David danced with Mick, Angie danced with Bianca.

Brian Wilson made his first full length stage appearance in 12 years, when he appeared at The Beach Boys' Anaheim Stadium concert in 1976, before an audience of over 74,0000 people. The concert was filmed for a national TV show.
Atlanta Pop Festival, in 1969, featured Johnny Winter, Janis Joplin, Chuck Berry, Creedence Clearwater Revival, Blood Sweat and Tears, amongst many others.
Atlanta Pop Festival, in 1970. Over three days 40,000 people saw The Allman Brothers, B. B. King, Captain Beefheart, Country Joe and The Fish, Ginger Baker's Airforce, Jimi Hendrix, Sly and The Family Stone and many others.
The Newport Jazz Festival, in 1969, included rock for the very first time and featured Ten Years After, James Brown, Jeff Beck, Jethro Tull, O. C. Smith, The Mothers Of Invention, Johnny Winter, B. B. King, John Mayall and Blood Sweat and Tears. Festival ran until July 6.
Byrds "Mr. Tambourine Man" entered UK charts to make No. 1 in 1965.
The Beatles play Barcelona Bullring, Spain, in 1965.
Count Von Zeppelin makes the first flight in a rigid airship in 1900.

JULY 4

Independence Day in the USA.

Al "Blind Owl" Wilson, of Canned Heat, born in Boston, Massachusetts. He performed on vocals, piano, harmonica and guitar until he died in late 1970.

LOUIS ARMSTRONG / PHOTO: LONDON FEATURES INTERNATIONAL

Louis Armstrong born in New Orleans, in 1900. One of the first to popularize New Orleans jazz, inventor of "scat" singing when he lost the words to one of his songs in 1927.

Jeremy Spencer, vocals and slide guitar with Fleetwood Mac, born in 1948. At the height of the band's success, during a February 1971 tour of the USA, he disappeared and was later found to have become one of the Children Of God in Los Angeles. Little has been heard of him since. He made one solo album consisting of rock'n'roll oldies, faithfully reproduced.

Bill Withers born in Slab Fork, West Virginia in 1938. This ex-computer operator's debut single was a million-seller "Ain't No Sunshine" in 1971 but he could not maintain the sales after his US No.1 in 1972 with "Lean On Me".

Donald McPherson, lead singer with The Main Ingredient, dies of leukemia in 1971.

The Beatles play Manila, Araneta Colosseum, in 1966. After refusing special invitations to appear at the Presidential Palace they are denied police protection from fans at the airport and are severely harassed George Harrison says that the only thing that would make him return to Manila would be to drop an 'A'-Bomb on it.

Rolling Stones appear as the jury on BBC-TV "Jukebox Jury" program in 1964, and in 1972 their Washington D.C. concert draws a crowd of 48,000, causing sixty-one arrests.

Marcel Proust begins work on "Remembrance Of Things Past", his lifetime's work in 1899.

Lewis Carroll tells story of "Alice in Wonderland" to Alice in 1862.

Steven Foster born in 1826. The first pop composer.

Gina Lollobrigida born in 1928.

JULY 5

St. Zoe. The name means life and is perpetuated in honor of Eve.

Jaime Robbie Robertson born in 1943. Songwriter and lead guitarist of The Band. Originally backing Ronnie Hawkins (The Hawks) they toured Britain with Bob Dylan in 1966, and recorded the "Basement Tapes" at Big Pink with him in 1967. Their first album has achieved classic status in music circles.

Andy Ellison born in 1950. First with John's Children (with Marc Bolan) then with Jet.

Knebworth Pop Festival near London in 1975. 100,000 people attend to see Pink Floyd, Captain Beefheart and Steve Miller.

Rolling Stones give free concert in London's Hyde Park in 1969. Jagger reads from Shelley in memory of Brian Jones.

"Hello Suzie" by Amen Corner, enters UK charts in 1969.

Drugs. Lord Stonham reports to the House of Lords in 1967: "In 1966 there were at least sixty cases of pharmacy-breaking in London, thirty-five in Manchester, twenty-five in Lancashire and fourteen in Liverpool. Well over half a million tablets were stolen".

Thunderclap Newman's "Something In The Air" reaches UK No. 1. Group discovered and produced by Pete Townshend, were not ready for fame.

JULY 6

Jet Harris (Terence Harris), leader of The Shadows, born in Kingsbury, London, in 1939. "Apache", their first release, made UK No. 1 in July 1960. They had another twenty-seven hit singles in the next seven years. Harris was an early rock casualty and left the group to be replaced by Brian Locking.

Gene Chandler (Eugene Dixon) born in Chicago, in 1937. "Duke of Earl" was a great US hit in January 1962.

Richard Elswit, guitarist with Dr. Hook and The Medicine Show, born in New York in 1945.

Jan Bradley born in 1944. Her big US hit was "Mama Didn't Lie" which reached No. 4 in February 1963.

Louis Armstrong dies of severe heart and lung disease, in New Orleans, in

1971. He had been unable to blow a trumpet for many years which resulted in him turning more to vocals towards the end of his life.

Queen release their first single, "Keep Yourself Alive"/"Son And Daughter" in 1973. Both tracks appeared on their first album.

The Jefferson Airplane form in 1965 and play their first gig at Marty Balin's Matrix Club in San Francisco.

"Hard Day's Night", The Beatles' first film, had its Royal premiere at the London Pavilion in 1964.

Brian Jones hospitalized suffering from strain, in 1967.

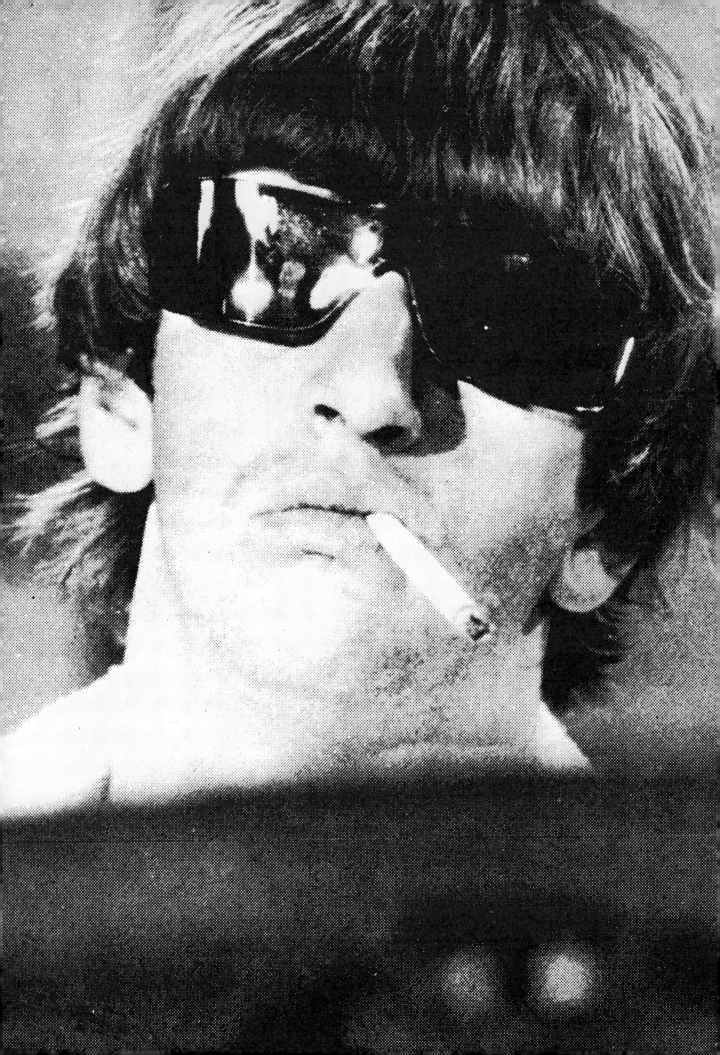

JULY 7

Japanese Festival of The Stars.

Ringo Starr (Richard Starkey) born in Dingle, Liverpool, in 1940. "We're unassuming, unaffected and British to the core. Someone asked me once why I wore rings on my fingers, and when I told him it was because I couldn't get them on my nose, he didn't believe me."

Mary Ford (Colleen Summer), of Les Paul and Mary Ford, born. "Mocking Bird Hill" with Paul's advanced guitar sound was a hit in February 1951.

Rob Townshend, drummer with Family, born in 1947. Jimmy Miller and Dave Mason produced the group's first album in 1968, "Music In A Doll's House".

Jim Rodford, bass player with Argent, born in 1945. "Argent" in 1970 was their first album and included the hit "Liar".

Joe Zawinul born in Vienna in 1932. Originally pianist with Miles Davis and Cannonball Adderley, he formed the jazz-rock band Weather Report with Wayne Shorter in 1971.

Larry Rheinhardt, guitarist with Iron Butterfly, born in 1948. Together with Mike Pinera, he replaced Eric Braunn after the incredibly successful "In A Gadda Da Vidda" album, but the album "Metamorphosis" did not reach the same standard and the group split in 1972.

Keith Richard charged in 1975, with possession of an offensive weapon and reckless driving in Arkansas. Hundreds of teenage girls besieged the jail where Richard and Ron Wood were held. He was cleared on August 15.

Doors reach US No. 1 with "Light My Fire" in 1967. Underground rock goes onto the AM wavelengths.

Rolling Stones begin recording sessions in Los Angeles in 1965.

First British Disc Jockey was Christopher Stone, who broadcast his record round-up from the BBC's studio at Savoy Hall, in 1927.

JULY 8

Jai Johnny Johanson, one of the two drummers in The Allman Brothers Band, born in 1944. Joined the band when Duane Allman formed it in Macon, Georgia, in 1969.

Steve Lawrence (Leibowitz) born in Brooklyn, New York, in 1935. His "Go Away Little Girl" was US No. 1 in 1962.

Billy Eckstine (William Clarence Eckstine) born in Pittsburgh, in 1914. He was last in the charts with "The Bitter And The Sweet" in 1956.

The Beatles hold a party to celebrate the premiere of the film "A Hard Day's Night" in 1964. The Rolling Stones are among the guests. "I was 62 the day they had the premiere of "Hard Day's Night" and we all went to the Dorchester. Then Paul handed me a big parcel— and I opened it and it was a picture of a horse. So I said "Very nice"—but I thought, what do I want with a picture of a horse ? Then Paul must have seen my face because he said 'It's not just a picture dad. I've bought you the bloody horse'."—James McCartney.

Percy Bysshe Shelley dies in 1822.

JULY 9

Brian Jones funeral in the parish church in his home town of Cheltenham Spa, in 1969.

Donald McPherson born in 1941. Originally known as The Poets before becoming The Main Ingredient in 1966. A number of hits in 1970 and 1971 with "I'm So Proud", "Spinnin' Around" and "Black Seeds Keep On Growing" before Donald died of leukemia in July 1971.

David Hockney born in Bradford, England, in 1937. British pop artist. Was the subject of the film "A Bigger Splash" in 1975.

The Kinks' "Sunday Afternoon" reached UK No. 1 in 1966.

WATTS, RICHARD, ANDREW OLDHAM & JACK NITZSCHE IN AN L.A. STUDIO IN 1965 / PHOTO: GERED MANKOWITZ

ARLO GUTHRIE/PHOTO: U.P.I.

JULY 10

St. Secunda Rufina.

Arlo Guthrie born in Coney Island, New York City, in 1947. Son of Woody Guthrie. "Alice's Restaurant" was his first and biggest selling album and was made into a film, pioneering the multi-media exploitation of "product" with the book of the film, the cook-book of the film of the album, and a restaurant franchise.

Jelly Roll Morton, ragtime piano player and composer dies in Los Angeles in 1941.

The Beatles release single

and album "A Hard Day's Night" in 1964.

Dave Smally, guitarist with The Raspberries, born in 1949. In 1975 they disbanded after their best album "Starting Over".

Cher petitions for divorce from Greg Allman after ten days of marriage in 1975. Greg reportedly fell into his spaghetti a few days before, splashing Cher with tomato sauce.

Marcel Proust, French novelist, born in Paris, in 1871.

JULY 11

Tab Hunter (Arthur Andrew Kelm) born in 1931. "Young Love" was a February 1957 hit in the US and the UK. He also had a TV series in the early

Sixties and is now a TV actor.

Terri Garthwaite, vocals and guitar with Joy Of Cooking, born in 1938. She and Toni Brown formed the group at the University of Berkeley in 1970 and their first album, named after the group, was released that year. She cut a solo album 1975.

George Gershwin dies, during an operation for the removal of a cystic tumor in 1937, at a Maryland hospital.

Yul Brynner born in 1916. "The King And I" brought him and his bald head to fame and fortune.

Margot Fonteyn and Rudolph Nureyev busted at a "pot party" in 1967.

JULY 12

Minerva, Goddess of Wisdom.
St. Jason (Mnason) Disciple, identified with the leader of the Argonauts.

Swamp Dogg (Jerry Williams Jr.) born in 1942. Recorded as Little Jerry and under his own name for the first twenty-five singles, before Swamp Dogg was born to reach fame in 1975.

Blind Faith make their US debut at Madison Square Garden, New York, in 1969.

Janis Joplin performs first gig with her new band Full Tilt Boogie, to a four thousand-strong crowd in Louisville, Kentucky, in 1970.

Elvis Presley has his first UK No. 1 with "All Shook Up" in 1957.

Coasters' "Yakety Yak" reaches US No. 1 in 1958.

R. Buckminster Fuller, "design-scientist", born in Milton, Massachusetts, in 1895. Developer of the geodesic dome, and many other additions to twentieth-century technology, such as the Dymaxion house and car.

Smoke rings. The greatest number of smoke rings blown from a single puff of a cigarette is one hundred and sixty-nine, a record set by one Keith Harraway of Essex, England, in 1974.

JULY 13

Beginning of the four-day Japanese Festival of Lanterns, in honor of the Ancestors.

Jim McGuinn born in Chicago, in 1942. Changed his name to Roger as part of his Subud religion.

JANIS JOPLIN/PHOTO: KEITH MORRIS

ROGER McGUINN

The Everly Brothers announce, in 1973, that they are breaking up. Between 1957 and 1965 they had 9 million-selling single hits and a total sale of over 35 million singles and albums world-wide.

Founded The Byrds and owns the name. The line-up has changed time after time, but always features McGuinn's current interest, from space rock to country and western.

After several unspectacular solo albums he formed his own band but in 1976, after touring with Dylan's Rolling Thunder Review, he teamed up with brass player Rob Stone from the Review.

Billy The Kid shot by Pat Garrett in 1881.

Assassination of Marat by Charlotte Corday, in 1793.

Jay Uzzell, lead of The Corsairs, born in 1942. ''Smoky Places'' reached US No. 12 in January 1962.

Queen release their first album, ''Queen'', in 1973. They had rehearsed for 18 months previously.

Longest spit, At the 1973 International Spittin' Belchin' and Cussin' Triathalon held at Central City in Colorado, Harold Fielden spat thirty-four feet and one quarter of an inch.

The first anti-conscription riots begin in New York City, in 1893. They lasted three days and over 1,000 were killed.

JULY 14

Bastille Day in France, commemorating the 1789 event.

Woodrow Wilson (Woody) Guthrie born in 1912. Composer of many classic folk songs and an enormous influence on Bob Dylan, as well as Joan Baez, Ramblin' Jack Elliott, Pete Seeger, Phil Ochs, and many more.

''This Land Is Your Land'' stands as his most remembered song.

Vince Taylor born in London, in 1939. ''I'll Be Your Hero'' was a UK hit in 1960.

Jerry Rubin born in Cincinnati, Ohio, in 1938. Together with Abbie Hoffman he founded the Youth International Party: Yippie. After the 1968 Democratic Party Convention the Yippies were accused of conspiring to cause a riot, resulting in the famous ''Chicago 8'' trial. Rubin and Hoffman were finally ousted from the party by a more 'militant' wing and Rubin now spends his time quietly studying ecology, alternative technology and organic living.

Tsar executed by Revolutionaries in Russia, in 1918.

JULY 15

Linda Ronstadt born in 1946. After singing with The Stone Poneys where she had a hit with Mike Nesmith's "Different Drum", she made a series of solo albums. None of which were successful until Peter Asher produced her "Heart Like A Wheel" album.

Tommy Dee born in 1940. He wrote "Three Stars" in March 1959, after the deaths of Buddy Holly, Richie Valens and The Big Bopper.

George Gershwin has two simultaneous funeral services in 1937, one in Hollywood and the other in New York City, where the body was.

John Lennon's mother dies in a road accident in Liverpool, in 1958. "The copper came to the door, to tell us about the accident. It was just like it's supposed to be, the way it is in the films. Asking if I was her son, and all that. Then he told us, and we both went white. It was the worst thing that ever happened to me."—John Lennon.

JULY 16

The Hegira, the famous journey of Mohammed.

Thomas Boggs, of The Box Tops, born in Memphis, Tennessee. "The Letter" was their biggest hit.

Mindy Carson born in New York City, in 1927. "My Foolish Heart" was one of her early Fifties hits.

Newport Folk Festival, in 1969, included Led Zeppelin among the traditional folk line-up.

The First A-Bomb was exploded at 5.32 am, in Alamagordo, New Mexico, in 1945.

Watergate. James McCord, born 1924 (he claims the date was October 9, 1918, the date of birth of E. Howard Hunt, but the records state as above). Ex-CIA man, convicted of the break-in of June 17th, 1972, McCord broke silence to allege facts of a White House cover-up.

JULY 17

Crab Ceremony.
Japanese Festival in honor of Susa-No-O, The Moon God begins today, ends on July 24.

Spencer Davis born in Swansea, in 1941. The Spencer Davis Group formed in 1963 and was very advanced for its time, particularly their first album "Their First Album" in February 1965. The group went through a radical change in line-up in 1967

and in 1969 Davis moved to California. The group featured Stevie Winwood on guitar and his brother Muff on bass.

Billie Holiday (Elenora Holiday) dies of heroin overdose in 1959. Policemen were waiting outside her door in the hospital to bust her had she recovered. Her best recordings were between 1935 and 1943, when she played with a small combo. Diana Ross portrayed her in the film of her life "Lady Sings The Blues".

Geezer Butler, bassist of Black Sabbath, born in 1949. Consummate masters of heavy metal rock, they have defied bad criticism to make many gold albums.

Moody Blues open their 24/32-track studio in West Hampstead, London, in 1974. The first quadrophonic studio in Britain.

Hollywood Argyles' "Alley-Oop" reaches US No. 1 in 1960.

Haile Selassie born in 1891. Emperor of Ethiopia, Lion of Judah and Spiritual head of Rastafarianism, the religion subscribed to by many Jamaicans, notably Bob Marley and The Wailers, Toots and The Maytals, Burning Spear, and many other Reggae artists.

The Beatles "Yellow Submarine" film premiered at the London Pavilion, in 1968. The voices on the cartoon film are not theirs, but they did provide four new songs. Their producer George Martin scored the background music. The complete soundtrack was released as an album.

James Cagney born in New York City, in 1899. Was a Vaudeville dancer before moving to Hollywood, where he was known for his tough-guy portraits.

JULY 18

Brian Auger, Jazz-blues-rock organist, born in London, in 1939. The Brian Auger Trinity came to fame when they performed with

JULIA LENNON & SON JOHN

Julie Driscoll and had a hit with "Wheels Of Fire" in 1968. Group finally broke up in 1970, and he formed Oblivion Express. Auger played with many rock and blues stars, and is featured on Sonny Boy Williamson's last album "Don't Send Me No Flowers".

Screamin' Jay Hawkins (Jalacy Hawkins) born in 1929. In 1956 his classic "I Put A Spell On You" was released. Once notorious for jumping into the audience dressed only in polka-dot underwear.

Martha Reeves, of Martha and The Vandellas born, in Detroit, Michigan, in 1941. They had big hits with "Heatwave" which made US No. 2 in August 1963 and "Quicksand" US No. 8 in 1963, and the classic "Dancing In The Street" which made US No. 2 in August 1964. Early in 1976 she had a solo hit with "Memories".

Tim Lynch, of Flamin' Groovies, born in San Francisco, in 1946. Only fully appreciated during the 1975 punk-rock revival.

Danny McCullock, of The Animals, born in Shepherds Bush, London, in 1945. He was with the group in their early, pre-psychedelic line-up.

Wally Bryson, guitarist with The Raspberries, born in 1949. "Starting Over" in 1975 was their final album and their first that the critics liked.

Dion (Dion DiMucci) born in The Bronx, New York. "Lonely Teenager" was a US hit in October 1960. "Runaround Sue" was a transatlantic hit in November that year.

JULY 19

Clarence White, guitarist with The Byrds during their mid-career line-up, dies after being in a coma for

several days, after he was hit by a car in Lancaster, California, in 1973.

Elaine "Spanky" McFarlane born in Peoria, Illinois. Leader of Spanky and Our Gang who had the first of many hits with "Sunday Will Never Be The Same" in May 1967, in the US.

Bernie Leadon born in 1945. A member of the Flying Burrito Brothers, until he and three members of Linda Ronstadt's backing group joined together in 1971 to form The Eagles. From their first album they were a success, but their "Desperado" album in 1973 is their best.

Brian Harold May, guitarist with Queen, born in Hampton Hill, Twickenham, near London, in 1947. In 1963-4 he built his own electric guitar, which he continued to use in concerts and recordings with Queen.

George Hamilton IV born in Winston-Salem, North Carolina, in 1937. His first hit was "A Rose And A Baby Ruth" in October 1956, but he is best known to Country and Western audiences. He spends a great deal of time in England, in the Country and Western clubs.

JULY 20

St. Margaret of Antioch. Swallowed by a dragon which she destroyed by the Sign of the Cross, emerging unharmed, thereafter becoming a patron of Childbirth.

"Like A Rolling Stone". Bob Dylan's single released in 1965. He regarded this as his most advanced statement, dropping plans for the publication of his novel "Tarantula".

Lovin' Spoonful release their first single "Do You Believe In Magic" in 1965.

Jo-Ann Campbell born in Jacksonville, Florida, in 1938. "Kookie Little Paradise" was her biggest US hit, in 1960.

Roy Hamilton dies after a stroke in 1969. His last US chart entry was "You're Gonna Need Magic" in May 1961.

"Why Do Fools Fall In Love" by Frankie Lymon and The Teenagers reaches UK No. 1 and stays for three weeks, in 1956.

John Lodge, bass and vocals with The Moody Blues, born in 1943. A Birmingham group formed in 1964, "Days Of Future Passed" was one of the first concept albums.

Jan and Dean's "Surf City" makes US No. 1 in 1963. Recorded while they were still at high school in Los Angeles, during their lunch break.

Sir Edmund Hillary, conqueror of Everest, born in 1919.

Jane Asher announces that her engagement to Paul McCartney is off, when she appears as a guest on BBC-TV's "Dee Time" in 1968. McCartney, watching the program at a friend's home was taken by surprise at the news.

JULY 21

Cat Stevens (Steve Georgiou) born in 1947. Son of a Greek restaurateur and a Swedish mother. First record "I Love My Dog" (1966) went nowhere in the UK, but his second **"Matthew And Son"** (1967) made No. 2 and he was away. But he contracted TB and spent a year recuperating, writing the songs which turned him into the singer-songwriter. "Mona Bone Jakon" contained his hit single "Lady D'Arbanville" in 1970. Since then he has produced a series of albums in the same genre and has established a faithful following. His records are produced by ex-Yardbird Paul Samwell-Smith.

Ernest Hemingway, founder of the hairy-chest school of literature, born in Oak Park, Illinois, in 1899.

Bed of Nails. In 1975 a new record was claimed by Barrie Wall, who lay on his bed for thirty-three hours in a shop window in Bournemouth, England.

JULY 22

Alexander The Great born 356 BC.

Estelle Bennett, of The Ronettes, born in 1946. One of Phil Spector's great early Sixties groups.

Don Henley born in 1946. Drummer in Linda Ronstadt's backing group who, together with two others, left in August 1971 to form The Eagles. Their first album, "Eagles" was a hit, containing the chart single "Take It Easy" and they have enjoyed continued success.

George Clinton born in 1940. Founder-member of Funkadelic, the extraordinary alter ego of the group Parliament, that was founded in Detroit in the mid-Fifties. They had a number of hard-driving funk hits in the early Seventies.

Chuck Jackson born in Winston Salem, North Carolina, in 1937. Among his mid-Sixties hits were "I Don't Want To Cry", "Any Day Now" and "Since I Don't Have You". He worked with Maxine Brown and in 1965 made "Something You Got" with her.

Terence Stamp born in 1940. His first film was "Billy Budd" in 1962, but he is most famous for the showcase role in "The Collector" of 1965. "Pete Townshend's favorite actor" (also brother of the Who's manager, Chris Stamp).

Aretha Franklin arrested in Detroit, in 1969, for causing a disturbance in a parking lot. She was taken to the police station, posted at $50.00 bail bond and ran down a road sign while leaving.

Pied Piper strikes in Hamlin in 1376. Takes away children when town won't pay him for rat-catching activities. Donovan played the part in the English film.

Scandal. The Profumo affair reaches the Old Bailey in 1963, starring Stephen Ward, Christine Keeler and

Mandy Rice-Davies. Godsend to the flowering satire boom of the early Sixties.

JULY 23

Sun enters Leo, ruled by the Sun, but associated with Jupiter by the Romans. St. Apollinaris and St. Appolonius, celebrated on this date appear to be forms of Apollo, the Sun God.

Tony Joe White born in Mississippi River swamplands of Oak Grove, Louisiana, in 1943. Wrote "Polk Salad Annie" (recorded by Elvis Presley), which gave him a high US chart entry in early 1968. Records produced by Billy Swan.

Madeline Bell born. One-time member of Blue Mink, but mainly known for her session work, including that with the Rolling Stones.

Dino Danelli, drummer with The Rascals, born in 1945. Originally The Young Rascals, they dropped the "Young" on reaching the age of 20.

Andy Mackay, saxophone and oboe player with Roxy Music, born in 1946. It was Mackay who introduced Eno to the group. Roxy being essentially a loose group, Mackay released first a solo album "In Search Of Eddie Riff" and then wrote the UK No.1 album taken from the successful TV series "Rock Follies".

David Essex (David Albert Cook) born in Plaistow in East London, in 1947. He changed his name to Essex in December 1964, but it wasn't until 1971, when he landed the part of Christ in "Godspell" that he achieved any success. September the same year his single "Rock On" made UK No. 1, but it took until March 14th, 1974 for the same thing to happen in the USA.

Cleveland Duncan, lead with The Penguins, born in 1935. "Earth Angel" was in the US charts in November 1954. Years later, Frank Zappa was to write "Memories Of El Monte" for them.

"Get Away" by Georgie Fame reaches UK No. 1 in 1966.

Raymond Chandler born in 1888. "There was nothing in that for me, so I let it drift with the current."

Lif Ras Tafari Mekonnen, crowned Haile Selassie I. 225th Emperor of Ethiopia, King of Kings, Lord of Lords, and Conquering Lion of the House of Judah, born in 1891. The focal point of Rastafarianism, the philosophy followed by most modern Jamaicans and the basis of Reggae music.

Telstar communications satellite launched in 1962.

JULY 24

Pythagoras born.

Heinz (Heinz Burt) born in Hargen, Germany, in 1942. Had 1963 hit in UK with "Just Like Eddie". Part of the mid-Sixties British rock scene. Famous peroxide blonde.

Chris Townson, drummer with John's Children and later with Jet, born in 1950. Marc Bolan came out of John's Children, which was an early English flower power group.

Drugs. "The Times" in 1967, carries a full page advertisement placed by the SOMA organization, advocating the legalization of marijuana. It was signed by all four Beatles, as well as by Nobel prizewinners such as Bernard Crick, discoverer of the DNA code.

Rolling Stones play Empress Ballroom, Blackpool, in 1964. The audience mobs the stage and they have to run for safety. In 1972 they play at Madison Square Garden, New York City.

"We've Gotta Get Out Of This Place" by The Animals enter the UK charts in 1965.

Bobby Ramirez, drummer with White Trash, dies in a bar fight in Rush Street, Chicago. One of the three men who attacked Ramirez turned himself in and was charged with first degree murder. Ramirez was twenty-three.

Simon Bolivar born in 1783. Liberator of South America.

JULY 25

St. Christopher, giant who carried Christ across a stream. Christianised form of Atlas, who supported the heavens on his shoulders.

Steve Goodman born in Chicago in 1948. This diminutive songwriter had a great reception from audiences at festivals in Britain in 1972 and 1973, but in USA has never had any national exposure, despite two fine solo albums. He wrote "The City Of New Orleans", the Arlo Guthrie Top Twenty hit.

Jim McCarty born in 1943. Founder member and drummer of The Yardbirds, who took over the Rolling Stones' residency at the Crawdaddy Club, Richmond, London, in 1963. After The Yardbirds' break-up in 1968, McCarty formed the duo Together with Keith Relf. This turned into Renaissance.

Mark Clarke, early bass player with Uriah Heep, born in 1950, Finally replaced by Gary Thain in 1972.

Walter Brennan born in Lynn, Massachusetts, in 1894. "Old Rivers" was US No. 5 in April 1962. Plays Granpappy Amos in "The Real McCoys".

Neil Young joins Crosby Stills and Nash and they play Fillmore East in 1969. He and Stephen Stills were both in Buffalo Springfield.

Tom Dawes, of The Cyrkle, born in 1944. Originally The Rondells, a New York vocal group, they were renamed by Brian Epstein. They had a US No. 1 with "Red Rubber Ball" in 1966.

"Cheap Thrills" album by Big Brother and The Holding Company released in 1968. They get a gold record on advance sales. Janis Joplin's first album.

Beach Boys' "I Get Around" enters the UK charts in 1964.

John Sinclair, information Minister for the White Panther Party and manager of MC5, given nine and a half to ten years for possession of two joints of marijuana. John Lennon campaigned on his behalf.

ANDY MACKAY & ENO IN ROXY MUSIC / PHOTO: BYRON NEWMAN.

JULY 26

Michael Philip Jagger born in Dartford, in 1943. "I see a great deal of danger in the air . . . teenagers are not screaming over pop music any more, they're screaming for much deeper reasons. We are only serving as a means of giving them an outlet. Pop music is just the superficial tissue to it all . . . When I'm on stage, I sense that the teenagers are trying to communicate to me, like by telepathy, a message of some urgency. Not about me or about our music, but about the world and the way we live . . . Teenagers the world over are weary of being pushed around by half-witted politicians who attempt to dominate their way of thinking and set a code for their living. They want to be free and have the right of expression, of thinking and living aloud without any petty restrictions. This doesn't mean they want to become alcoholics or drug-takers or tread down on the parents. This is a protest against the system. I see a lot of trouble coming in the dawn."

Roger Meddows Taylor born in Kings Lynn, Norfolk, in 1949. Founder member and drummer of Queen, he formed the group in 1972, with guitarist Brian May after they disbanded Smile. Old friend Freddie Mercury joined them as vocalist and they auditioned for a bassist, getting John Deacon in after six months. After 18 months solid rehearsal they launched themselves

with considerable success, appealing to teenyboppers and progressives alike, and their superbly produced records filled the charts by 1976. Their "Bohemian Rhapsody" was the most expensive single ever to record.

Bob Dylan appears at the Newport Folk Festival in 1963, along with Peter Paul and Mary, Tom Paxton, Phil Ochs, Joan Baez, Ramblin' Jack Elliott and many others. There were over 70 performers and a crowd of 37,000. Dylan sang "Blowin' In The Wind" solo and was joined by Pete Seeger for "Ye Playboys And Playgirls". With Joan Baez he did "With God On Our Side".

Aldous Huxley born in Godalming, Surrey, in 1894. Author of "radical" novels but "Brave New World" caused a greater impact.

George Bernard Shaw born in 1856. Novelist, playwright, socialist and vegetarian.

JULY 27

St. Joseph of Arimathea. Took part in the burial of Jesus. Brought the Holy Grail to Britain.

Bobby Gentry born in Chickawaw County,

Mississippi, in 1944. "Ode To Billy Joe" took her to US No. 1 in 1967.

Lightnin' Slim dies in 1974. His real name was Otis Hicks and he was born in St. Louis sometime in 1915. Recorded many fine blues such as "Can't Live This Life No More", "Don't Start Me Talkin' ", "Baby Please Come Back" and "Have Mercy On Me Baby". Back in 1954 he recorded the obscure title "Bugger Bugger Boy" on the Feature label.

Kim Fowley born in Los Angeles, in 1942. His long career in pop began with such songs as "Stranded In The Jungle" which he wrote and produced for The Jayhawks. He continued with "Nut Rocker" by B. Bumble and The Stingers, "Cherry Pie" by Skip and Flip, "Alley Oop" by the Hollywood Argyles and The Rivingtons' "Papa Oom Mow Mow". His many singles and albums of his own work have created a cult following for him. In 1976 he launched a group

of 16-year-old girls called The Runaways.

Nick Reynolds, of The Kingston Trio, born in Coronado, California, in 1933. They made the most of the folk boom in the early Sixties with sixteen hits beginning with "Tom Dooley" in 1958.

Pirate Radio. First reading of the Marine Broadcasting Offences Act, in 1967. The Act aimed at silencing the pirate radio stations off the British coast.

Drugs. Beginning of the Opium War between China and Britain, in 1839, after Chinese authorities seize and burn British cargoes of opium.

Sexual Offences Act becomes law in the UK in 1967. The first piece of legislation to legalize homosexual behavior between consenting adults in private.

JULY 28

Rick Wright, keyboards and vocals with The Pink Floyd, born in London, in 1945. The development of multi-media quadrophonic sound has meant that the Pink Floyd no longer really need to appear at their concerts. Their amazing album "Dark Side Of The Moon" has been in the UK album charts ever since it was released early in 1973.

Steve Peregrine Took born in London, in 1949. He formed Tyrannosaurus Rex with Marc Bolan in 1967. They became an underground cult group in the Summer of Love, making three albums of flower-power philosophy.

Ned Kelly film, with Mick Jagger, premiered in Glenrowan, near Melbourne, Australia, in 1970 (near where Ned Kelly lived). Australia did not take kindly to a middle class English rockstar playing a native hero.
Watkins Glen Festival in 1973. 600,000 people attended. The only casualty was a skydiver whose parachute caught fire.

Jackie Onassis born in Southampton, Long Island, New York, in 1929.

Peter Doyle, of The New Seekers, born in Melbourne, Australia, in 1949. Among their MOR hits was the Coca-Cola jingle "I Want To Teach The World To Sing" in 1972. They disbanded in 1974.
George Cummings, guitarist and steel guitarist with Dr. Hook and The Medicine Show, born in 1938.
Gary Glitter's first UK No. 1 in 1973, "I'm The Leader Of The Gang". His parents used to stand backstage signing autographs as "Mum and Dad Glitter".
Rock Marathon. The endurance record for continuous rock and roll is held by a four-piece called The Animation, who in 1974 finished their gig of one hundred and forty hours and thirty-four minutes, at St. Andrew's Church Hall in Liverpool.
Drugs. William Deedes reported to the House of Commons in 1867, "There are 7,000,000 Egyptians addicted to hashish, and the Egyptian Government are at their wits end to know what to do about it."
Beatrix Potter born in 1866. Her animal drawings and stories have contributed to the peculiarly English nostalgia for the nursery.

JULY 29

Bob Dylan crashes his Triumph motorcycle near Woodstock in 1966, breaks his neck and goes into retirement for an extended period. Horror rumors circulate.

Cass Elliott dies in London, in 1974. Major solo artist as well as member of The Mamas and Papas, she dies of natural causes, aged thirty-three.
The Beatles' film "Help" has Royal premiere performance at the London Pavilion in 1965.

JULY 30

Euclid, Father of Geometry.

Jeffrey Hammond-Hammond born in 1946. Bass guitarist with Jethro Tull, replacing Glen Cornick .

B. B. Dickerson, bass player with War, born in 1949. Through the Sixties they played under various names until, as The Night Shift, they joined up with Eric Burdon. They became War and finally cut loose from him to make it alone.
Edward "Kookie" Byrnes born in 1938. Star of the 1959 TV series "77 Sunset Strip". He was famous for combing his hair and made single "Kookie Lend Me Your Comb".

Paul Anka born in Ottawa, Ontario, in 1941. His first hit was "Diana" in the summer of 1957.
Rolling Stones let it be known in 1970, that Allen Klein and his ABKCO Industries no longer represent them. Massive law-suits follow.
"Out Of Time" by Chris Farlowe reaches UK No. 1

in 1966. A Jagger and Richard composition.

"Wild Thing" by The Troggs reaches UK No. 1 in 1966. Later immortalized by Jimi Hendrix.

Benjamin Botkin, the folklorist dies, in 1975 at his home in Croton-on-Hudson, New York. He was seventy-four. He spent more than thirty-five years collecting and publishing songs.

JULY 31

Jim Reeves dies in 1964. On The Grand Ole Opry circuit from 1955 onwards, he had hits with "Four Walls" in 1957 and in 1960 with "He'll Have To Go".

James Taylor reaches US No. 1 in 1971 with "You've Got A Friend" on which Carole King played piano. She later recorded it with Taylor on her "Tapestry" album.

Lord Chief Justice hears Mick Jagger and Keith Richard appeal their drug sentences in 1967. Keith's conviction is quashed and Mick is given a conditional discharge, as a result of the press and public outcry to their jailing.

Rolling Stones play Belfast in 1964. The show is stopped after only twelve minutes because of rioting fans.

The Miami Show Band, an Irish pop group, are ambushed and murdered by Protestant gunmen in 1975, near Newry in Northern Ireland.

"Last Exit To Brooklyn" trial begins at the Old Bailey in 1969.

Franz Liszt dies in 1886.

AUGUST 1

Lammas or Gule of August. Celtic Festival to Lugh. St. Fides Pistis, St. Spes (Elpis), and St. Charitas (Agape) Faith, Hope and Charity, called daughters of St. Sophia, who also had temples in Pagan Rome.

Johnny Burnette, of "You're Sixteen" fame, falls off a ferry boat and drowns while going fishing, in 1964.

Denis Payton, saxophone player with The Dave Clark Five, born in London, in 1943. First called "The Tottenham Sound", coming as it did on the heels of the "Mersey Sound", the group came from that suburb of London. "Glad All Over" was a 1963 UK No. 1 but though "Bits And Pieces" and "Everybody Knows" both reached No. 2, they could never again repeat that initial success.

The Concert for Bangla Desh held in Madison Square Garden, New York City, organized by George Harrison. Eric Clapton, Bob Dylan, Ringo Starr, Billy Preston, Ravi Shankar, Leon Russell, Badfinger and numerous others played at this benefit for Bangla Desh victims in 1971.

"Performance" premiered in 1970. The film starred Mick Jagger, James Fox and Anita Pallenberg. It was made in 1968, and was not released due to problems with the distributors and the content. The scene in which Jagger has intercourse with Anita Pallenberg and Michele Breton was cut, but eventually screened at the Amsterdam Wet Dream Festival.

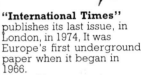

"International Times" publishes its last issue, in London, in 1974, It was Europe's first underground paper when it began in 1966.

Ringo Starr appears on BBC-TV show "Juke Box Jury" in 1964.

Herman Melville born in 1819. Author of "Moby Dick".

DDT invented in 1874.

AUGUST 2

Kwan-Yun, Chinese Buddhist Goddess.

Andy Fairweather-Low born. Originally with Amen Corner he formed the group Fairweather when they disbanded in 1970. They had a UK hit with "Natural Sinner" before breaking up. He then began a solo career having a 1976 hit with "Wide Eyed And Legless".

Jim Capaldi, vocals and drummer with Traffic, born in Evesham, Worcestershire, in 1944. Formed in 1967, Capaldi was in the original line-up and survived all the changes, but made a solo album in 1972 called "Oh How We Danced". Had a 1976 hit with "Love Hurts".

Garth Hudson, keyboards with The Band, born in 1937. They came together in the late Fifties as The Hawks, Ronnie Hawkins backing group. When Dylan went electric in 1965 he chose them as the backing group. They toured with him, first as The Hawks and then as The Band. The first Dylan single they play on is "Can You Please Crawl Out Your Window". They have been able to successfully combine their own work

with supporting Dylan largely because neither, Dylan, nor The Band, work very often.

Max Romeo's "Wet Dream" entered UK charts in 1969 and reached No. 10, despite being banned from airplay by the BBC.

Edward Patten, of Gladys Knight and The Pips, born in 1939.

Brian Cole, one of the original members of The Association, dies of an apparent heroin overdose in Los Angeles, in 1972.

AUGUST 3

Lenny Bruce (Leonard Alfred Schneider) dies of overdose of morphine, in 1966. The police posed his naked body with a syringe for the benefit of press photographers. "There's nothing sadder than an old hipster".

The Beatles appear at The Cavern Club in Liverpool, for the last time in 1963, in a Bank Holiday show, together with The Merseybeats and The Escorts.

The Doors reach US No. 1 with "Hello, I Love You" in 1968.

Rolling Stones in 1964, play Longleat House, home of the Marquis of Bath, during the third pop concert held there.

Tony Bennett (Anthony Dominick Benedetto) born in New York City, in 1926. Among his many hits was "I Left My Heart In San Francisco" August 1962.

John York, bass player with The Byrds from 1969 to 1971, born in White Plains, New York. Played on "Dr. Byrds And Mr. Hyde", among other albums.

The "Oz" Three sentenced to between fifteen and nine months at the Old Bailey in

London, in 1971. They had been charged with publishing an obscene magazine, the "School Kids Issue" of "Oz", the London underground magazine.

AUGUST 4

Maureen Starkey born in 1946. Her marriage to Ringo lasted until July 1975.

Elsberry Hobbs born in 1936. Bass with The Drifters from 1959.

Paul Leyton, of The New Seekers, born in Beaconsfield, England, in 1947. Their biggest MOR hit was the Coca Cola jingle "I Want To Teach The World To Sing" in 1972. They disbanded in 1974.

Bill Graham announced in 1969 that he was "finished with San Francisco", effective December 31st, when new owners took over the old Fillmore Auditorium.

Eddie Condon, jazz guitarist, dies at Mount Sinai Hospital, New York

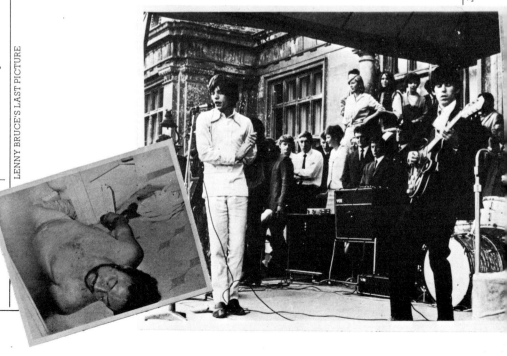

City, of a bone disease, in 1973, aged 67.

The Medicine Ball Caravan leaves San Francisco in 1970, on its journey across the US. Members include Wavy Gravy and The Hog Farm and seven tie-dyed tepees. They later form a band called Stoneground, visit the UK and make an album.

Percy Bysshe Shelley born in 1792. It was Shelley that Jagger read as Brian Jones' epitaph at the Rolling Stones free concert, in Hyde Park, in 1969.

Great Britain declared war on Germany, in 1914.

AUGUST 5

Nanak, Founder of Sikhism.

Jimmy Webb born in Elk City, Oklahoma in 1946. He met Johnny Rivers in 1966 and wrote "By The Time I Get To Phoenix" for him. He wrote "Up, Up And Away" for Fifth Dimension in 1967. Glen Campbell had three hits with Webb songs. He recorded his own work on three solo albums, dissatisfied with other people's versions.

David LaFlamme, electric violinist with It's A Beautiful Day, born. Their first album, named after the group, was released in 1968, it featured the acclaimed "White Bird".

The Beatles' album "Revolver" released in Britain, in 1966. The use of backwards tapes which began on the single "Rain" and was continued extensively on this album, caused great excitement.

"Cupid" by Sam Cooke enters UK charts in 1961.

The Pink Floyd's first album, "The Piper At The Gates Of Dawn" was released in the UK, in 1967.

Sammi Smith born in Orange, California in 1943. She had a string of country hits from 1968, and a Top Ten hit with Kris Kristofferson's "Help Me Make It Through The Night" in 1970. Regarded as "new wave" country.

Rick Huxley, guitarist with The Dave Clark Five, born in 1942. The group burst onto the scene with a UK No. 1 in 1963 "Glad All Over" and followed it with "Bits And Pieces", "Catch Us If You Can", "Everybody Knows" and several others, though they never again had No. 1 in Britain, because they tended to be forgotten as they spent much of their time touring the USA.

"American Bandstand" show on ABC-TV from Philadelphia, begins in 1957. Dick Clark was its host and it rapidly became the most influential music show in the country, introducing the whole Philadelphia sound before collapsing in the payola scandals. Clark's slogan was: "To reflect what's going on early enough to make a profit on it".

Jo Damita born in 1940. "I'll Be There" was her biggest US hit, in June 1961.

Joe Hill Lewis, the "Be Bop Boy", dies of tetanus in 1957.

AUGUST 6

Hiroshima Day.

Mike Sarne (Michael Scheur) born in Paddington London, in 1940. "Come Outside" was UK No. 1 in May 1962. He also directed the film "Joanna".

Memphis Minnie died in Memphis, Tennessee, in 1973. She recorded hundreds of powerful delta blues numbers in the Thirties.

Mike Elliott, sax player with The Foundations, born in 1929. Their first record "Baby Now That I've Found You" was a million seller in 1967. He left in 1968.

Isaac Hayes born in Covington, Tennessee, in 1938. Began recording in 1962. With David Porter wrote Sam & Dave's hit "Hold On I'm Coming" and in 1968 cut his own "Hot Buttered Soul" album, which was an instant success. Writing the score for "Shaft" finally established him as an international name and his "Black Moses" image continues today.

Stevie Wonder seriously injured in a car crash, in North Carolina, in 1973.

"Yippie Day" declared in Disneyland, California, in 1970. Yippies gathered at Sleeping Beauty's Castle and later chanted and cheered for Charles Manson and Ho Chi Mihn. They ran up the Viet Cong flag on Tom Sawyer's Island. Police closed the park six hours early.

The Beach Boys' "God Only Knows" enters UK charts, in 1966.

Troggs' "With A Girl Like You" reaches UK No. 1, in 1966.

Lucille Ball born in 1911.

The United States of America explodes 'A'-Bomb over Hiroshima, in 1945, killing 70,000 people.

Drugs. The massive seven-volume Indian Hemp Drug Commission Report, completed in 1894 for the British Government.

AUGUST 7

Andy Fraser born in 1952. He was the bass player and co-songwriter with Free until the group split up in 1971. He went on to form Peace. After a brief reunion to record "Free At Last" he left to form Sharks.

Jonathan Jackson killed in a shoot-out at the Marin County Courthouse, in 1970. A close friend of Angela Davis, he was trying to free James McClain, William Christmas, and Ruchell Magee. Davis was accused of supplying the guns, and became America's No. 1 Wanted Woman.

Charles Pope, of The Tams, born in Atlanta, Georgia, in 1936. "Untie Me" was a hit in 1962, in 1963 "What Kind Of Fool" reached the US Top 10. Their first UK hit was "Hey Girl Don't Bother Me".

Ron Holden born in 1939. "Love You So" was March 1960 hit in the US and a juke box classic in the UK for years afterwards.

Stan Freberg born in Los Angeles, in 1926. He first reached the US charts in January 1951, with "John and Marsha".

Homer, of Homer and Jethro, dies of a heart attack in 1971. They had a 1959 hit with "The Battle Of Kookamonga" in the US.

AUGUST 8

Joe Tex born in Baytown, Texas, in 1933. Author of James Brown's hit "Baby You're Right", he finally began to reach the charts himself in the mid-Sixties—after recording for ten years. Hits such as "A Woman Can Change A Man", "I Want To Do Everything With You", "A Sweet Woman Like You", enabled him to begin calling himself Soul Brother No. 1. It is said that Mick Jagger took much of his early stage act from watching Joe Tex perform.
Steve Perron, lead singer of Children, dies from inhaling vomit, in 1973. He wrote the ZZ Top hit "Francene".
John David, drummer of Dr. Hook and The Medicine Show, born in New Jersey in 1942. He was later replaced by John Wolters.

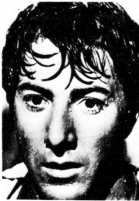

Dustin Hoffman born in 1937. "The Graduate" in 1967 shot him to fame as an actor and "Midnight Cowboy" confirmed it. He bought a brownstone in Greenwich Village, but The Weatherpeople, while making bombs, demolished the house next to his, in 1970, causing severe damage to Hoffman's new investment.
Rolling Stones play The Hague, in 1964. Audience riots and two girls get their clothes torn off.

AUGUST 9

Day of the Heroes or Demi-Gods of the Romans.

Steven Parent, Wociech Frykowski, Abigail Folger, Jay Sebring and Sharon Tate, who was eight months pregnant, murdered in the Roman Polanski-Sharon Tate residence in Beverly Hills, in 1969. Victims of the Charles Manson Family. The court case opened up a Pandora's Box of murders and weirdness, which extended well beyond the Manson Family, into the whole bizarre outgrowths of the sex, drugs, mysticism of "the summer of love", and some interesting interpretations of Beatle lyrics. The remains of the underground initially supported Manson, with the LA Free Press running a regular column written by him in prison, and The Weathermen praising him in one of their bulletins, but the final details of his case repelled almost everyone.

Lillian Roxon, Australian rock journalist, dies of a severe asthma attack in New York City, in 1973. She was the author of "Rock Encyclopedia" and had columns in everything from "Oz" Magazine to "Oui." Her regular columns in "Mademoiselle" magazine and the "New York Sunday Times" established her following in the USA. She was 41.
"Ready Steady Go", British TV's influential rock and roll program, first went on the British airwaves in

CATHY McGOWAN OF 'READY STEADY GO' & FRIEND

1963. Compered by Cathy McGowan the show covered all sides of the pop music scene, with a studio packed full of guests and stars who'd dropped by to chat or perform. The show introduced all the new dances, the new clothes and the new British rock music. It finally closed on 23rd December, 1966.

Bob Dylan is introduced on stage at a Joan Baez concert, in Forest Hills, New York, in 1964. He sings three numbers with her.
"Cannonball" Adderley, alto-sax jazz-player, dies aged 46, in Gary, Indiana, after an illness following a heart attack. Adderley had his own combo in New York City in the mid-Fifties, and played with Miles Davis and George Shearing.
Paul Anka's "Lonely Boy" enters UK charts to reach No. 3, in 1959.

Barbara Mason born in Philadelphia, in 1947. Her first recording was in 1964, but it was "Yes I'm Ready", her 1965 US Top 10 hit, that established her reputation. Other hits were "Sad Sad Girl" and "I Need Love".
Lord Melchett, 26-year-old Labor member of the House of Lords, is named as head of a Government working party to investigate rock festivals in the UK. He was co-author with Jonathon Green of the "I.T. Book Of Drugs".
Atomic bomb dropped on Nagasaki, in 1945, by USA.

AUGUST 10

Yashodhara, wife of Gautama Buddha. Buddhist Nun.

Ronnie Spector (nee Veronica Bennett) born in New York City, in 1947. Another Phil Spector discovery, whom he later married. "Be My Baby" was US No. 2 and UK No. 4 in October, 1963, for the Ronettes.

Ian Anderson born in Edinburgh in 1947. Formed Jethro Tull, (named after the inventor of the seed drill) and well known for playing the flute while standing on one leg. His concept albums began with "Aqualung" in 1971 and progressed through "Thick As A Brick" which was loved, "Passion Play", which was not and "Too Old Too Rock And Roll, Too Young To Die" in 1976.
Eric Braunn, guitarist with Iron Butterfly, born in 1950. When Braunn left the group in 1971 they replaced him with two new guitarists, but were unable to repeat the success of "In A Gadda Da Vidda", the heavy metal album which has sold more copies than any other album on the Atlantic Records catalogue.
Bobby Hatfield, of The Righteous Brothers, born in 1940. The Phil Spector production "You've Lost That Loving Feeling" made US and UK No. 1 in December 1964.
Michael Mantler born in Vienna, Austria, in 1943. Married to Carla Bley. Recorded "No Answer" with words by Samuel Beckett, featuring Jack Bruce and Don Cherry. Has done a great deal of work in the Jazz Composers Orchestra.
Eddie Fisher born in 1928. Minor film star, night club owner and Elizabeth Taylor's fourth husband.
Jimmy Dean (Seth Ward) born in 1928. "Big Bad John" was US No. 1 in 1961.
Mick Jagger fined £32 in Liverpool, in 1964, for driving with no insurance.
Shirley Watts presents prizes at the North Wales Sheepdog Trials, in 1975. Meanwhile the husband Charlie is on tour with the Rolling Stones in America. The Watts breed Welsh sheepdogs at their home in the south of France.

AUGUST 11

Lou Reizner born in Chicago, in 1938. Originally with The Skyliners, he became a record producer. "Tommy", with The London Symphony Orchestra, and orchestrated versions of "Layla" are his responsibility.
Eric Carmen, born in 1949. Originally vocalist, piano and bass with The Raspberries. A typical early Seventies group, they looked back to the Sixties for musical direction with such albums as "Fresh" and "Starting Over". In 1976 Carmen went solo with the hit single "All By Myself" and an album.
Jeff Hanna, guitarist of The Nitty Gritty Dirt Band, born in 1947. Their triple album "Will The Circle Be Unbroken" is accepted as the peak of their success. They also had a Top Ten hit in 1970 with "Mr Bojangles".
Buster Brown born in Criss, Georgia, in 1914. "Fannie Mae" was in the US charts in February 1960.
Eric Brann, singer, guitarist and songwriter with Iron Butterfly, born in Boston, Massachusetts. One of the biggest mid-Sixties heavy metal groups.
Neil Sedaka makes US No. 1 in 1952, with "Breaking Up Is Hard To Do".
"Cheech and Chong Day" in San Antonio, Texas. The two comedians had donated a concert in a high-school voter registration contest, in 1972.
The Watts Riots begin in Los Angeles, in 1965.
Enid Blyton born in 1897. Her children's books are the world's biggest sellers, though educationalists object to them.

AUGUST 12

Sam Andrew, guitarist with Big Brother and The Holding Company, born in 1941. Their first album, in 1967, was the only one that presented them as a group, since after that they fell very much in the shadow of Janis Joplin. In 1969 she left them and was replaced by Nick Gravenites, but they never recaptured the old excitement.
Buck Owens (Alvin Owens) born in Sherman, Texas, in 1939. His earliest appearances are as a session man, including some of Gene Vincent's records. With his group, The Buckeroos, he has sold 10 million albums in The

Country and Western market, but has more recently turned his attention toward right-wing politics.
Joe Jones born in 1926. ''You Talk Too Much'' was a US hit in 1960.
Rod Bernard born in 1940. ''This Should Go On Forever'' made the US charts in March 1959.

Buddy Holly enters US charts in 1957 with ''That'll Be The Day''.

Fleetwood Mac make their first public appearance at the National Jazz and Blues Festival, in 1967. Their leader, Peter Green, was originally with John Mayall's Bluesbreakers.

Francis Lea, of The Vernons Girls, born in 1939. They made regular appearances on Jack Goode's early BBC-TV programs.
The Beatles begin a US tour at the Chicago Amphitheater in 1966.
Cecil B. de Mille born in 1881.
William Blake dies in 1827.

AUGUST 13

St. Hippolytus. Torn to pieces by wild horses like the son of Theseus of the same name Hippolytus. Patron of Horses.

King Curtis stabbed to death by Juan Montanez, in 1971, in a fight outside an apartment building owned by Curtis in New York City. It was Friday the thirteenth.
The Jefferson Airplane make their first appearance. It was at The Matrix Club, in 1965, owned by Marty Balin (who started the group). They were the first of the many San Francisco groups and started a new wave of music which culminated in the flower-child ''Summer of Love'' in 1967.

Craig Douglas born in Newport, Isle of Wight, in 1941. ''100 Pounds Of Clay'' made No. 4 in the UK charts in 1961, but ''Only Sixteen'' in 1959 was the No. 1.

Fidel Castro born in Mayari, Oriente Provence, Cuba, in 1927.
Alfred Hitchcock born in 1899.

John and Yoko Ono Lennon give two Madison Square Gardens concerts in 1972 and raise $250,000 for retarded children. ABC-TV paid $300,000 for a film of the event. In addition to the concert John and Yoko donated $60,000 of their own money.
Lovin' Spoonful's ''Summer In The City'' makes US No. 1 in 1966. A classic summer rock song.

AUGUST 14

David Crosby born in Los Angeles, in 1941. First with The Byrds, in their original line-up, he left to join Steve Stills and Graham Nash in their triumvirate, after an argument with McGuinn about the group recording Carole King's pop numbers ''Wasn't Born To Follow'' and ''Goin' Back'', which he felt weren't political

enough. He has made a solo album, and duo albums with Graham Nash, with whom he plays on concert dates from time to time. Carole King joined them on their 1976 tour.

Steve Stills arrested in a motel room outside San Diego, in 1970. The manager found him "crawling down a hallway" and later "incoherent" on his bed when the police arrived. He was released on $2500 bail.
Family Dog, Chet Helms' rock venue, finally closed in 1970. The official end of the San Francisco scene.

Bertolt Brecht, dies, in 1956. Many of his songs, written with Kurt Weill, reached the pop and rock worlds, such as "Mac The Knife" and modern groups like Henry Cow still list him as a major influence. The Doors recorded his "Whiskey Bar" song from "Mahogony".

Gladys Presley, Elvis's mother, dies of a heart attack, in 1958.

Big Bill Broonzy (William Lee Conley Broonzy) dies in Chicago, in 1958. First recordings date to 1945. Famous for songs such as "Hard Headed Woman", "Blue Tail Fly" and "See See Rider".
Buddy Greco (Armando Greco) born, in 1926. "Mr. Lonely" was his biggest hit, in 1962.
Pirate Radio, Britain's first pirate station, Radio Caroline, makes its last broadcast, in 1967.

Sonny and Cher reach US No. 1 with "I Got You Babe", in 1965.
The Beatles begin American Tour and tape an Ed Sullivan TV show in 1965, with Cilla Black.
V-J Day. USA ends war with Japan in 1945.

AUGUST 15

Tommy Aldridge, drummer with Black Oak Arkansas, born in Nashville, Tennessee, in 1950. "High On The Hog" was their first gold album of southern boogie.
Woodstock Music and Art Fair opens on Max Yasgur's dairy farm, near Bethel, New York, in 1969. 450,000 gathered to hear some good music, some fantastic music, to wallow in mud, become the "Woodstock Nation" and be the unpaid cast in

one of the most successful rock movies ever.
Buddy Holly marries Maria Elena Santiago, in Lubbock, Texas, after two weeks of dating, in 1958. He was killed in February the next year.
Peter York, drummer with The Spencer Davis Group, born in Birmingham, in 1942. In the original group, he stayed on after Stevie Winwood, left but finally went his own way with Eddie Hardin, keyboards.
Bobby Helms born in 1933. "Jingle Bell Rock" was in the US charts in Christmas 1957, 1958, 1960, 1961 and 1962. "My Special Angel" was a 1957 hit.

Floyd Ashton, of The Tams, born in 1933. Their first hit was "Untie Me" in 1962 but they didn't reach the UK charts until 1971, when a reissue of "Hey Girl Don't Bother Me" reached No. 1.
Sylvie Vartan born in Iskretz, Bulgaria. French pop singer who appeared with The Beatles at the Paris Olympia and appeared in early Christmas shows with them.
Shan Palmer, of The Kaye Sisters, born in Hull in 1938. "Paper Roses" was a hit in 1960.
Craig Douglas enters UK charts with "Only Sixteen", which reaches No. 1, in 1959.

Abbie Hoffman and Jerry Rubin arrive in Chicago, in 1968, and give interviews about Yippie activities planned for the Democratic Party Convention: "100 greased pigs released one day at The Loop", "Yippie studs whose job is to seduce the delegates' wives and daughters . . .", "Yippie girls dressed as whores . . . they're going to pick up convention delegates and slip acid into their drinks . . ." all these suggestions and more were taken seriously by Mayor Daley and his police force.

The Beatles play Shea Stadium, New York City, in 1965.
Lawrence of Arabia born, in 1888.
Napoleon Bonaparte born, in 1769.
Thomas de Quincey born, in 1785. Author of "Confessions of an English Opium-Eater"

AUGUST 16

Eydie Gorme born in 1931. "Too Close For Comfort" was a March 1956 hit for her and "Blame It On The Bossa Nova", in 1963, reached US No. 7.

Kevin Ayers born in Herne Bay, Kent, in 1945. After leaving the Soft Machine he formed The Whole World, before going solo. He lives much of the time in France, where he has met with great success. Hardly heard of in the US until 1976, he produces very English, highly original, if slightly eccentric, music.
Gary Loizzo, vocals and guitar with The American Breed, born in 1945. "Bend Me, Shape Me" was a US No. 5 in 1967. The group, after line-up changes, later became Rufus.
Al Hibbler born in 1915. "He" was a US No. 7 in 1955.
Barbara George born in 1942. "I Know" reaches US No. 3 in 1961.
Terry Dene's "Start Movin' " entered UK charts, in 1957.
Gordon "Snowy" Fleet, drummer with The Easybeats, born in Australia, in 1945. He was replaced by Tony Cahill. "Friday On My Mind" was a UK No. 6 in November 1966.

AUGUST 17

Paul Williams, of the original Temptations, found dead, in 1973, in his car in Detroit, with a bullet in his head and holding a gun.

"My Girl" was US No. 1 in 1965 and they hit the top again in 1972 with "Papa Was A Rollin' Stone", with many chart entries in between.
Mae West born in 1892. "Night After Night" in 1932 was one of her best films, "Go West Young Man" in 1936, and "The Heat's On" in 1942. She returned to films in 1970, with "Myra Breckinridge". She also made an album of rock'n'roll songs, released in the mid-Sixties.

Pete Townshend clubs Yippie Abbie Hoffman over the head with his guitar, when Hoffman leaps on stage during The Who set at the Woodstock Festival, in 1969.
Gary Talley, of The Box Tops, born. "The Letter" in 1967 was their biggest hit.
"Fire" by The Crazy World of Arthur Brown reaches

UK No. 1 in 1968. Their only chart entry despite huge "underground" popularity.
Freddie and The Dreamers enter UK charts with "I'm Telling You Now", in 1963. A Brian Epstein group.
Davey Crockett born in 1786, inventor of famous hat.

AUGUST 18

Carl Wayne, guitar and vocals for The Move, born in Nether Writace, near Birmingham, in 1944. "Flowers In The Rain" in 1968 had the most "underground" appeal at the time. The group even got sued by Harold Wilson for some libelous advertising. They had nine chart entries in the UK before breaking up.

Cisco Houston born in 1918. Woody Guthrie's great friend and fellow folk-singer.
Nona Hendryx born in 1945. Originally a member of the Del Capris she joined Patti Labelle in The Blue Belles in 1962. In 1972 they became Labelle.

Muhammad Ali marries his second wife, Belinda Boyd, in 1967. Her father is a member of Fruit Of Islam, the Karate-trained section of the Black Muslims.

MICK JAGGER & MARIANNE FAITHFUL IN AUSTRALIA 1969

achieving superstardom and in January 1970, he formed Ginger Baker's Airforce. In January 1973, he opened a recording studio in Akeja, Nigeria and led a Nigerian band called Salt for a short time. Started a trans-Saharan trucking company in 1975.

Jason Starkey, son of Ringo and Maurene Starkey, born at 3.25 pm, at Queen Charlotte's Hospital in Hammersmith, London, in 1967.

Marianne Faithfull attempts suicide, in 1969, in Australia when she and Mick Jagger were over there for the filming of "Ned Kelly", which featured Jagger in the lead role.
Barbara Harris, of The Toys, born in Elizabeth City, North Carolina, in 1945. "Lovers' Concerto", their 1965 million-seller was a rearranged Bach melody.

him together with a Manchester group, The Dakotas. As Billy J. Kramer and The Dakotas they had a UK No. 1 with "Bad To Me" in 1963 and "Little Children" in 1964. Four of their six UK Top 20 hits were Lennon-McCartney compositions.
Ginger Baker born in

Lewisham, London, in 1939. Played with Acker Bilk and Terry Lighfoot's jazz bands, before joining Blues Incorporated in 1962. In February 1963, he joined the Graham Bond Trio, later the Graham Bond Organisation, then in 1966, came Cream. He was in Blind Faith in 1968, after

John Richard Deacon, bass guitarist with Queen, born in Leicester, in 1951. He was chosen after six months of auditions in 1972. Queen were the first real supergroup to emerge in the Seventies.
Orville Wright born in 1871. First co-pilot.

AUGUST 19

Johnny Nash born in Houston, Texas, in 1940. "I Can See Clearly Now" was US No. 1 in 1972.
Billy J. Kramer (William Ashton) born in Liverpool, in 1943. Brian Epstein put

AUGUST 20

Mohammed born in 570.
Robert Anthony Plant born in Worcestershire, in 1948. Originally with the Birmingham group Band Of Joy (together with John Bonham), he was recruited by Jimmy Page for his New Yardbirds, after the old group split up in 1968. "Whole Lotta Love" on their second album, "Zeppelin II", has become the epitome of "heavy metal" rock and its success was in part due to the strength of Plant's vocals. As part of the second wave British invasion of the USA they created a storm,

GINGER BAKER / PHOTO: BARRIE WENTZELL

ROBERT PLANT / PHOTO: CAMERA PRESS

commercial market, he stands with Duke Ellington as one of the best of the jazz big band sounds.

Sam McGee dies in a tractor accident on his farm in Franklin, Tennessee, in 1975. He was 81 years old and one of the oldest members of The Grand Ole Opry, having joined it during the show's first months in 1925.

Bob Dylan is re-signed to Columbia Records by Clive Davis, in 1966. He was first signed by their A & R chief John Hammond, where he was known as "Hammond's folly", until his records took off with the "protest" boom.

Christopher Robin born in 1920. As a child he was written into A. A. Milne's "Winnie The Pooh" books, as the little boy that Pooh Bear visited. Christopher Robin became a bookseller and spent most of his time trying to avoid publicity. Brian Jones bought A. A. Milne's house, and it was there that he died.

AUGUST 22

quickly gathering a cult following which soon numbered millions. They are one of the biggest selling bands in the world and are renowned for their three and even four-hour shows.

Jim Pankow, trombone player with Chicago, born in 1947. The group got together in 1969 as The Chicago Transit Authority.

Rolling Stones' "Satisfaction" released in Great Britain, in 1965.

George Jackson murdered in 1971, shot down by warders in San Quentin Prison. Bob Dylan was moved to write and record his first political song in five years about him.

Leon Trotsky murdered by Stalin's assassination squad, in Mexico City, in 1940. He

DAILY NEWS FINAL

TROTSKY IS DEAD

was attacked by Ramon Mercader with an ice-pick and died the following evening at 7.25 pm.

"G.I. Slayings Tied To Drugs" reports the "Baltimore Sun" of 1970. "A former Army psychiatrist told a Senate sub-committee today that marijuana caused some American soldiers to shoot their comrades".

AUGUST 21

Jackie DeShannon born in Hasel, Kentucky, in 1944. A singer-songwriter, her biggest hit was "Put A Little Love In Your Heart", in June 1969.

Count Basie born in 1904. For more than forty years, William Basie led one of the greatest jazz big bands. He relied heavily on the twelve bar blues form, his band always enjoying a surfeit of brilliant soloists. Although his later records were aimed more at the

Fred Milano, of The Belmonts, born in 1939. They continued after Dion left and had hits with "Tell Me Why" (1961), "Come On Little Angel" (1962) and many others.

Bob Flanigan, lead of The Four Freshmen, born in 1926. ''Graduation Day'', in 1956, was their best-known hit.

Joe Chambers, of The Chambers Brothers, born in Scott County, Mississippi, in 1942. They were the only soul group to successfully introduce elements of the experimental West Coast Rock into their music. Their hits include US No. 11, ''Time Has Come Today'' in 1968, ''I Can't Turn You Loose'' and ''Funky'' in 1971.

Dave Berry and The Cruisers reach UK No. 1, in 1964, with ''The Crying Game''.

Dale Hawkins (Delmar Allen) born in 1938, in Goldmine, Louisiana.

Rock'n'roller and author of the much imitated ''Suzie Q'', featured by the Rolling Stones on their first album.

The Beatles play Empire Stadium, Vancouver, in 1964, and in 1965, play Portland Coliseum. Allen Ginsberg wrote a poem about it which appears in his book ''Planet News''.

Kalin Twins reach UK No. 1 spot, in 1958, with ''When''.

George Frederic Handel began to compose ''The Messiah'' in 1741. He said ''I believe I have been inspired''. He finished the work on September 14th.

Television. BBC-TV begins regular transmissions in 1936.

AUGUST 23

Sun enters Virgo, ruled by Mercury, but associated with Ceres by the Romans. Nemesis, Goddess of Fate.

Keith Moon born in Wembley, London, in 1947. The Who were formed in 1964 and ''discovered'' in a Shepherds Bush pub by Kit Lambert and Chris Stamp, who managed them, after studying how to run a record company by examining the mechanics of distribution in the biscuit trade. Moon's drumming became a major feature of The Who, particularly in their stage act. The only member of the group to continue their auto-destructive image.

Rudy Lewis born in 1936. He was with The Drifters between 1961 and 1964, during the period of such great hits as ''Up On The Roof'' (1962) and ''On Broadway'' (1963).

John Lennon and his art school friend, Cynthia Powell, are married at Mount Pleasant Register Office in Liverpool, in 1962. Paul McCartney is the best man.

Yippies organize a ''Be-In'' in Lincoln Park, Chicago, during the 1968 Democratic Party Convention. The evening broke up peacefully, when Allen Ginsberg and Ed Sanders of The Fugs led a dance through the streets of Old Town.

Watchfield Free Festival near Swindon, Wiltshire, starts in 1975. Over 150 groups were on the bill, the festival being the successor to the Windsor Free Festival, broken up a year before by police violence.

Rolling Stones fans have water hoses turned on them by security guards, outside Manchester TV studios, in 1965.

The Greek Colonels are sentenced to death, in 1975.

QUICKSILVER MESSENGER SERVICE

AUGUST 24

Herculaneum and Pompeii destroyed when Vesuvius erupted in 79. St. Bartholomew's Massacre of the Huguenots in Paris in 1572.

John Cipollina, guitar with Quicksilver Messenger Service, born in Berkeley, California and . . .

David Freiberg, bass with Quicksilver Messenger Service, born in Boston. One of the first San Francisco groups, they formed in 1965, did free concerts at the height of flower power. ''Happy Trails'' album in March 1969, was a success for them. For a time Nicky Hopkins was a member of the band.

William Winfield, lead with The Harptones, born in 1929. ''Sunday Kind Of Love'' in 1953 and ''Life Is But A Dream'' a year later, continue to be played on oldies shows.

Ernie Wright, of Little Anthony and The Imperials, born in 1939. The first of many hits in the US was ''Tears On My Pillow'' which made No. 4 in 1958.

Ken Hensley, keyboards with Uriah Heep, born in 1945. They made their first album in 1970 ''Very 'eavy, Very 'umble''.

Mason Williams, author, composer and ''happenings'' artist, born in Abilene, Texas.

Billy J. Kramer and The Dakotas ''Bad To Me'' reaches UK No. 1 in 1963.

Rolling Stones, in 1965 meet US financial manager Allen Klein for the first time, at the London Hilton.

Demonstrators in Lincoln Park, Chicago, during the 1968 Democratic Party Convention, are cleared from the park into Clark Street by the police, who charged—first at the newsmen and then at the rest of the crowd. ''Time'' and ''Newsweek'' got the worst of the beating.

Aubrey Beardsley born in 1872. In his lifetime, he was heavily censored for the sexual content of his work.

Capt. Webb is the first man to swim the English Channel, in 1875.

AUGUST 25

Wayne Shorter born in New Jersey in 1933. He played saxophone with Miles Davis and Art Blakey before forming Weather Report, the jazz-rock group in 1971.

Little Eva reaches US No. 1 with ''Loco-Motion'' in 1962, written and produced by Gerry Goffin and Carol King.

Butch Trucks, drummer with the ill-fated Allman Brothers, breaks his leg in Macon, Georgia, in 1973, when his Mercedes hit another car.

Maharishi Mahesh Yogi bought a custom-built Bentley, with push-button controls for seat elevation and with stereo tape unit, in 1969. It cost his followers $26,500.

Leonard Bernstein born in Lawrence, Massachusetts, in 1918.

Karl Marx's ''Das Kapital'' first edition, published in 1867.

Chicago police, during the 1968 Democratic Party Convention, riot and attack peaceful demonstrations in Grant Park and Lincoln Park, breaking limbs and hospitalizing demonstrators. Police entered bars and restaurants and pulled patrons out into the street—no matter who they were. They even stopped cars and clubbed their occupants. Pacifist Tom Hayden was attacked by the police and his plainclothes police tail, before being arrested for allegedly spitting on a cop.

AUGUST 26

Ganesha, Hindu Elephant God of Wisdom.

Isle of Wight Pop Festival in 1970 begins. It lasted four days, and among the acts was Jimi Hendrix, who

played a strange, messy set. It was his last-ever performance. He died in London ten days later.

Georgia Gibbs born in 1926. Her first hit was with ''If I Knew You Were Comin' I'd've Baked A Cake'' in 1950.

Keith Allison born in San Antonio, Texas. He was the singer and guitarist with The Raiders and also had a number of solo Country and Western hits.

Vic Dana born in 1942. Of fifteen US chart entries, ''Red Roses For A Blue Lady'' was his biggest hit, in 1965.

The Beatles, Mick Jagger and Marianne Faithfull all go to Bangor, North Wales, in 1967, to see the Maharishi. They are

accompanied by a large number of newsmen. It was Patti Harrison's idea.

National Women's Strike in 1970, causes New York City telephone exchanges, TV stations and newspapers to close down.

1968 Chicago Democratic Party Convention, police attack and club 200 clergymen, who were counseling non-violence while sitting around a huge cross in Lincoln Park. In Grant Park, a larger crowd of demonstrators were beaten and clubbed in front of the Hilton Hotel. The police even entered houses and dragged people out into the street to club them.

Wellington-boot hurling. New Heights were reached in 1975, by shoe worker Christopher Smith, who at an annual contest at Wellingborough, Northamptonshire, England slung a rubber boot 134 feet

AUGUST 27

Iamblichus, preserved the Mysteries of the Egyptians.

Tim Bogert born in Richfield, New Jersey. Originally with Vanilla Fudge, he and Carmine Appice joined with Jeff Beck to form the unusually heavy group Beck, Bogert and Appice.

Brian Epstein found dead at his home, in 1967. Cause, given as accidental accumulation of Carbitol. The Beatles hurry back from Bangor, where they were on a retreat with the Maharishi Mahesh Yogi.

Phil Shulman born in Glasgow in 1937. With his brothers Ray and Derek, he was a member of Simon Dupree and The Big Sound before the three of them formed Gentle Giant in 1969. They had their first US success in 1973 with "Octopus" after which Phil left. His tenor sax and trumpet made a large contribution to their earlier albums.

Simon Kirke, drummer with Free, born in 1949. When the group broke up in 1971 he continued working with Paul Kossoff for a bit, before finally forming Bad Company together with Paul Rodgers, also from Free's original line-up.

"Highway 61 Revisited" released in USA, in 1965. It was Bob Dylan's sixth album.

Police riot outside the Chicago Hilton during the 1968 Democratic Party Convention. Throwing women through the plate glass windows of the Haymarket Bar and running amok in the hotel lobby, clubbing down anyone who they thought might be a demonstrator, until the carpet ran with blood. The McCarthy campaign office, on the 15th floor, was turned into an emergency hospital to handle the casualties of police violence. People kneeling in prayer were clubbed to the floor, as was a British member of Parliament who had to have a number of stitches in her head. Jerry Rubin was arrested when his bodyguard turned out to be an undercover police agent.

Haile Selassie, Emperor of Ethiopia from 1929 to 1974, dies in 1975. The spiritual head of the West Indian Rastafarians, notably Bob Marley, Toots and The Maytals, I. Roy, U. Roy, and Big Youth.

AUGUST 28

St. Hermes. Christianized form of Hermes (Mercury).

Dan Serephine, drummer with Chicago, born in 1948. The band numbered their albums Chicago I through

CHICAGO DEMOCRATIC CONVENTION 1968

VIII from their first album in 1969.

Wayne Osmond born in 1951. One of the five brothers and one sister act whose teenybopper appeal finally began to decline in 1975.

Rolling Stones announce, in 1965, that they are to be co-managed by Allen Klein and Andrew Loog Oldham. They sign a new five-year contract with Decca, on the same day, for an undisclosed enormous sum, as their single ''Satisfaction'' enters the UK charts.

Bob Dylan booed off stage, at Forest Hills Stadium, New York, in 1965, for playing electric guitar.

Democratic Convention in Chicago in 1968. Riot police gas, charge, beat and arrest demonstrators. And in 1973 . . .

Abbie Hoffman, king of Yippie media-freaks and star of the 1968 Chicago Convention riots, arrested at 6.45 pm, on the 10th floor of a Times Square hotel New York City, together with three friends. The charge was for allegedly selling three pounds of cocaine to two undercover NYPD agents. Hoffman later jumped bail and went underground.

Billy Grammer born in 1925. ''Gotta Travel On'' reached US No. 4 in 1958.

Mary McCartney, daughter of Paul and Linda McCartney, born in London, in 1969.

Funeral of ''Chocolate George'' Hendricks brings out the Hells Angels in force, in 1967. Hendricks had been run over and killed by a tourist in the Haight-Ashbury. The Grateful Dead and Big Brother play for the wake.

The Beatles play The Dodger Stadium, Los Angeles, in 1966. Their second-to-last live performance ever.

AUGUST 29

Thoth. Egyptian form of Mercury. Egyptian New Year.

The Beatles give their last ever live performance, anywhere in the world, at Candlestick Park, San Francisco, in 1966.

George Harrison joins The Quarrymen, in 1958, whose members already include Paul McCartney and John Lennon. They were playing at the opening night of The Casbah Club in Heyman's Green, Liverpool. A club run by Mrs. Best, mother of Pete Best who was later their drummer (before being replaced by Ringo Starr).

Charlie Parker born in 1920. ''Bird'' originated the be-bop style of jazz saxophone, playing at Minton's Club in New York City. He injected new life into Forties jazz, creating a revolutionary new music. But he was unable to gain any commercial success and died of a heroin

overdose in 1955. Amongst those he played with were Dizzy Gillespie, Thelonious Monk, and the teenage Miles Davis.

Dinah Washington (Ruth Jones) born in Tuscaloosa, Alabama, in 1924. In July 1949, ''Baby Get Lost'' was released. Her biggest pop hit was ''What A Difference A Day Makes'' in 1959, and she followed the same year with ''Unforgettable'', ''Love Walked In'' (1960), and ''September In The Rain'' (1961). Her last chart entry was ''Soulville'' in 1963, the year that she died.

Dick Halligan, organist, piano, flute and trombone with Blood Sweat and Tears, born in Troy, New York.

Chris Copping, bass player, born in 1945. Originally with Robin Trower and Gary Brooker in the Southend R & B group, The Paramounts, which had a minor hit with ''Little Biddy Pretty One'', before breaking up in 1966. When Dave Knights left Procul Harum, Copping replaced him in time to record ''Broken Barricades'' in 1971. He switched to organ when Alan Cartwright joined the group on bass.

Michael Jackson, of The Jackson Five, born in Gary, Indiana, in 1958.

Ingrid Bergman born in 1915.

Chicago police raid the McCarthy office on the 15th floor of the Hilton Hotel, dragging dozens of helpers down to the Hotel lobby and beating them, ''to teach, them a lesson'', after they had used their offices as an emergency hospital during the police riot two days before, during the 1968 Democratic Party Convention.

AUGUST 30

John Phillips, guitar and vocals with The Mamas and The Papas, born in Parris Island, South Carolina. ''Monday Monday'' was No. 1 in 1966, three months after ''California Dreamin' '' had made No. 4 in the US charts. When they broke up in 1968, he released a well-received solo album. An attempted reunion in 1971 was short-lived.

The Beatles first record on Apple label released. ''Hey Jude'' goes straight to No. 1 in 1968. It has the

VAN MORRISON / PHOTO: STEVE BERRY

longest-ever fade-out on a single.

Chuck Colbert, bass with The American Breed, born in 1944. ''Bend Me, Shape Me'' was a US No. 5, and other chart records included ''Step Out Of Your Mind'' and ''Green Light'' in 1968.

Huey Long's Birthday, celebrated in Louisiana.

AUGUST 31

Van Morrison born in Belfast, in 1945. Formed Them in 1963. ''Here Comes The Night'' and ''Baby Please Don't Go'' were their biggest successes. The former was written by Bert Berns, who sent Morrison a plane ticket to the US when Them disbanded in 1967. He recorded for Berns' Bang label, but his solo career only really took off after he had signed to Warner Brothers.

Bob Dylan plays the Isle of Wight Pop Festival in 1969. He gets £38,000 in cash for playing for one hour. In the audience were assorted Beatles, Rolling Stones, Who and other rock luminaries. He was backed by The Band.

John Gage, guitarist, originally arranger for Geno Washington's Ram Jam Band, born in 1947. Made an album in 1971 while with Dada, before joining Vinegar Joe.

Angels reach US No. 1 with ''My Boyfriend's Back'' in 1963.

James Coburn born in 1927. Best known for his role in ''The Magnificent Seven'' in 1960, and as Sam Peckinpah's ''Pat Garrett'' with Bob Dylan, in 1973.

SEPTEMBER 1

Labor Day in the USA.
Festival of the Hungry Ghosts in
Singapore.

Barry Gibb born in 1946.
The Bee Gees first record
was "Spicks And Specks"
released in 1967 and which
went nowhere. But
success came later that
year with "New York
Mining Disaster 1941."
Roy Head born in Three
Rivers, Texas, in 1941.
Formed The Traits in 1958.
After a few R & B revivals,
he had a 1964 hit with
"Treat Her Right" which
got to No. 2. At first thought
to be a white soul singer,
later records showed him
to be a talented rockabilly
performer, but his early
success was never matched
in the Seventies.
Tommy Evans born in
1927. He sang bass with The
Drifters during 1956-1957,
when they recorded
"White Christmas" and
"Fools Fall In Love".
Nelson Rockefeller's
Draconian anti-drug laws
took effect in New York
State at 1.00 am, in 1973. A
first offender could be sent
to prison for life, for
possession of as little as
twenty-five micrograms of
LSD, five grams of a
stimulant, any amount of
heroin no matter how small.
An ounce of marijuana could
get the offender up to
fifteen years jail.
Tokyo and Yokohama
devastated by earthquake,
in 1923.

SEPTEMBER 2

Ceres, Goddess of Corn. The Greater
Eleusinian mysteries, dedicated to her,
were celebrated September 2 until
September 10.

Rosalind Ashford born in
Detroit, in 1943. As one of
Martha and The Vandellas,
she had numerous hits with
Martha Reeves and Annette
Sterling, perhaps the
greatest of which were
"Heatwave" in 1963 and
"Dancing In The Street" in
1964. She left the group
when Martha fell ill, in 1970.
Jimmy Clayton born Baton
Rouge, Louisiana, in 1940.
"Just A Dream" was his

biggest hit, reaching US
No. 4 in July 1958, though
"Venus In Furs" in 1962, is
better known. (Not to be
confused with Lou Reed's
song of the same name.)
Robert Lee Dickey
(Bobby Purify) born in
Tallahassee, Florida, in
1939. Together with cousin
James had a US Top 10 hit
with "I'm Your Puppet" in
1966.
Joe Simon born in
Simmesport, Louisiana.
"Teenager's Prayer" in
1966, "Nine Pound Steel" in
1967, "You Keep Me
Hanging On" in 1968 and
"The Chocking Kind" in
1969.
**John Ronald Reuel
Tolkien** dies in Oxford, in
1973, at age 81. His "Lord
Of The Rings" trilogy
captured the imagination of
youth in the middle and late
Sixties, creating a Tolkien
cult. Various albums were
released of readings from
the books, music inspired

by the books, and music on
similar themes to the books.
He was professor of Middle
English at Oxford.
Horace Silver, jazz pianist,
born in 1928.

Rod Stewart reaches UK
No. 1 with "You Wear It
Well" in 1972.

SEPTEMBER 3

Al Jardine born in Los
Angeles, in 1942. A friend
of the Wilson brothers, he
was one of the founder
members of the Beach
Boys when they started in
1961. After their initial
concerts under the names
of The Pendletones, Carl
and The Passions and
finally The Beach Boys,
Jardine left to pursue his
studies at dental college.
However, when The Beach
Boys surfing music became
popular he rejoined the
group, replacing the Wilson
Brothers' neighbor, David
Marks, who had filled his
place.
Memphis Slim (Peter
Chatman) born in Memphis,
Tennessee, in 1916. His first
hit was "Beer Drinking
Woman" in 1940, but later
found role as blues
interpreter for white
audiences. Has lived in fame
since mid-Fifties.
Gary Walker (Gary Leeds),
of The Walker Brothers, born
in Glendale, California, in
1944. When the Walker
Brothers split in 1967, he
reverted to his real name
and formed a group called
Rain.
Mike Harrison, keyboards
with Spooky Tooth, born in
1945. When the band broke
up, made an unsuccessful
solo album before reforming
for two more albums.
Don Brewer, drummer of
Grand Funk Railroad, born
in 1948. The group had 10
million albums before
turning to producers such
as Todd Rundgren and
Frank Zappa.
George Biondo born in
1945. Steppenwolf was

formed in 1967, from the
Canadian blues band
Sparrow. Trying to mix
blues with heavy rock was
difficult but it gave them
three US Top Ten hits,
notably "Born To Be Wild"
which perpetuated their
hard, bike-boy image when
it was used in "Easy Rider".
They disbanded in 1972,
but re-formed in 1974.

Al "Blind Owl" Wilson, of
Canned Heat, found dead
with a bottle of downers in
fellow group member Bob
Hite's garden, in Topanga
Canyon, Los Angeles,
California, in 1970. He
played guitar, piano and
harmonica, as well as
singing with the group. It is
his voice on "On The Road
Again".

Woody Guthrie dies of
Huntingdon's Corea, in 1967,

after fifteen years of paralysis. The legendary folk singer, the man behind Pete Seeger, Ramblin' Jack Elliott and Bob Dylan. ''This Machine Kills Fascists'' was the slogan on his guitar.

Donovan has his first US No. 1, ''Sunshine Superman'' in 1966. ''This Machine Kills'' was the slogan on his guitar.

Britain enters World War II, in 1939.

Oliver Cromwell's ''lucky day''. On this day were fought the battles of Dunbar (1650) and Worcester (1651) and on this day he died, in 1658.

SEPTEMBER 4

Gene Parsons, of the Byrds, born in Los Angeles, California. Drummer with the group on ''Dr. Byrds And Mr. Hyde'' (1969), ''The Ballad of Easy Rider'' (1970) and later albums.

Gary Duncan, lead singer with Quicksilver Messenger Service, born, and . . .

Greg Elmore, drummer with Quicksilver Messenger Service, born on the same day. The two other members of the group were also born on the same day, August 24th.

Merald Knight, Gladys Knight's brother and one of The Pips, born in 1942.

The Who have their van stolen after leaving it parked outside Battersea Dogs' Home in London, while they went in to buy a guard dog, in 1965. They got the van back but lost £5,000-worth of equipment.

SEPTEMBER 5

St. Herculanus, possible form of Hercules.

Buddy Miles born in Omaha, Nebraska, in 1946. Drummer with The Electric Flag, he formed his own group from Flag members when the group broke up in 1968. The Buddy Miles Express opened at The Hollywood Whiskey A Go-Go and attracted a great deal of attention. Hendrix played on ''The Buddy Miles Express'' album in 1968 and wrote the sleeve notes. Joined Hendrix's Band of Gypsies and, after Hendrix died, formed The Buddy Miles Band. Has also worked with Carlos Santana.

Dave 'Clem' Clempson born in 1949. Originally in Colosseum he replaced Peter Frampton in Humble Pie. His arrival heralded a period of much ''heavier'' music, until the group broke up in 1974.

Joe ''Speedo'' Frazier, lead with The Impalas, born in 1943. ''Sorry (I Ran All The Way Home)'' was US No. 2 in 1959.

Josh White dies during heart surgery, in 1969. Blues singer, famous for his rendition of ''See See Rider'' and ''One Meat Ball' which he wrote. He was 61.

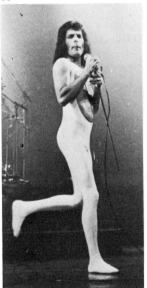

FREDDIE MERCURY/PHOTO: CHALKIE DAVIES

Freddie Mercury (Frederick Bulsara), vocalist of Queen, born in 1946, in Zanzibar. The group shot to fame in 1973 with their first concert. Firmly established at the top of the UK charts, their ''Hungarian Rhapsody'' was a 'mini' opera within a single, and justified the record company's expenses on its complex production, by being one of the biggest selling singles of the Seventies.

Loudon Wainwright III born in Chapel Hill, North Carolina in 1946. His starkly humorous music first emerged in the late Sixties. Now more mellow, his harsh voice and guitar have

an added backing group. He is married to Kate McGarrigle.

Dean Ford born in 1946. Marmalade originally appeared as Dean Ford and The Gaylords, a leading Scottish group. Marmalade had a UK No. 1 in 1968, with the cover version of ''Ob La Di Ob La Da'', with Dean Ford as lead vocalist. He released a solo album in 1975.

John Mitchell, Watergate defendant, born in 1913. ''Jeeesuss! All that crap, you're putting it in the paper? It's all been denied. Katie Graham's gonna get her tit caught in a big fat wringer if that's published. Good Christ! That's the most sickening thing I ever heard.''

Lynette ''Squeaky'' Fromme makes symbolic assassination of President Ford, in Sacramento, California. She never pulled the trigger. A Manson supporter, she held Ford responsible for his imprisonment.

LOUDON WAINWRIGHT III / PHOTO: PETER HOJAR.

ROGER WATERS & HIS WIFE JUDY/PHOTO: GEORGE WILKES

SEPTEMBER 6

Roger Waters, bass and vocals with Pink Floyd, born in Great Bookham, in 1947. Originally played lead guitar when the group was known as the Ab-Dabs, changing to bass when Syd Barrett joined. Premier "psychedelic-rock" band to emerge from British Underground in 1966-67. Their first single "Arnold Layne" was banned by pirate radio for being "too smutty". When Barrett left, the group changed to long, drawn-out compositions on both stage and record. "Dark Side Of The Moon" was in the album charts for over two years.

Bob Dylan plays his first gig at the Gaslight Cafe in Greenwich Village, in 1961. This was one of the regular venues for him in his early days as a folk singer. On the same day in 1967, the documentary of his 1965 UK tour was premiered in New York, "Don't Look Back" by D. A. Pennebaker.

SEPTEMBER 7

Buddy Holly (Charles Hardin Holley) born in Lubbock, Texas in 1936. A genuine rock stylist, his first record was "That'll Be The Day" in June 1957. "Peggy Sue" (November 1957) was written about the girlfriend of Crickets, drummer, Jerry Allison. He died aged 23 when his plane crashed in 1959, but his songs were recorded by The Beatles, Rolling Stones, and many others. His own records still sell in large quantities.

Little Milton (James Campbell) born near Inverness, Mississippi in 1934. Blues guitarist and singer, he was discovered in 1953 by Ike Turner for Sun Records. He went on to record many blues numbers. Highly adaptable, he could play in any blues style and subsequently R & B and Soul, gaining popularity equal to that of his fellow Sun recording artist Howlin' Wolf.

Al Caiola born in 1920. He had hits with movie and TV themes "The Magnificent Seven" and "Bonanza".

Grandma Moses born in 1860. Famous American "primatif" painter.

Smashing pianos A world record time was set in 1968, by a team of six Irishmen who demolished an upright piano, and passed the wreckage through a circle nine inches in diameter, in two minutes and twenty-six seconds.

London "Blitz" began with a German air raid on the docks in 1940.

SEPTEMBER 8

Ronald McKernan (Pigpen) born in San Bruno, California, in 1945. Keyboards, harmonica and vocals with The Grateful Dead. He died after a long period of ill health. His best work is found on the Dead's earlier albums, "Grateful Dead" (1967) and "Anthem Of The Sun" (1968). "I began singing at 16. I wasn't in school, I was just goofin'. I've always been singing along with records, my Dad was a disc jockey and it's been what I wanted to do".

Patsy Cline (Virginia Patterson Hensley) born in Winchester, Virginia in 1932. "Crazy" reached US No. 9 in 1961. She had ten US chart entries before her death in 1963.

Dante Drowty, lead of Dante and The Evergreens, born in 1941. Their version of "Alley Oop" went to US No. 15 in 1960.

Peter Sellers born in Southsea, in 1925. Best known for his films and work with "The Goons", radio show. He made a number of records including a highly successful spoken word album "Songs For Swinging Sellers" (1960). He made a Shakespearian version of The Beatles "Hard Day's Night", backed with "Help!" spoken as a church sermon.

Zeke Snodgrass Young born to Neil Young and Carrie Snodgrass, in 1972, at Neil's ranch near Santa Cruz, California.

Attica State Jail, New York, in 1971. Prisoners act to back-up their reform plan. Governor Rockefeller sends in army and kills hostages and prisoners. Medical reports faked to show that prisoners murdered hostages.

The first rocket bomb of World War II, fell on London in 1944.

Richard Coeur de Lion born in 1157.

SEPTEMBER 9

Chrysanthemum Festival of the Japanese. Janmashtami, Krishna's birthday.

Otis Redding born in Dawson, Georgia in 1941. A series of superb singles and albums from the early Sixties until his death in a plane crash in December 1967, included such hits as "I Can't Turn You Loose", "Satisfaction", and "Sittin' On The Dock Of The Bay". His appearance at the 1966 Monterey Festival, alongside Janis Joplin and Jimi Hendrix, won him the respect of white rock audiences.

IN LOVING MEMORY
OF OUR OWN
BUDDY HOLLEY
SEPTEMBER 7, 1936
FEBRUARY 3, 1959

Billy Preston born in Houston, Texas in 1946. He first played with Mahalia Jackson, featuring in the film ''St Louis Blues'' aged ten. He toured with Sam Cooke and Little Richard, but it was on tour with Ray Charles that The Beatles saw him. He played on ''Get Back'' and ''Let It Be'', and Apple released some solo singles. He was a guest on the 1975 Rolling Stones tour of America, and has made notable appearances on Sly Stone records.

Inez Foxx, born in 1942. Together with brother Charlie Foxx, ''Mockingbird'' was a June 1963 hit.

Jimmy Reed born in Mississippi, in 1925. One of the R & B greats, he was easily the most popular bluesman recording in Chicago, with a long string of hits over the years from the early Fifties. His style

directly influenced many blues artists in the Sixties, and British rock bands such as the Rolling Stones who featured ''Honest I Do'' on their first LP. Presley recorded ''Big Boss Man'', along with The Pretty Things and The Grateful Dead.

Doug Ingle, leader and organist for Iron Butterfly, born in Omaha, Nebraska, in 1945. One of the heaviest of the heavy metal psychedelic groups.

Luther Simmons, Jr. born in 1942. Originally calling themselves The Poets, the group changed their name to The Main Ingredient in 1966, and had a number of hits in the early Seventies. ''Everybody Plays The Fool'' was a million-seller in 1972.

Elvis Presley begins his first tour since 1958 in 1970.

Slade reach UK No. 1 with ''Mama Weer All Crazee Now'' in 1972.

The Flowerpot Men, the British Tin-Pan Alley answer to flower-power, enter UK charts with ''Lets Go To San Francisco'' in 1967.

SEPTEMBER 10

Arthur, King of Britain (approximate date of departure to Avalon).

Don Powell (Donald George Powell), drummer with Slade, born in Bilston, Staffordshire, in 1950. ''Coz I Luv You'' was their first UK No. 1 in 1971. Managed by ex-Animal and ex-Hendrix manager Chas Chandler.

Barriemore Barlow, drummer with Jethro Tull, born in 1949. He replaced Clive Bunker when he left to form the ill-fated Jude.

Danny Hutton, lead vocal of Three Dog Night, born in Buncrana, Ireland. One of the biggest selling US groups on the road. They began a series of best-seller, post psychedelic, heavy rock albums with ''Three Dog Night'' in 1969.

Jose Feliciano born in Lorez, Puerto Rico, in 1945. Blind from birth, he had a big hit with The Doors' composition ''Light My Fire'', making US No. 3 in July 1968.

Arthur Dyer Tripp born in 1939. Percussionist with the Cincinnati Symphony Orchestra, and drummer with The Mothers Of Invention on the ''Uncle Meat'' and ''Burnt Weenie Sandwich'' albums. Left during the line-up changes that occurred in late 1970, to join Captain Beefheart's Magic Band.

Rolling Stones play on ''Ready Steady Go'' TV Show in 1965. One of the most progressive programs on British television at the time, with imaginative lighting and camera effects, much admired by the Americans. Produced by Elkan Allan.

SEPTEMBER 11

Phil May born in 1944. Formed the Pretty Things

in 1963, with the Rolling Stones original bassist Dick Taylor, but they were always regarded as the poor man's Stones. Their early singles caught the R & B boom, but the group was always unstable with seemingly constant personnel changes. But May survived as the only original group member until he went solo in 1976. ''S.F. Sorrow'', a rock opera album, and ''Parachute'' were both highly regarded, but failed to make any commercial impact.

Great White Wonder, the first bootleg record, appeared in stores in Los Angeles in 1969. A two volume compilation of unreleased Bob Dylan tracks from ''The Basement Tapes'' and the ''Minneapolis Hotel Tapes'' of 1961. It sold at $6.50 a set. The double album was soon available in New York City and London, in locally pressed editions.

Bernie Dwyer, drummer with Freddie and The Dreamers, born in 1940. The group's biggest hit was ''I'm Telling You Now'' which was US No. 1 in 1963.

''Satisfaction'' by the Rolling Stones makes UK No. 1 in 1965. It was this song that firmly established

Jagger and Richard as songwriters to be reckoned with. Mick Jagger: ''We cut ''Satisfaction'' in Los Angeles when we were working there. We cut quite a lot of things and that was just one—contrary to some newspaper reports it only took us just half an hour to make. We like it but didn't think of it as a single . . . I get the idea for a lyric quite separately from the songs. And Keith gets his ideas quite separately from my lyrics. Keith may play a phrase and it fits with one of my ideas for a lyric. In the case of ''Satisfaction'' we thought of a phrase and the riff first and worked from there.''

Kinks reach UK No. 1 with ''You Really Got Me'' in 1964. Their first chart entry.

SEPTEMBER 12

Gerry Beckley born in 1952. One of the three Americans living in London who formed the band America and had a million selling single "A Horse With No Name" in 1971. They followed this with "I Need You" in the same year but since then have moved away from the obviously commercial pop format—and away from the charts.
Jay Osmond, one of The Osmonds, born in 1955. The appeal of this Mormon teenybopper group finally began to decline in 1975 . . .
Donny Osmond, born the same day as his elder brother Jay.
Andrea Simpson born in Barnet, Hertfordshire, in 1945. The Caravelles "You Don't Have To Be A Baby To Cry" was a US and UK hit in 1963.
Woody Guthrie Memorial Concert with Bob Dylan, Joan Baez, Jack Elliott, Arlo Guthrie and 18,000 others, held at Hollywood Bowl in 1970.
UN Convention relating to the Suppression of the Circulation of Trade in Obscene Publications concluded in 1923.

SEPTEMBER 13

Peter Cetera, bass and vocals with Chicago, born in 1944. The group began in 1969 as The Chicago Transit Authority before changing on their second album to the simpler Chicago.
Plastic Ono Band play debut gig at The Toronto Peace Festival, in 1969. John Lennon playing in

concert for the first time in four years: "All the people were singing 'Give Peace A Chance' and it was fantastic", he said. The concert was a rock'n'roll revival and also featured Chuck Berry, Little Richard, Bo Diddley and Gene Vincent. The Plastic Ono Band consisted of Lennon and Eric Clapton on guitars, Klaus Voorman on bass, and Alan White (of Yes) on drums. They had never played together before the concert.
Zak Starkey, son of Ringo and Maureen, born at 8.00 am, in Queen Charlotte's Hospital, Hammersmith, London, in 1965. Ringo's first child.

SEPTEMBER 14

Paul Kossoff, guitarist of Free, born in Hampstead, London, in 1950. The band was formed in 1968 and "discovered" by Alexis Korner. Kossoff survived the first line-up split but finally left the band in late 1973. He then formed "Back Street Crawler", but died in 1976. He was discovered dead from a drug overdose, when the group's plane arrived in New York from a gig in Los Angeles.
The Pope canonized America's first native-born saint in 1975, Elizabeth Bayley Seton (1774-1821).

SEPTEMBER 15

St. John the Dwarf's Day.

Julian "Cannonball" Adderley born in Florida, in 1926. Cannonball was a mid-fifties jazz alto-sax star. He had his own combo in New York City, and later played with Miles Davis and George Shearing.
Les Braid, bass player of the Swinging Blue Jeans, born in Liverpool, in 1941. Their only three Top 10 entries were covers of American material; best known for "Hippy Hippy Shake".

B.B. KING/PHOTO: KEITH MORRIS

Lee Dorman, bass player with Iron Butterfly, born in 1942. "In A Gadda Da Vidda" was the biggest grossing album on the Atlantic Records catalogue.
Jimmy Gilmer born in Chicago, in 1940. "Sugarshack" was his 1962 hit.
Gary Thain, bass player with Uriah Heep receives almost fatal electric shock at a concert in Dallas, Texas, in 1974. He retired.
Four Seasons' "Sherry" made US No. 1 in 1962.

SEPTEMBER 16

B. B. King born in the Mississippi Delta, in 1925. His first record was "Miss Martha King" released in 1949. Legendary blues guitarist, hero of Eric Clapton and most of the younger blues guitarists of the Sixties.
Kenny Jones, drummer with The Small Faces and later The Faces, born in Stepney, East London, in 1948. The real "mod" band of Sixties London. The Faces had a hit with their first single "Whatcha Gonna Do About It?", in September 1965. When Steve Marriott left the group in 1968,

Jones was among those who formed the new Faces with Rod Stewart and Ron Wood.
Bernie Calvert, bass player with The Hollies, born in 1944. He joined the group as a replacement for Eric Haydock.

Betty Kelly, of The Vandellas, born in Detroit in 1944. She replaced Annette Sterling, who left to marry after ''Heatwave'' Betty's first hit was ''Quicksand'' followed by ''Livewire'' and the US No. 2 hit ''Dancing In The Street'' in 1964, which didn't hit the British charts until 1969, when a reissue took it to No. 4. Betty left the group in 1969.

SEPTEMBER 17

Hank Williams born in Mount Olive, Alabama, in 1923. His first recording was in 1946, as a honky-tonk band leader, but it was as a composer of country and western standards that he is best known. ''Love Sick Blues'', ''Your Cheatin' Heart'', ''There'll Be No Teardrops Tonight'' and ''(I Heard That) Lonesome Whistle'' are among his greatest songs. He died on New Year's Day, 1953, of alchohol and chloral hydrate.

First 33 1/3 rpm LPs and players were launched in 1931, by RCA Victor at a demonstration held at the Savoy Plaza Hotel in New York City.

SEPTEMBER 18

Frankie Avalon (Francis Avallone) born in Philadelphia, in 1939. An archetypal American teen-idol of the late Fifties. He began as a trumpet-playing child prodigy, but ''De De Dinah'' established him in January 1958, alongside Fabian and Bobby Rydell. In the UK it was ''Venus'' which was his big hit a year later.

Patricia Hearst arrested in 1975, in San Francisco, a year after the FBI had put her on their wanted list for armed robbery with the Symbionese Liberation Army.

Jimi Hendrix dies in London, in 1970. St. Mary Abbott's Hospital, Kensington, pronounced him dead on arrival, after he had collapsed at Monika Danneman's Notting Hill flat. The verdict of the autopsy was that he had drowned on his own vomit.

Tiny Tim announced his engagement to Miss Vicki Budinger, in 1969, at The New Jersey State Fair. ''I was so moved I shed a tear and put it in an envelope that I always keep in my ukulele''.

Greta Garbo born in 1905.

John Barry's ''Walk Don't Run'' enters the UK charts in 1960. Inspired by middle period Buddy Holly, it formed the basis of the ''new sound'' of the Sixties.

SEPTEMBER 19

Thoth, Egyptian form of Mercury.

John Coghlan, drummer with Status Quo, born in 1946. A heavy metal working-class oriented group, they first achieved Top Ten success in the UK in 1968 with ''Pictures Of Matchstick Men''.

Brook Benton (Benjamin Franklin Peay) born in Camden, South Carolina, in 1931. ''It's Just A Matter Of Time'' went to US No. 3 in January 1959. Benton's ballad style filled the gap between rock'n'roll and the rock of the mid-Sixties.

Application Number .3.0.1.7......

The fee for this certificate is 8s. 0d. When application is made by post, a handling fee is payable in addition.

CERTIFIED COPY   **OF AN ENTRY**

CAUTION:—Any person who (1) falsifies any of the particulars on this certificate, or (2) uses a falsified certificate as true, knowing it to be false, is liable to prosecution.

QDX 004124

DEATH   Entry No. **7**

Registration district   Kensington   Administrative area Royal Borough of Kensington and Chelsea

Sub-district   St. Mary Abbots

1. Date and place of death   Eighteenth September 1970 St. Mary Abbots Hospital, Kensington

3. Sex   Male

2. Name and surname   Jimi HENDRIX otherwise James Marshall HENDRIX

4. Maiden surname of woman who has married   —

5. Date and place of birth   27th November 1942 United States of America

6. Occupation and usual address   a musician, 507/508 Cumberland Hotel Great Cumberland Place, Marylebone.

7.(a) Name and surname of informant   Certificate received from G. Thurston. Coroner for Inner West London. Inquest held 28th September 1970

(b) Qualification

(c) Usual address

8. Cause of death   Inhalation of vomit Barbiturate intoxication (quinalbarbitone) Insufficient evidence of circumstances open verdict

9. I certify that the particulars given by me above are true to the best of my knowledge and belief   Signature of informant

10. Date of registration   Twentyninth September 1970

11. Signature of registrar   E. M. Fisher   Registrar

CERTIFIED to be a true copy of an entry in the certified copy of a register of Deaths in the District above mentioned. Given at the GENERAL REGISTER OFFICE, SOMERSET HOUSE, LONDON, under the Seal of the said Office on 8th September 19.72..

This certificate is issued in pursuance of the Births and Deaths Registration Act 1953. Section 34 provides that any certified copy of an entry purporting to be sealed or stamped with the seal of the General Register Office shall be received as evidence of the birth or death to which it relates without any further or other proof of the entry, and no certified copy purporting to have been given in the said Office shall be of any force or effect unless it is sealed or stamped as aforesaid.

JIMI HENDRIX'S DEATH CERTIFICATE

BRIAN EPSTEIN IN THE CAVERN CLUB/PHOTO: CAMERA PRESS

Lovin' Spoonful, coming from the New York club scene of the early Sixties. Their first hit "California Dreamin'" popularized the flower-power philosophy, and a dozen more followed. But, caught in a rut, the group split in 1968 and Cass Elliott went solo. She died in London in 1974, while over for a series of concerts.

Gram Parsons dies in 1973, while on holiday at the Joshua Tree Motel in the Joshua Tree National Monument. He died of "multiple drug use", liquor, morphine, amphetamines and cocaine all being found in his body after death. He was 26 and had first made his name with the International Submarine Band, later joining The Byrds, forming The Flying Burrito Brothers and finally cutting two solo albums with Emmylou Harris. His coffin was stolen from Los Angeles International Airport by his roadie and a road worker, who cremated him in the desert at the base of Cap Rock, an outcrop of quartz monzonite in the National Monument, in accordance with his wishes. "If I go, I want to be in Joshua Tree and my ashes scattered there". His roadies were charged with theft of the coffin and fined $300 each.

Brian Epstein born in Liverpool, in 1934. He ran a record shop in Liverpool and "discovered" The Beatles after noticing the demand for their German single "My Bonnie". After signing them, he enlarged his management side to include Gerry and The Pacemakers, Cilla Black and many other Merseyside groups. "It wasn't so much that Brian Epstein discovered The Beatles but that The Beatles discovered Brian Epstein".—Paul McCartney.

Twiggy born in 1949. One of the most famous models of the "Swinging Sixties". She starred in "The Boy Friend" by Ken Russell, and later took up a singing career in variety and television. Released a solo album in July 1976.

David Bromberg born in Tarrytown, New York, in 1945. One of Bob Dylan's friends on the folk circuit in New York, his own albums have never met with much success.

Mick Massi, of The Four Seasons, born in 1935. "Sherry" was a US No. 1.

Tommy Steele (Tommy Hicks) "discovered" playing at the Two I's coffee bar in Old Compton Street, Soho, in 1956. His first record "Rock With The Caveman", made two days after his recording test, established him as one of Britain's first rock'n'rollers. He moved on into variety in later years.

Cass Elliott born in Alexandria, Virginia, in 1943. Originally with John Sebastian in The Mugwumps, she formed a quarter of The Mamas and The Papas. The group, shrewdly managed by Lou Adler, was closely associated with Sebastian's

Bill Medley, of The Righteous Brothers, born in 1940. They had a local hit in "Little Latin Lupe Lu" in 1963. Jack Good discovered them for his "Shindig" TV Show. Phil Spector produced their "You've Lost That Lovin' Feelin'" which was a 1964 transatlantic No. 1. In 1968 they split up and Medley recorded solo with no success. In 1974 they reunited and reached the US Top Ten with "Rock'n' Roll Heaven" and "Give It To The People".

Jimi Hendrix described as "A key figure in the development of pop music" in the headline to his obituary in the London "Times", in 1970.

SEPTEMBER 20

Romulus, Founder and first King of Rome.

John Dankworth born in Woodford, Essex, in 1927. Premier British big band leader and also smaller combos. Married to Cleo Laine the jazz singer.

Jim Croce dies in 1973, along with five other people, when their single engine plane hit a tree on take off from Natchitoches, Louisiana. "Photographs And Memories" was one of his greatest hits, along with "Bad Bad Leroy Brown", which was also recorded by Frank Sinatra.

Jim Morrison found not guilty in Miami, in 1970, of "lewd and lascivious behavior" but guilty of "indecent exposure and profanity".

Blind Faith album entered UK charts to reach No. 1 in 1969. The ill-fated prototype supergroup never really meshed, and this album showed it well. **"Bad Moon Rising"** by Creedence Clearwater Revival reaches No. 1 in UK charts. It made No. 2 in the USA in 1969.

SEPTEMBER 21

Don Preston (Donald Ward Preston), keyboards with The Mothers of Invention, born in Flint, Michigan, in 1932. He was with the group from its formation in 1965 until 1970.

Dickey Lee born in Memphis, Tennessee, in 1940. He wrote the Country and Western classic "She Thinks I Still Care" and had a hit with "Patches" in 1962 and "Laurie" in 1965.

Herbert George Wells born in 1866. His "War Of The Worlds" caused panic when it was broadcast as a radio play by Orson Welles, in the US in the Thirties. His "Kipps" was the basis for Tommy Steele's "Half A Sixpence".

Leonard Cohen born in Montreal, Canada in 1934. At first a novelist ("Beautiful Losers" 1966), his first two albums were very successful, and "Sisters Of Mercy" and "Suzanne" became classics. A major figure in the "bedsitter" singer-songwriter league.

Betty Wright born in Miami in 1953. Started working on recordings at the age of 11. She had a string of romantic soul hits from 1968 until the funky "Clean Up Woman" in 1971

SEPTEMBER 22

Virgil.
St. Silvanus, slightly Christianized form of the God of Forests.

George E. Chambers, of The Chambers Brothers, born in Flora, Mississippi in 1931. Their stoned black hippie image appealed to white audiences in the late Sixties. Previously they had a minor success with their rough versions of soul material in the mid-Fifties, but in 1968 they made No. 11 in the US with "Time Has Come Today".

Leroy Holmes born in 1913. His orchestral themes entered the US charts three times in the Fifties.

Joni James (Joan Carmella Babbo) born. "Why Don't You Believe Me" was US No. 1 in 1952. She was in the charts all through the Fifties.

Bilbo and Frodo Baggins born, according to J. R. R. Tolkien.

Bob Dylan appears at a Carnegie Hall "Hootenanny" in 1962, and did five numbers including his "Talking John Birch Society Blues".

SEPTEMBER 23

Autumnal Equinox. Sun enters Libra, ruled by Venus, associated with Vulcan by the Romans.
Japanese Festival of Equinox in honor of Buddha.
Chinese festival of Buddha in name of Fo.

Tim Rose, composer and singer, born in Washington DC, in 1940. Originally with The Big Three (along with

Mama Cass Elliott) he went solo and made the ''Tim Rose'' album in 1967, with a version of ''Hey Joe'' (which probably introduced the song to most other people who recorded it at that period).

Bruce Springsteen born in 1949. Hailed as ''the new Dylan'', Columbia records nearly ended his career by their overkill publicity. An individual, stylish performer, his ''Born To Run'' album of 1975 was ruined by over production, but it was an American hit.

Ray Charles (Ray Charles Robinson) born in Albany, Georgia, in 1932. Blind at six, he studied music in Florida until 1947, when he was orphaned. He moved to Seattle, and formed a trio blatantly copying Nat King Cole. Signed to Atlantic, he was often in the US charts with his ''soul-gospel'' sound. ''What'd I Say'' is his most basic hit, and he dominated the Rhythm and Blues, and often the pop charts, throughout the Sixties. The most influential black musician of the decade.

Roy Buchanan born in Ozark, Arkansas in 1939. Propelled into the ranks of guitar superheroes by a Polydor recording contract in 1971, having earlier backed such as Dale Hawkins and The Hawks.

Joe Hill Louis born in Whitehaven, Tennessee in 1921. Known as The Be Bop Boy on his blues program for WDAIA, which began in 1949.

Barbara Allbut, of The Angels, born in 1940. On the same day as her sister . . . **Phyllis ''Jiggs'' Allbut**, also in The Angels, born in 1942. ''My Boyfriend's Back'' was a US No. 1 in June 1963.

Robbie McIntosh, drummer with The Average White Band, overdoses with heroin in 1974, thinking it was cocaine, in a North Hollywood motel room. The Courts thought it was murder, and a man later confessed to it as a revenge killing.

Gil Turner, former member of New World Singers and close friend of Bob Dylan in Greenwich Village days, died in San Francisco in 1974.

Paul McCartney rumored dead, for the first time, in an article in the ''Northern Star'', the Illinois University newspaper, in 1969. headlined ''Clues Hint At Beatle Death''.

Ron Busby, drummer with Iron Butterfly, born in 1941. ''In A Gadda Da Vidda'' was the prototype heavy metal album.

''The Letter'' by The Box Tops reaches US No. 1 in 1967. Their only major hit, the group was among the few white acts to achieve success from soul-oriented Memphis, but ''Cry Like A Baby'' did make No. 2 in 1968.

Rick Valence ''Tell Laura I Love Her'' reaches UK No. 1, despite a BBC ban, in 1960.

SEPTEMBER 24

Anthony Newley born in Clapham, London, in 1931. ''Why'' and ''Strawberry Fair'' were UK hits in 1960. His style was directly copied by the young David Bowie.

Gerry Marsden, of Gerry and The Pacemakers, born in Liverpool, in 1942. ''You'll Never Walk Alone'' was their third record and their third UK No. 1 in 1963.

John Lennon given reprieve to remain in the United States for the birth of baby by Yoko in 1975. It was later proved that the campaign to have Lennon deported was initiated by the Nixon administration.

Jerry Donahue, guitarist with the 1975 line-up of The Fairport Convention, born in 1946.

RAY CHARLES ON STAGE./PHOTO: ANNIE LEIBOVITZ

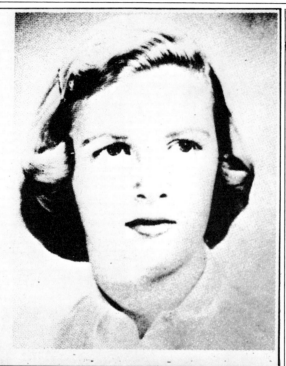

LINDA L. EASTMAN
Advertising Club 4;
Chorus 1, 2, 3, 4;
Pep Club 3, 4.
"Strawberry Blonde"
....Yen for men
....Shetlandish.

Linda McCartney (nee Eastman) born in 1942. When she married ex-Beatle Paul, newspapers said she was the heiress to the Eastman photographic fortune. In actual fact, her father was a lawyer and was soon working for Apple. His original name was Epstein but he had changed it earlier by deed poll.

Daddy at the Beverly Hills Tennis Club

F. Scott Fitzgerald born in 1896. "An author ought to write for the youth of his own generation, the critics of the next and the schoolmasters of ever afterwards."

SEPTEMBER 25

John Locke, pianist with Spirit, born in Los Angeles. in 1943. A curious group with an almost cult following. Locke played keyboards with the group for the first four albums, before leaving when the group split up. When they reformed he was not in the line up.
Joseph Russell, of The Persuasions, born in Henderson, North Carolina, in 1939. The group began in New York in 1968.
Barry McGuire's "Eve Of Destruction" makes US No. 1 in 1965. His was the lead vocal on New Christy Minstrel hits such as "Green Green", but "Eve Of Destruction" gave him success in the wake of Dylan's protest songs.
Charlie Monroe dies of cancer in 1975. He was 72 and began his country music career back in the Twenties, as lead singer and guitarist of The Monroe Brothers.

"The Twist" by Chubby Checker makes US No. 1 in 1960. Hank Ballard, who wrote the song as a B-side, had had a hit with it himself in March 1959. It began the whole twist craze.

SEPTEMBER 26
American Indian Day.
St. Cyprian, Astrologer and Magician.

Bryan Ferry born in Washington, County Durham, in 1945. Originator of the art school rock group Roxy Music, he began in 1973 to also pursue a solo career, recording "Those Foolish Things" and "Another Time Another Place". Exaggerated themes of decadence and romantic nostalgia permeate his work, whereas Roxy have moved into an area of ironic self parody and sardonic humor.

Bessie Smith dies in a car crash near Coahoma, Mississippi, in 1937, through loss of blood after being turned away from a whites-only hospital. Hundreds of classic records such as "Empty Bed Blues" put her in a class of her own, a source of inspiration to all jazz and blues singers.
Brian Jones fined £50 with £105 costs after being found guilty of possession of marijuana in 1968.
George Gershwin (Jacob Gershwin), born 1889, at 242 Snediker Avenue, New York City.

HECKSTALL-SMITH, KORNER, JACK BRUCE, JAGGER & CYRIL DAVIES IN 1961.

Henderson, North Carolina. First sang with The Crowns, which in 1959 became The Drifters. Their No. 1 in the US was ''Save The Last Dance For Me'' in September 1960.

Helen Shapiro born in Bethnal Green, London, in 1946. Her first record and big hit, ''Don't Treat Me Like A Child'' was recorded when she was 14 years old, in 1960. Her first No. 1 was '''You Don't Know''. The Beatles first toured as her support act in 1963.

Dick Heckstall-Smith, sax player born, in 1934. First with Alexis Korner's Blues Incorporated, then John Mayall, the New Departures Big Band and with John Hiseman's Colosseum.

Joe Bauer born in 1941. An ex-jazz drummer, he joined The Youngbloods in 1966, formed by Jesse Colin Young. Essentially an East Coast good-time band, their version of ''Get Together'' launched them into the West Coast. They folded in 1973, after they had produced a number of notable albums, including ''Elephant Mountain'' and ''Rock Festival'', and having formed their own record company, Raccoon.

three years of marriage, he left her for Liz Taylor.

First gramophone, or disc-player, was patented in 1887, by Emile Berliner, a German immigrant living in Washington, DC.

George Chambers, of The, Chambers Brothers, born in 1931. The first of the ''psychedelic soul'' groups of the mid-Sixties.

T. S. Eliot born in St. Louis Missouri in 1888. 'Human kind cannot bear very much reality.''

SEPTEMBER 27

Rory Storme overdoses on sleeping pills, in 1972. His mother kills herself on the same day.

Don Nix born in Memphis, Tennessee in 1942. He has produced albums by John Mayall, Jeff Beck, Delaney and Bonnie, Skin Alley, as well as being an original member of The Bar-Keys and making his own solo albums.

Alvin Stardust born, in Muswell Hill, London in 1942. His real name is Bernard William Jewry, but he changed his name, first to Shane Fenton and then finally to Alvin Stardust.

SEPTEMBER 28

Ptah, Egyptian form of Vulcan.
St. Wenceslaus, King, Patron of Bohemia.

Ben E. King (Benjamin Nelson) born in 1938, in

Jimi Hendrix's death said to have been caused by ''suffocation from inhalation of vomit due to barbiturate intoxication'', reported the pathologist at the official inquest held in 1970, in London.

Mary Hopkin's ''Those Were The Days'' reaches UK No. 1 and stays six weeks in 1968. Paul McCartney produced the song, after Twiggy had discovered her on the British TV talent show ''Opportunity Knocks''. Her father acting as her manager stipulated in her contract with Apple that at least two songs on every album should be in her native tongue of Welsh.

Eddie Fisher and Debbie Reynolds married in 1955. Debbie had a US No. 1 in 1957 with ''Tammy'' and Eddie's string of hits ran from 1950 to 1967. After

RORY STORME & THE HURRICANES WITH DRUMMER RINGO STARR (RIGHT)

JERRY LEE LEWIS ON BRITISH TV ROCK SHOW "WHOLE LOTTA SHAKIN"

SEPTEMBER 29

Jerry Lee Lewis born in Ferriday, Louisiana, in 1935. His first record was "Crazy Arms" in 1957. In May 1957, he recorded "Whole Lotta Shakin' Goin' On" and in November his classic "Great Balls Of Fire" was released, both of which sold six million copies. His marriage to his 14-year-old cousin, Myra Brown almost cost him his career in bad publicity but the marriage lasted until "We were married for thirteen years and one day Myra just upped and walked out".

Mark Farner, guitarist and vocals with Grand Funk Railroad, born in 1948. A group with ten million–selling albums whose later albums were produced by Todd Rundgren, "We're An American Band", and by Frank Zappa.

Mike Pinera, guitarist with Iron Butterfly, born in 1948. He joined the group in 1971, replacing Eric Braunn. Pinera later joined Cactus when the group folded in 1972. The album "Metamorphosis" did not attract the critical attention or the sales of the earlier "In A Gadda Da Vidda".

Freddie King (Billy Myles) born in Longview, Texas, in 1934. No relation to B. B. or Albert. He first recorded under his own name in 1956, having jammed with many bands including Muddy Waters. Eventually Leon Russell signed him to his Shelter label.

Rolling Stones play the Granada, Shrewsbury, in 1965, and in 1963, they opened their first British tour with The Everly Brothers and Bo Diddley, at The New Victoria, London.

Bob Dylan plays harmonica on Caroline Hester's first album for Columbia Records in 1961, produced by John Hammond who signed Dylan on the strength of his playing.

Brigitte Bardot born in 1934.

SEPTEMBER 30

Mike Harrison, keyboards for Spooky Tooth, born in Carlisle, in 1945. Their first album "It's All About" was released in 1968. They disbanded in 1973, having had a faithful Underground following.

Frankie Lymon born in New York City, in 1942. "Why Do Fools Fall In Love" made US No. 7 in January 1956, when he was only 12 years old. He died of a heroin overdose in 1968.

Sylvia Peterson, of The Chiffons, born in 1946. Carole King played piano on "He's So Fine", in 1963.

THE WRECK OF JAMES DEAN'S PORSCHE, 1955.

James Dean dies in a car crash in 1955. He had made only three films : ''East Of Eden'' (1954), ''Rebel Without A Cause'' (1955) and ''Giant'' (1955). Later deified, his image of the misunderstood teenage rebel has never faded.

Jill Corey (Norma Jean Speranza) born in 1935. Of her five US chart entries ''Love Me To Pieces'' was the biggest in 1957.

Truman Capote born in 1924. The man who called Jack Kerouac's work ''just typing . . .'' and wrote ''Breakfast at Tiffany's'' and ''In Cold Blood''.

Johnny Mathis born in San Francisco, in 1935. His white-aimed schmaltz made him the first black American millionaire.

Christine Gail Hinton, David Crosby's girlfriend was killed in a car crash, when her VW bus was involved in a head-on collision with a school bus in Novato, north of San Francisco Bay, in 1969.

Bee Gees' ''Massachusetts'' enters UK charts to reach No. 1 in 1967.

Columbia Records closed their four Hollywood recording studios in 1972, firing their twenty-eight recording engineers. It seems that groups preferred to use the small independent studios.

Dewey Martin born in Chesterville, Ontario, in 1942. First a folksinger and then with The Dillards before becoming the drummer with Buffalo Springfield, when they got together in Los Angeles in 1966.

Gus Dudgeon born in 1942. Elton John's producer and a director of his Rocket Records. Among other acts he has produced, are David Bowie, Kiki Dee, Joan Armatrading and The Strawbs.

OCTOBER 1

National Day, Republic of China.

Scott McKenzie born in Arlington, Virginia, in 1944. Originally a member of Journeymen with Mama and Papas founder John Phillips, it was he who persuaded McKenzie to join him in LA in 1967. McKenzie established himself in the folk-rock genre and his ''San Francisco (Be Sure To Wear A Flower In Your Hair)''

became a international hit and the hippie anthem. It caused many pilgrimages to the city, and McKenzie (sincere about his love-and-peace philosophy) stopped recording when the flower power summer ended, apart from one country album in 1970.

Richard Harris, singer and actor, born in Limerick, Ireland. ''MacArthur Park'' was a US No. 2 in 1968. Usually cast as a rebel, a part he tries to play in real life.

Herbert Rhoad, of The Persuasions, born in Bamberg, South Carolina, in 1944. The group first formed in 1968 and were on Zappa's short lived Straight label for a while.

Rolling Stones play the Palace of Sports in Milano, in 1970. Police use tear gas to disperse two thousand fans unable to get in. Sixty-three arrested.

Barbara Parritt, of The Toys, born in Wilmington, North Carolina, in 1944. ''Lovers Concerto'', their 1965 million-seller was a rearranged Bach melody.

The Pink Floyd arrive in the USA in 1967, for their first tour.

The Beatles sign a five year management contract with Brian Epstein, in 1962.

Charles Manson removed from the courtroom at his trial in 1970, after singing ''Old Grey Mare'' to the Judge. When told to stop, he retorts ''You won't let me make noise, you've ordered me to stop living.''

Mao Tse-Tung and the Red Army enter Peking in 1949 in triumph.

Sex. Abbotsholme School, England introduces sex education into the curriculum in 1889, the first ever to do it.

OCTOBER 2

Durga, Wife or Shakti of Siva. Celebrated by some Hindus today as the day she destroyed a buffalo-headed monster. Rama marched against Ravanna. Aristotle.
Public Holiday in India.
Goose Fair in Nottingham, England.

Don McLean born in New Rochelle, New York, in 1945. "American Pie" suddenly shot him into fame in 1971 though he'd been playing the folk scene since 1963.

Michael Rutherford born in 1950. The bassist of Genesis and one of its founder-members, being one of the group of song-writing enthusiasts who formed the band at a London private school. Their melodramatic rock has brought them much success in Europe.

The Grateful Dead. Eight narcotics agents raid their communal house at 710 Ashbury Street, San Francisco, in 1967. Pigpen, Bob Weir and nine others were arrested. Police had no warrants and entered by breaking down the door.
"Hang On Sloopy" by The McCoys make US No. 1 in 1965.
Alex Raymond born in 1909. The man who drew Flash Gordon.
Graham Greene born in 1904. "Fame is a powerful aphrodisiac."
Groucho Marx born in New York City, in 1898.
Mahatma Gandhi born in 1869. Pacifist figurehead of Indian freedom.

OCTOBER 3

Dipamkara Buddha, most celebrated of the Tathgatas, or Seven Heroic Buddhas Of The Past.

Eddie Cochran born in Albert Lea, Minnesota in 1938. His first US chart entry was "Sittin' In The Balcony" in March 1957, but it was "Summertime Blues" in August 1958 which made him a real star. He became a legend after his death in a car wreck in England.

Chubby Checker (Ernest Evans) born in Philadelphia, in 1941. His first record, "The Class" was released in May 1959. But "The Twist" made No. 1 in summer 1960 and again in summer 1961 and really made him. In December 1963 he married Catharina Lodders from Holland, Miss World 1962.
Andrea Carroll (Andrea Lee DeCapite) born in 1946. "It Hurts To Be Sixteen" was a US hit in July 1963.
James Darren (James Ercolani) born in Philadelphia, in 1936. "Goodbye Cruel World" went to US No. 3 in October 1961.
Mexico City riots in 1968, prior to Olympic Games. Twenty students shot by police.

Charles Manson sings "That Old Black Magic" to the Judge at this trial in 1970. His three fellow-defendants shout "Hail Caesar" as the Judge walks in. They are all removed from the court, Manson shouting, "It's your judgment day, not mine".

OCTOBER 4

Janis Joplin dies from an overdose of heroin at the Landmark Hotel, Hollywood, in 1970. She had just completed "Pearl", her third album. The girl from Port Arthur, Texas came to fame at the Monterey Festival of August 1967. Managed by Albert Grossman, her first album sold a million in the US. Her great love for Bessie Smith showed throughout her brief career.
Bessie Smith buried in 1937. The greatest female

jazz-blues singer of all-time. Mortally injured in an auto crash, her arm being severed. She was refused admission to a whites-only hospital and died of loss of blood.
Jim Fielder, bass player, born in Denton, Texas. Formerly with The Mothers Of Invention, he later joined Blood Sweat and Tears.
Buster Keaton born in 1895. One of the great comedians of Hollywood. Began his career in 1917, in

two-reelers with Fatty Arbuckle, and continued making films until his death in 1966.

Patti Labelle (Patricia Holt) born in 1944. Originally The Blue Belles, The Patti Labelle and The Bluebells, the group finally transformed into Labelle in 1972 and had a million–selling hit with "Lady Marmalade".
Sputnik launched by USSR in 1957, the first satellite.

OCTOBER 5

The Beatles first single, "Love Me Do" released in the UK in 1962. It reached No. 16 in the UK charts.
Billy Lee Riley born in Pocahontas, Arkansas, in 1933. He recorded under the names of Billey Riley, Skip Wiley, Darren Lee, Lightnin' Leon, and was also with The Jivin' Five, The Megatons, The Rockin'. Stockin's and Sany and The Sandstones, among others.
Carlo Mastrangelo, of The Belmonts, born in 1938. They made some hits after lead singer Dion left, such as "Tell Me Why" in 1961.

Charles Manson dragged out of trial courtroom in 1970, after attacking the Judge with a sharpened pencil. Manson shouted, "I'm gonna have you removed if you don't stop. In the name of Christian justice I'm going to cut your head off."

Arlene Smith, of The Chantels, born in 1941. "Look In My Eyes" was their highest US chart entry in September, 1961.
Abi Ofarim born. With Esther they had a UK hit with "Cinderella Rockafella" in 1968, and were also involved in the early management of the German rock group Can.
George Jones Jr, lead with The Edsels, born in 1936. "Rama Lama Ding Dong" made the US charts in May 1961, though it was originally recorded in 1958.
Jose Jimenez (Bill Dana) born in 1924. His comedy record "The Astronaut" was a summer 1961 US hit.
The Fourmost enter UK charts in 1963 with "Hello Little Girl",
Jack Ford, twenty-three-year-old son of President Gerald Ford, admits, in 1975, to smoking marijuana.
Marijuana. Oregon becomes, in 1973, the first US state to decriminalize grass.
Diane Linkletter, an aspiring actress and daughter of American TV performer and author, Jack Linkletter, falls to her death after an attempt to fly from a sixty-floor window, allegedly on LSD, in 1969.

OCTOBER 6

Cecrops, founder of classical Greek culture.

Millie (Millicent Small) born in Jamaica, in 1947. "My Boy Lollipop" was a UK hit in April 1964 and reached No. 2 in both US and UK.

The Tornadoes "Telstar" reaches UK No. 1 in 1962.
Radio Station KPFT-FM in Houston, Texas is bombed for the second time in 1970, by right-wing extremists. The station broadcast advertisement-free news and was opposed to the Vietnam War.
Funeral Service for "Hippie, loyal son of Media" held in 1967, by the Diggers. It was a date that was, in effect, arbitrary. The "Summer Of Love" was long since dead, lost to the succeeding epidemics of methedrine and then heroin, that in turn devastated Haight Ashbury.
LSD declared illegal in 1966 by the US Government.

OCTOBER 7

Janis Joplin cremated in 1970.

Johnny Kidd killed in a car crash in Lancashire, in 1966. Johnny Kidd and The Pirates had their first hit with "Shakin' All Over" which made UK No. 3 in 1960.
Mario Lanza dies of a heart attack in Rome, in 1959. Famed for his popular operatic recordings of the Fifties.
Gary Puckett, of Gary Puckett and The Union Gap born in Hibbing, Minnesota, Bob Dylan's home town. They first entered the charts with "Woman Woman" in November 1967, in the US, perhaps best known for "This Girl Is A Woman Now" of 1969.
Tony Sylvester born in 1941. The Main Ingredient were originally known as The Poets in the late Fifties, changing their name in 1966. The early Seventies gave them a number of hits including the million-seller "Everybody Plays The Fool" in 1972. Sylvester left to become a producer in 1974.

OCTOBER 8

Confucius, founder of Confucianism.

Pete Drake born in Augusta, Georgia in 1933. One of the first and best steel guitar players. A very busy Nashville sessionman he has worked with many, notably Bob Dylan. He plays on "John Wesley Harding", "Nashville Skyline", and "Self Portrait". He has also produced for Ringo Starr.
Ray Rowyer, guitarist of Procul Harum, born in 1945. Replaced by Robin Trower after the hit single "Whiter Shade Of Pale" but before their first album.

Buzz Clifford (Rees Francis Clifford III) born in Berwyn, Illinois, in 1942. "Baby Sittin' Boogie" was his 1961 US hit.
Doc Green born in 1934. He sang baritone with The Drifters from 1959 onwards and was on such hits as "Save The Last Dance For Me" which was US No. 1 in 1960.
The Great Chicago Fire of 1871.
President Johnson has gall bladder operation in 1965. Goes on TV to show his scar to the waiting world.

L.B.J. PLEASE STAY

OCTOBER 9

John Winston Lennon born in Woolton, Liverpool, in 1940. "Rock and roll is the music that inspired me to play music. There is nothing conceptually better than rock and roll. No group, be it The Beatles, Dylan or The Stones have ever improved on 'Whole Lotta Shaking' for my money. Or maybe like our parents: that's my period and I'll dig it and never leave it."

Sean Ono Lennon born in New York, in 1975. The only child of John and Yoko Lennon, after Yoko having suffered two miscarriages.

John Lennon wins his legal battle against deportation from the United States. Judge Irving Kaufman ruled that a marijuana conviction in Britain was not sufficient reason for deporting

Che Guevara shot by Bolivian authorities in 1967, against the wishes of the CIA who wanted to question him first.

Pat Burke, saxophone player with The Foundations, born in 1937. "Baby Now That I've Found You" launched the group in 1967.

O. V. Wright (Overton Vertis Wright) born in Memphis, Tennessee, in

1939. He made the original recording of "That's How Strong My Love Is" in 1964 and released fine, but commercially unsuccessful, records throughout the Sixties.

John Alex Entwhistle born in Chiswick, London, in 1946. In addition to his bass and horn work with The Who, he leads his sometime

band, John Entwhistle's Ox.

Elvis Presley and his wife Priscilla get divorced in Santa Monica, California in 1973. She took with her considerable property, $750,000 and an extra $4,200 for twelve months, $4,000 for her daughter Lisa, half the proceeds from the sale of the Presley Los Angeles home and 5% of

the total stock in two music publishing companies. They left court arm in arm and kissed before Elvis drove away without her.

The Beatles begin their fourth British tour at The Gaumont, Bradford, in 1964.

Rolling Stones play The Odeon, Leeds, in 1965 and in 1964 announce the cancelation of their South African tour, because of The Musicians Union anti-apartheid embargo.

E. Howard Hunt, born in 1918. As "Eduardo", Hunt had been a CIA organizer in the abortive "Bay of Pigs" invasion of Cuba and was co-leader of Watergate "Plumbers". Writing as John Baxter and Gordon Davies, Hunt is a top-selling thriller writer, as well as a prisoner for his part in Watergate.

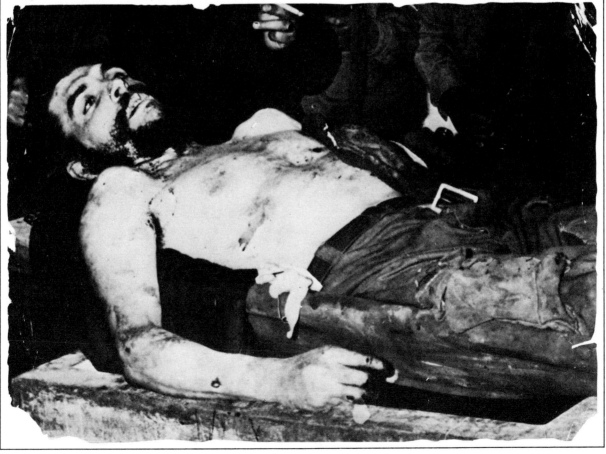

GRACE SLICK IN 1966.

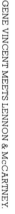
GENE VINCENT MEETS LENNON & McCARTNEY.

OCTOBER 10

Plotinus, Alexandrian philosopher and mystic.
Anniversary of Chinese Revolution.

Grace Slick born in 1939. She joined the Jefferson Airplane in 1966, replacing Signe Anderson, who left to have a baby. Slick had before that fronted Great Society, another San Francisco group. After four years the Airplane began to split up. Having originally written the group's first two hits "White Rabbit" and "Somebody To Love", she recorded an album with guitarist, Paul Kantner "Sunfighter", in 1971. Her child by Kantner was named God, but she later

changed it to China. The Airplane reformed as Jefferson Starship, with Slick as vocalist.
Keith Reid born in 1946. He joined with Gary Brooker to form Procul Harum in 1967. Their first single, "A Whiter Shade Of Pale" was a world wide hit for them in 1967, and Reid's lyrics have been a mainstay for the group through many changes in line up.
Alan Cartwright born in 1945. Came in on bass with Procul Harum when Chris Copping switched to organ after their "Broken Barricades" album in 1971.
Frank Zappa's solo album, "Hot Rats", released in US in 1969. The cover featured the late Miss Christine of the GTO's.
Bobby "Boris" Pickett and The Crypt-Kickers reach US No. 1 with "Monster Mash" in 1962. Another song the BBC banned.
Harold Pinter, British playwright, born in Hackney, East London, in 1930.
Spiro Agnew sacked as Vice-President of the USA in 1973.

OCTOBER 11

Cadmus, Greek culture hero.

Edith Piaf dies near Grasse, France, in 1963. The "Little Sparrow", the greatest of

all the chanteuses, had 40,000 mourners at her funeral.
Muddy Waters seriously injured and three others killed, in a car crash in Illinois in 1969.

OCTOBER 12

Columbus Day in USA.

Sam Moore born in Miami, Florida, in 1935. Joined with Dave Prater in 1958 to form Sam and Dave. Success was a long time coming but finally in 1966 "You Don't

Know Like I Know" and "Hold On I'm Coming" were big chart entries and in 1969, they had a US No. 2 with "Soul Of Man" which sold over a million.
Rick Parfitt, guitarist and vocals with Status Quo, born in 1948. Their first UK Top 10 hit was "Pictures Of Matchstick Men" in 1968. Became a heavy metal, working-class group with a following in Britain.
Aleister Crowley (Edward Alexander Crowley) born in Leamington, Warwickshire at 11.00 pm, in 1875. "The Great Beast", "The Wickedest Man Alive". His motto was "Do What Thou Wilt". One of his novels was entitled "Diary Of A Drug Fiend". He died in 1947.
Gene Vincent dies in 1971 from a seizure attributed to

a bleeding ulcer. His 1957 recording of "Be-Bop-A-Lula" is a rock'n'roll classic, but his career was dogged by mismanagement, and by 1958 he was an outcast in a rock scene, dominated by clean-cut boys like Fabian and Rick Nelson. He attempted a comeback but by 1969 alcoholism had turned the wild rocker into a portly middle-age. He appeared at the Toronto Rock Festival the year before his death.
Johnny Ray's "Just Walking In The Rain" enters UK charts to stay for eighteen weeks and reach No. 1 in 1956.
Phil Spector's "Warner-Spector" label launched in 1974.
Brian Poole and The Tremeloes' "Do You Love Me" reaches UK No. 1 in 1963.
Belly Dancing. Pamela Ness, aged twenty-two, set up an all-time record of twenty-seven and a half hours of continuous wiggling. Immediately after the event she was taken to a hospital in Missouri, suffering from "faintness and aching feet".

PAUL SIMON IN NEW YORK CITY, 1975.

OCTOBER 13

St. Edward The Confessor, King of England.

Paul Simon born in Newark, New Jersey, in 1941. He and Art Garfunkel grew up, went to school together, and formed Tom and Jerry. As Simon and Garfunkel, they reached No. 1 with "The Sound Of Silence" in the US in 1966 and later albums such as "Bridge Over Troubled Waters" (1970) still enjoy enormous sales. As a solo artist, he has achieved continuing success with a series of impeccably produced albums.

Chris Farlowe (John Deighton), born in London in 1940. Began with The John Henry Skiffle Group then moved into rock and roll as Chris Farlowe and The Thunderbirds. At this time, he recorded "Buzz With The Fuzz". When he met Mick Jagger, who wrote and produced for him, he had a hit with "Out Of Time" which made UK No. 1 in 1966. Made comeback in 1976.

Lenny Bruce born in 1925. "If you believe there is a God, a God that made your body, and yet you think that you can do anything with that body that's dirty, then the fault lies with the manufacturer."

Janis Joplin's ashes scattered at sea off Stinson Beach, Marin County, California, in 1970.

The Beatles appear on ABC-TV program "Sunday Night At The

London Palladium'' in 1963.
Robert Lamm born in 1944. In 1968 he formed The Chicago Transit Authority at the time when large jazz-rock bands were the in thing, Lamm played keyboards and wrote many of their lyrics. Chicago led the way for such groups as Blood Sweat and Tears in the charts.

Marie Osmond, the only girl in the six piece Osmonds. A Mormon teenybopper group whose appeal finally began to decline in 1975.

Goldfish Swallowing. In 1975 Leonard McMahon swallowed five hundred and one goldfish in four hours, at Oakland, California, beating the previous best of three hundred.

Emmeline Pankhurst holds the first Suffragette meeting in 1905, at the Free Trade Hall, London. The first utterance of the famous battle-cry ''Votes For Women''.

Hard living got the better of him.

Watergate. John Wesley Dean III born in 1938. Dean, the baby-faced success story, who was Nixon's Chief Domestic Counsel until his firing on April 30, 1973, blew the whole Watergate cover-up wide open.

King Harold of England shot in the eye at the Battle of Hastings by a Norman arrow, in 1066. The High altar of Battle Abbey was built on the exact site.

Robert Parker born in New Orleans, in 1930. Played saxophone on Professor Longhair's 1949 sides, and with Joe Tex, Ernie K Doe on ''Mother In Law''. In 1966 he had a US No. 4 with ''Barefootin'''.

''International Times'' published in London, in 1966. It was the first underground newspaper in Europe and only the fifth in the world. The print run was 5,000 copies.

in the US and No. 3 in the UK in 1965.

David Carroll born in Chicago in 1913. ''Melody Of Love'' was a 1954 instrumental hit.

Keith Richard and Anita Pallenburg given suspended sentences and fined £500 in Nice, on drug charges in 1973.

Country Joe and The Fish give out their first record at the protest march to Oakland in 1965. It was an EP called ''Fire In the City''/''Superbird''.

Howlin' Wolf suffers a severe heart attack in 1969, but he survived another six years.

The Pink Floyd appear together with The Soft Machine, at the launching party in 1966 for ''International Times'', the London underground newspaper. It introduces them for the first time to a large audience.

P G Wodehouse, born in Guildford, Surrey in 1881. Creator of Bertie Wooster and Jeeves.

Oscar Fingal O'Flahertie Wills Wilde born in 1854.

Derek and The Dominoes begin tour of USA in Trenton, New Jersey, in 1970.

Moratorium Day in the USA in 1969. In Viet Nam, GI's patrol with black armbands while in the US, a million Americans march against the war.

US Army in 1970 awards a Silver Star for Valor to Brigadier General Eugene P. Forrester in Viet Nam. It is later revealed that his acts of heroism were invented by enlisted men under orders.

Kent State Grand Jury indicts, in 1971, twenty-five members of the University and praises the National Guard's killing of four students when they opened fire on an unarmed crowd, holding a small demonstration against the US invasion of Cambodia.

Friedrich Nietzsche born in Rocken, Prussian Saxony.

OCTOBER 16

Bob ''Ace'' Weir (Robert Hall Weir) born in 1947. Played jug and kazoo with Mother McCree's Uptown Jug Champions, the band which grew first into The Warlocks and finally The Grateful Dead. Weir began by taking guitar lessons from Jorma Kaukonen and played guitar with The Dead, making a solo album ''Ace'' in 1972.

Dave Lovelady, drummer with The Fourmost, born in 1942. They had previously been The Four Jays and the Four Mosts, before Brian Epstein changed their name. ''A Little Lovin''' made UK No. 6 in 1964.

Emile Ford born in 1937. ''Counting Teardrops'' was a UK hit in 1960.

Leonard Chess, one of the founders of the famous

Chess record label, dies in Chicago of a heart attack, in 1969. He was fifty-two.

Berkeley anti-war rally, with Kesey and his Merry Pranksters and the Instant Action Jug Band (to become Country Joe and The Fish), held in 1965.

''A Tribute To Dr. Strange'' is the title of a dance given at the Longshoreman's Hall in San Francisco, in 1965. It started the long series of ''psychedelic'' weekly dances and featured the first of Ken Kesey's public ''Acid Tests''. The venue later became Bill Graham's Fillmore West.

Eugene O'Neill born in 1888. Playwright who got sucked into Hollywood.

OCTOBER 14

Cliff Richard (Harry Roger Webb) born in Lucknow, India, in 1940. Lauded as the British Elvis, his first record was ''Move It'' in September 1958. He became a show-biz institution, smothering early promise in a shower of corn, not helped by his clean-cut, evangelical image.

Charlie Watts marries Shirley Ann Shepherd in Bradford, in 1964.

Bill Justis, composer and performer of ''Raunchy'', born in 1926.

Joe Cocker and six members of his band busted for drugs in Adelaide, Australia, in 1972.

Drugs. The Comprehensive Drug Abuse Prevention and Control Act of 1970, passed by the United States Congress. It reclassified marijuana offenses as misdemeanors.

Errol Flynn dies in 1959.

OCTOBER 15

Richard Carpenter born in New Haven, Connecticut in 1945. With his sister Karen he formed Spectrum, which was heard by Herb Alpert, who signed the two to A & M. Since, as The Carpenters, they have recorded many highly commercial versions of pop standards and some of their own compositions, having an unbroken string of hits.

Tito Jackson, of The Jackson Five, born in Gary, Indiana, in 1953.

Chris Andrews born. ''Yesterday Man'' made UK No. 3 in October 1965. Robert Wyatt recorded it in 1974 as a single, but it was never released.

Marv Johnson born in 1938. ''You Got What It Takes'' in 1959 was his first US Top 10 hit.

Barry McGuire born in Oklahoma in 1935. ''Eve Of Destruction'' reached No. 1

"Anna Christie" was made in 1923 with Blanche Sweet and again in 1930, starring Greta Garbo.

Watergate. Charles Colson born in 1931. Special Counsel to President Nixon, he ran the "Dirty Tricks" department of the White House. Colson's motto "If you've got them by the balls, their hearts and minds will follow" was backed only by his insistence that he "would walk over my grandmother, if necessary" for Nixon. He walked, and fell, and was later converted to Jesus.

OCTOBER 17

Japanese Gods of Harvest festival. October 17-23 Tibetan Festival of Ancestors.

Cozy Cole born in 1928. His drum solo record "Topsy II" reached US No. 3 in September 1958.

Manfred Mann's "Do Wah Diddy Diddy" reaches US No. 1 in 1964.

Drugs. First major publicity on drugs to result in legal action, came from a series of stories in the New Orleans "Morning Tribune" of 1926, when a group of reporters described the "marijuana menace" threatening the city.

Gary Glitter reaches UK No. 1 with "I Love You Love Me Love" in 1973.

Arthur Miller born in 1915. Playwright and scriptwriter. "Death Of A Salesman" is one of his most famous plays. He wrote the screenplay for "The Misfits" starring his wife Marilyn Monroe.

A. S. Neill, born in 1883. Progressive educationalist, analyzed by Wilhelm Reich. Very influenced by Reich's concepts of the meaning of freedom, he set up his progressive school Summerhill, to try and put theory into practice. Joan Baez is among those who later helped him with his work.

OCTOBER 18

Thanksgiving Day in Canada.

Chuck Berry (Charles Edward Anderson Berry) born in San Jose, California, in 1926. "Maybellene", his first record, was released in July, 1955. Best known for his car and school songs "Like I didn't write 'School Days' in a classroom. I wrote it in the Street Hotel, one of the big, black, low-priced hotels in St. Louis."

Russ Giguere, lead with The Association, born in Portsmouth, New

Hampshire. "Along Comes Mary" was their first US Top 10 entry in 1966. "Cherish" (1966) and "Windy" (1967) both made US No. 1.

Ronnie Bright, bass with The Coasters, born in 1938. He replaced Will "Dub" Jones in the Sixties.

Al Green, soul singer, is scalded on his bare back, when a girlfriend, Mary Woodson, throws boiling grits at him before shooting herself, in 1973.

Richard Nader presented the first of his Rock 'N' Roll Revival Shows at the Felt Forum in New York City in 1969. Starring Bill Haley, Chuck Berry, The Platters and The Shirelles.

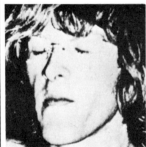

Paul Kantner, Jefferson Airplane's guitarist, busted in Oahu, Hawaii in 1969, for possession of marijuana. Police said Kantner was caught crawling through bushes with a joint between his lips. The Airplane had a different story.

John Lennon and Yoko Ono subject of a police raid at their flat in Montagu Square, London, and are remanded on bail for possession of cannabis. He was fined £150 with £21 costs.

John Lennon's first solo film appearance "How I Won The War" premiered at the London Pavilion in 1967, and in 1968

"Sugar Sugar" by The Archies makes US No. 1 and enters UK charts. An assemblage of studio musicians shown only as cartoons on TV.

The Grand Ole Opry founded in 1925.

OCTOBER 19

Peter "Tosh" McIntosh, of the original Wailers, born in Church Lincoln, Jamaica in 1944. A songwriter responsible for some of the Wailers' best material, but he left the group saying publicly that he would never work for Island Records again.

David Guard born in San Francisco in 1934. He was replaced in The Kingston Trio by John Stewart in May, 1961. They had many folk oriented hits such as "Tom Dooley".

Wilbert Hart, of The Delfonics, born in Philadelphia in 1947. The Philly Groove label was started for the group by their manager Stan Watson.

Larry Chance (Larry Figueiredo), lead with The Earls, born in Philadelphia, in 1940. "Remember Then" was their biggest US hit in 1962.

George Gates born in 1911. He made the US charts with film themes such as "Moonglow" and "Theme From Picnic" in 1956.

CIA in 1970, claims that thirty thousand Communist agents have infiltrated the Saigon Government.

OCTOBER 20

Ric Lee, drummer with Ten Years After, born in Gannock, Staffordshire, in 1945. First album "Ten Years After" was in 1967. The group has done more British tours than any other band.

LaVern Baker recorded "Tweedle Dee" in New York City, in 1954. Ahmet Ertegun and Jerry Wexler producing.

PETER TOSH

Wanda Jackson born in 1937. "Right Or Wrong" and "In The Middle Of A Heartache" made the US Top 40 in 1961.

Earl Bostic, bandleader, dies in 1965. Among the many greats in his various line-ups was John Coltrane.

Rolling Stones play their first show in Paris, at the Olympia, in 1964. One hundred and fifty arrests, £1400 damage to the Olympia.

Arthur Rimbaud born in 1854.

OCTOBER 21

Manfred Mann born in Johannesburg, South Africa, in 1940. Formed Mann-Hugg Blues Brothers in 1963, but later renamed the group Manfred Mann. Their third single "5-4-3-2-1" was an early 1964 UK hit. "Do Wah Diddy Diddy" made US No. 1 and established the band there. Bob Dylan remarked favorably on their versions of his "Mighty Quinn" and "If You Gotta Go, Go Now".

Steve Cropper, legendary guitarist with Booker T and The MGs, born in Willow Springs, Missouri, in 1941. "Green Onions" was their only hit. Now produces records including those of the Staple Singers.

Lee Loughnane, trumpet and flugelhorn player with Chicago, born in 1946. The band began in 1969 as The Chicago Transit Authority before changing to the much simpler Chicago on their second album.

Eric Faulkner, guitarist with The Bay City Rollers, born in Edinburgh in 1955.

Jade Jagger, daughter of Mick and Bianca, born in the Belvedere Nursing Home in Paris, in 1971.

Dr. Ross (Isaiah Ross) born in Tunica, Mississippi, in 1925. Early blues and boogie man who led Dr. Ross His Jump and Jive Boys in the early Fifties and Dr. Ross and His Orbits in the late Fifties. "Cat Squirrel" is one of his classics.

Sheila Jones, of The Kaye Sisters, born in Peckham, in 1936. One of the few British all-girl groups of the time.

Norman Wright, lead of The Del-Vikings, born in 1937. "Come Go With Me" made the US charts at No. 5 in 1957.

Buddy Holly's last studio session at the Pythian Temple Studios in New York City, in 1958. He recorded "It Doesn't Matter Any More" and "True Love Ways" among other tracks, using strings which his fans found hard to accept.

Astrella Celeste Leitch, daughter of Donovan and Linda Lawrence, born in 1971. Donovan and Linda were married in October 1970. Her son Julian attended the wedding; his father was Brian Jones.

Bill Black, of The Bill Black Combo dies in 1965. Their first chart entry in US was "Smokie Part 2" in 1959, but they had sixteen other chart entries.

The Beatles play Glasgow in 1964.

Jon Mark of Mark/Almond loses finger when falling out of a tree in Hawaii, in 1972.

Jack Kerouac, Beat Generation author of "On The Road" and "Dharma Bums" dies of a hernia in 1969. Allen Ginsberg, Gregory Corso and other old friends all attend the funeral in Lowell, Massachusetts, even though he had disassociated himself from them all years before.

Drugs. Drug Abuse Prevention Week begins in 1973, a scheme instituted by President Nixon.

Lady Chatterly's Lover obscenity trial began at Old Bailey in 1960. The publishers, Penguin Books, were later acquitted.

Pillar-Box Squatting. A world record number of twenty-nine, was set by a group of students from the City of London College in 1971.

Nelson wins the Battle of Trafalgar in 1805.

OCTOBER 22

Timothy Leary born in 1920. LSD pioneer and inventor of "Turn On, Tune In, Drop Out". He followed his own advice, leaving Harvard and setting up the Millbrook psychedelic community. Busted many times and eventually jailed, for possession of two joints. Released from jail in 1976.

Annette Funicello, of The Mouseketeers, born in Utica, New York, in 1942. Great TV personality.

Tommy Edwards dies in Virginia, in 1969. "It's All In The Game" was his biggest hit.

The Who rejected by EMI in 1964, after submission of recordings from a test session.

Jefferson Airplane give their first concert at University of California in Santa Barbara, in 1966.

Eddie Brigati, vocalist with The Rascals, born in 1946. Originally The Young Rascals, they dropped the "Young" on reaching the age of 20. "Good Lovin'" was a US No. 1 in 1966.

OCTOBER 23

Sun enters Scorpio, ruled by Mars. The swallows leave Capistrano.

Charlie Foxx, of Inez and Charlie Foxx, born in Greenboro, North Carolina, in 1939. A brother and sister act, they had a million-seller in 1963 with "Mockingbird". After several more hits, Inez left to go solo in 1969.

Ellie Greenwich born in 1939. Together with Jeff Barry she wrote many of Phil Spector's greatest hits, such as "Be My Baby" and "Then He Kissed Me".

The Drifters "Save The Last Dance For Me" by Pomus and Shuman reached US No. 1 in 1960.

Al Jolson dies in 1950. The first man to sing on film in "The Jazz Singer".

E.M.I. RECORDS LTD

Controlled by Electric & Musical Industries Ltd—the greatest recording organisation in the World

E.M.I. HOUSE · 20 MANCHESTER SQUARE · LONDON W.1

22nd October, 1964.

Kit Lambert, Esq.,
113 Ivor Court,
Gloucester Place,
London, N.W.1.

Dear Mr. Lambert,

I have listened again and again, to the High Numbers' white labels, taken from our test session and still cannot decide whether or not they have anything to offer.

You may, of course, in the meantime, have signed with another company, in which case, I wish you all the luck in the world. If you have not, I will be very interested to hear any other tapes you may have, featuring the group.

Yours sincerely,

BURGESS
Assistant to NORMAN NEWELL
Artistes & Repertoire Manager

Greg Ridley, bass with Spooky Tooth in their original line-up, also played with Humble Pie, born in Cumberland, in 1941. He plays on the ''It's All About'' (1968) and ''Spooky Two'' (1970) albums.

Drugs. Vice-Consul of the Colombian Consulate, General Jose Alvaro Cordoba Bojassen busted in 1970, when he arrived at Kennedy Airport with thirty-five pounds of pure cocaine, worth $5 million. Bail set at $75,000.

OCTOBER 24

United Nations Day.

Bill Wyman (William Perks), Lord of the Manor of Gedding and Thormwoods, born in Penge, Kent, in 1936. His father played piano accordion and Wyman was in his church choir for 10 years. He began piano at 4 years old and at 14 could play the organ and clarinet as well. He served two years in the Royal Air Force. In 1959 started his own group The Cliftons, but in 1962 answered an advertisement in ''The Melody Maker'' for a new bass player for The Rolling Stones. He passed the audition.

Paul and Barry Ryan born in Leeds, in 1948. ''Don't Bring Me Your Heartaches'' was their first UK hit in November 1965. Barry later went solo with songs written by twin brother Paul and had a No. 2 with ''Eloise'' in February 1968.

Dale ''Buffin'' Griffin born in 1948. Drummer of Mott The Hoople. David Bowie wrote their first hit ''All The Young Dudes'' when they re-formed in 1972. They broke-up again but with a new line-up, re-formed as Mott.

Edgar Broughton (Robert Edgar Broughton) born in Warwick in 1947 and formed the Edgar Broughton Band in 1969. They became a cult band in what remained of the English underground. ''Out Demons Out'', a chant taken largely from The Fugs was their biggest crowd pleaser. Edgar played guitar and did vocals.

Ricky Brook, of The Brooks Brothers, born. ''Ain't Gonna Wash For A Week'' was a UK hit in 1962.

Jerry Edmonton, drummer with Canadian psychedelic group, Steppenwolf, born in 1946.

Ted Templeman, of Harpers Bizarre, born in 1944. Mid-Sixties West Coast harmony group, had hits with Paul Simon's ''The 59th Street Bridge Song'' and Cole Porter's ''Anything Goes'' which featured Van Dyke Parks on piano. Templeman joined Warner Brothers as a house producer when the group split in 1970.

Pornography. ''As long as I am in the White House, there will be no relaxation of the national effort to control and eliminate smut from our national life.'' President Nixon's statement in 1970, rejecting the Report of the Presidential Commission on Pornography.

Evening Standard

Girl friend also arrested in Cheyne Walk raid

ROLLING STONE RICHARD—GUN, DRUGS CHARGES

Keith Richard, fined £205 at Marlborough Street Court on charges of cannabis, heroin, mandrax and gun possession, in 1973.

Keele University, England. Five hundred students sit-in in 1970, demanding representation on Senate. Fifty break into and explore the files in the Registry.

Twenty-Three Black Panthers arrested after all-night siege of their Headquarters, by one hundred police in Detroit, in 1970.

Dutch Schultz (Arthur Fliegenheimer) gunned down in 1935. His last words, spoken in delirium, were taken down by the FBI. They later formed the basis of several books by William Burroughs.

Walking Backwards. In 1932, Plennie L. Wingo of Abilene arrived in Istanbul, after walking backwards for over a year and a half from the starting point, Santa Monica, California. Distance covered was eight thousand miles.

OCTOBER 25

Jon Anderson born in Accrington, Lancashire in 1944. A founder-member of Yes, the leading symphonic-rock band of the Seventies. Their first album was released in 1969, but it was not really until Rick Wakeman joined in 1971 that they met with great success, topping rock polls in Britain by 1976.

Nick Drake, folksinger, whose first records were produced by Joe Boyd, dies in 1974.

Paul Hancox, guitarist and drums with Wayne Fontana and The

BILL WYMAN, 1966 / PHOTO: GERED MANKOWITZ.

Mindbenders, born. ''Groovy Kind Of Love'' was a 1966 international hit for them.

Helen Reddy born in Melbourne, Australia, in 1942. Her first US No.1 was ''I Am Woman'' in 1972, but she has followed it with another No.1 ''Angie Baby'' in 1974 and other Top Ten hits.

Jeanne Black born in Mount Baldy, California, in 1937. ''He'll Have To Stay'' was an answer to Jim Reeves' ''He'll Have To Go'' in 1960.

John Hall, drummer with The Equals, born in 1947. The group had a UK No. 1 in 1968 with ''Baby Come Back''.

Jack Kerouac, Beat Generation writer, invents ''spontaneous prose'' (at least in America) in 1951, and writes in streams of consciousness and with no corrections from this date onwards.

John Lennon filed suit in 1973, at Manhattan Federal Court, that wiretaps and surveillance were used against him and his lawyer Leon Wildes in connection with his applications against deportation.

reformed again in 1974 to cut ''Avalanche''.

The Beatles invested with their MBE awards by The Queen at Buckingham Palace in 1965. ''We just smoked a joint in the Buckingham Palace lavatory'' said Lennon later.

Alma Cogan dies in 1966 of throat cancer. ''Dreamboat'' was UK No. 1 in 1955.

INTERIOR VIEW OF O. K. CORRAL

Gunfight at The OK Corral in 1881. Wyatt Earp and his brothers Morgan and Virgil, assisted by the gunfighting dentist Doc John Holliday, shot it out with Ike Clanton, Billy Clanton, Tom and Frank McLowery, all but Ike Clanton were killed.

Pablo Picasso born in 1881, in Malaga, Spain.

Johann Strauss, Austrian composer, born in 1825.

Geoffrey Chaucer dies in 1406.

OCTOBER 26

''**Village Voice**'' newspaper in New York City started by Edwin Fancher, Daniel Wolf and Norman Mailer, who put up some of the money, in 1955.

Leslie West, guitarist with Mountain, born in New York City in 1945. He formed Mountain in 1969 and after a brief interlude with West, Bruce and Laing, Mountain

LESLIE WEST.

Bob Dylan plays Carnegie Hall, New York City, in 1963. For the program notes

he wrote the poem ''My Life In A Stolen Moment''.

Leon Trotsky (Lev Davidovitch Bronstein) born in Yanovka, in 1879. Leader of the Red Army during the Russian Revolution. Murdered by Stalinist agents whilst in exile in Mexico.

Picasso dies at his home in the south of France, in 1975

OCTOBER 27

"Jesus Christ Superstar" album released with a presentation at St. Peter's Lutheran Church, New York City, in 1970. Tim Rice and Andrew Lloyd Webber stood at the lectern explaining the music as it filled the church.

Cleo Laine, British jazz singer married to John Dankworth, born in London, in 1927.

Floyd Cramer born in 1933. "Last Date" reached US No. 2 in October 1960.

Don Patridge, one-man band London busker, born. "Rosie" was a February 1968 hit for him.

Dylan Thomas born in Carmarthenshire, South Wales. "Under Milk Wood" is probably his most famous poetic work. Drank himself to death at the Hotel Chelsea, New York City. Bob Dylan took his name from the poet, and later himself stayed at the Chelsea.

Abortion Act becomes law in the UK, in 1967. Clarified the legal situation regarding abortion.

Watergate. Harry Robbins ("Bob") Haldeman, born in 1926. As Nixon's Chief of Staff, this ex-advertising executive was closest to the President's ear. "Every President needs his son-of-a-bitch; I'm Nixon's" was his boast. On April 30, 1973, he was forced to resign.

Charles Manson defense lawyer in 1970, announces the intention of calling John Lennon to the witness stand to explain the meaning of certain Beatles songs. Manson had become obsessed with "Helter Skelter", "Piggies", "Black Bird" and "Revolution No. 9" from the Beatles double album. He believed the Beatles were prophesying the doom of the white race. (Lennon in fact only wrote the last of these songs.)

OCTOBER 28

Hathor, Egyptian form of Venus.

Thelma Hopkins, one of the two women singers in Dawn, born in Louisville, Kentucky, in 1948. "Tie A Yellow Ribbon Round The Old Oak Tree" was their biggest hit in 1973.

Rickie Lee Reynolds, guitarist with Black Oak Arkansas, born in Manilla, Arkansas, in 1948. The band was together for six years before signing with Atlantic in 1970 and achieving success.

Wayne Fontana born in Manchester, in 1945. With The Mindbenders he first entered the UK charts with "Um Um Um Um Um Um"

in October 1964 and reached No. 2 with "Game Of Love" in February 1965.

Curtis Lee born in 1941. "Pretty Little Angel Eyes" was his biggest hit and that was in 1961.

Brian Epstein, serving in his record shop in Whitechapel, Liverpool, is asked for "My Bonnie" by The Beatles in 1961. He finds the record was only released in Germany and sets out to see the group himself.

Hank B. Marvin, lead guitar with The Shadows, born in Newcastle, in 1941. Backing Cliff Richard, they first entered the UK charts in 1958, with "Move It". They began their solo career with "Apache" which was UK No. 1 in July 1960. Neil Young claims him to have been his first influence.

HANK B. MARVIN IN ABBEY ROAD / PHOTO: RONNIE NEWMAN.

WAYNE FONTANA & THE MINDBENDERS.

OCTOBER 29

Duane Allman dies in a motorcycle crash in Macon, Georgia in 1971. He was twenty-four. The Allman Brothers, one of the biggest heavy rock groups on the road, had many chart successes including the live album "At Fillmore East" in 1971. Duane was regarded as one of the finest bottleneck slide guitarists. He played on Clapton's "Layla" album, and also played as session man on albums by Wilson Pickett, Clarence Carter, King Curtis, Aretha Franklin, Boz Scaggs, and others .

Peter Green born in Bethnal Green, London, in 1946. He formed Fleetwood Mac in the summer of 1967, after leaving Steampacket which included Rod Stewart on vocals. Then replaced Eric Clapton in John Mayall's Bluesbreakers. Fleetwood Mac had big hits "Black Magic Woman" and "I Need Your Love So Bad". In 1968 their first album, "Fleetwood Mac" reached UK No. 1 and stayed in the charts for more than a year. After releasing "The Green Manalishi" in 1970, he quit the band, his place being taken by Christine Perfect from Chicken Shack. Since then he has been slowly recovering from a serious illness.

Michael Holliday commits suicide as part of some kind of pact with boxer Freddie Mills in 1963. "Story Of My Life" was UK No. 1 in 1958. They were both featured on BBC television pop show "6-5 Special" in the late Fifties.

Denny Laine (Brian Arthur Haynes) born in Birmingham, in 1944. Leader of The Moody Blues until 1966. Did solo single "Say You Don't Mind". Joined Paul McCartney's Wings when they formed. A most under-rated guitarist.

Randy Jackson, of The Jackson Five, born in Gary, Indiana. The group had four No. 1s in a row in the US with "I Want You Back" (November 1969), "ABC" (March 1970), "The Love You Save" (June 1970) and "I'll Be There" (September 1970).

The Who release "My Generation"/"Shout And Shimmy" in 1965 which gets to No. 3 in the UK charts.

Chairman of EMI, Sir Joseph Lockwood, in statement to the "Sun" newspaper in 1966, said that even if state-sponsored commercial radio was introduced, he would refuse to allow his records to be played all day long.

Wall Street Crash in 1929.

OCTOBER 30

Mars, God of War, Symbol of Energy.

Eddie Holland born in Detroit in 1939. Had a Top 30 hit with "Jamie" in 1962, but soon teamed up with his brother Brian and Lamont Dozier to form the

songwriting/production team, Holland Dozier and Holland, writing and producing a succession of hits for The Supremes, Marvin Gaye, Martha & The Vandellas, The Four Tops, The Temptations and so on. In 1968 they quit Motown and formed their own labels.

Tim Schmit, bass player with Poco, born in Oakland, California, in 1947. Joined the group in time for their

second album "Poco" (1970).

Frank Ifield born in Coventry, in 1937. "I Remember You" released in the UK in June 1962 made No. 1, as did many of his other recordings.

Ray Smith born in Paducah, Kentucky, in 1935. His US chart hit was with "Rock Little Angel" in 1960.

Rolling Stones "Get Off My Cloud", their fifth consecutive No. 1 in the UK, enters charts in 1965.

Bob Dylan's "Rolling Thunder Review" opens in Plymouth, Massachusetts, in 1975.

Charles Atlas born in Acri, Italy, 1893. "The World's Most Perfectly Developed Man".

Muhammad Ali and George Foreman receive largest-ever purse in 1974 for a boxing match. They received over $4,500,000 for a fight in Kinshasa, Zaire.

Ezra Pound born in Hailey, Idaho, in 1884. After moving to London he published the seminal literary magazine "Blast". During the Second World War he lived in Rome and broadcast regularly for the fascist government, on Rome radio. After many years in detention in the USA he was finally released and moved at once back to Italy, where he lived until his death, working on the final versions of his monumental "Cantos".

OCTOBER 31

Halloween.

Tom Paxton born in Chicago, Illinois, in 1937. Part of the early Sixties

folk boom and refused to change his style. He played at the 1969 Isle of Wight Festival in Britain and received a standing ovation which brought tears to his eyes. Best known for his "The Last Thing On My Mind", "Ramblin' Boy".

Russ Ballard born in 1947. Guitar and vocals with The Roulettes and then Unit 4+2. He was founder member of Argent and stayed throughout their most productive period, appearing on "Argent" in 1970, which included the hit "Liar" and only leaving after the double live album "Encore" which appeared in 1974. He left to go solo and was replaced by John Grimaldi and John Verity.

Kinky Friedman born in Rio Duckworth, Texas in 1944. He and his band the Texas Jewboys developed a highly original mixture of C & W, humor and ballads. Billy Swan and Waylon Jennings are among the top Nashville men who have worked with him.
Wayne Fontana and The Mindbenders enter UK charts for the first time, with "Um Um Um Um Um Um" in 1964.
"War Of The Worlds", Orson Welles' Mercury Theater radio presentation in 1938, scares America into believing a Martian landing is taking place. Welles was twenty-three years old at the time.
Drugs. The New Orleans

Medical and Surgical Journal of 1931, reports: "The dominant race and most enlightened countries are alcoholic, whilst the races and nations addicted to hemp and opium, some of which once attained to heights of culture and civilization, have deteriorated both mentally and physically."

Brian Jones sentenced to nine months in jail on drug charges in 1967. Released on bail pending appeal.
Talking. Victor Villimas of Cleveland, Ohio, who lapsed into silence in 1967 after talking continuously for five days and eighteen hours, setting an unbeaten record.
Mary Patricia McCartney, Paul McCartney's mother, dies in Liverpool in 1956.
Dale Evans born 1912. Wife of Roy Rogers.
John Keats born in 1795.

Bob Dylan appears at Philharmonic Hall, New York City, in 1964. This concert is sometimes known as his Halloween Concert. In return for Joan Baez helping him with his career he brought her onstage to sing three duets with him, and to do a solo version of "Silver Dagger".
"Bohemian Rhapsody"/ "I'm In Love With My Car" by Queen released in the UK in 1975. The single remains at No. 1 in the charts for eight weeks. The longest that any record had stayed there for twenty years.

Ric Grech born in Bordeaux, in 1945. Played bass with Family, the seminal London underground group. Left to join the 1969 supergroup, Blind Faith, with Eric Clapton, Steve Winwood and Ginger Baker.
Family plays its debut gig in 1967. Formed in Leicester in 1966 by the amalgamation of two local bands. Life-style featured in Jenny Fabian's "autobiography" "Groupie". Regarded as an important underground group in Sixties London.

Rolling Stones first record, "I Wanna Be Your Man"/ "Stoned" released in 1963. The A-side was especially written by John Lennon and Paul McCartney.
Elvis Presley back in the charts in 1969, as "Suspicious Minds" reaches US No. 1.
The Beatles open for 14-day season at The Star Club in Hamburg, in 1962.
"Oz" Magazine publishes its last issue in 1973. Started by Australian Richard Neville in 1967, it was the world's only full-color underground magazine.
"Let's Loot The Supermarket" by The Deviants was released in 1968. Possibly the most satisfactory of their records. It didn't get anywhere. Singer Mick Farren is now an editor of the English music paper "New Musical Express".

Dave Pegg, bass player with The Fairport Convention, born in 1947. He replaced Ashley Hutchings when he left to form Steeleye Span. Pegg has been one of the most consistent members of the line-up.

Keith Emerson born in 1944. Leader of The Nice who first came together to back P. P. Arnold, but soon broke loose on their own. Emerson's powerful organ dominated the group until they disbanded in 1970 and he went on to form Emerson Lake and Palmer. ELP was enormously successful and they started their own label, Manticore, promoting groups in the same musical area, including the Italian bands PFM and Banco.

Earl Carroll, lead of The Cadillacs, born in 1937. It is of Earl that "Everybody Calls Me Speedo, But My Real Name is Mr. Earl". "Speedo" was their first big hit in October 1955. In 1958, Speedo joined The Coasters (or in 1960, depending on which book you read).

Bruce Welsh, rhythm guitarist with The Shadows, born in Bognor Regis in 1941. Constantly in the UK charts throughout the Sixties.
Jay Traynor, lead with Jay and The Americans, born in 1938 in Brooklyn. Four US Top Ten hits in the Sixties including "Come A Little Bit Closer" in 1964.

Mississippi John Hurt dies in hospital in Granada, Mississippi, after a short illness. He was 74. He first recorded in 1928 but by 1929 he went back to farming. He was "rediscovered" in 1963 during the folk revival.

Bob Dylan's "Rolling Thunder Review" plays Lowell, Massachusetts, in 1975. Dylan and poet Allen Ginsberg pay a visit to the grave of Jack Kerouac who was from Lowell. Dylan is filmed playing white-face mime on the grave while Ginsberg improvises poetry.

NOVEMBER 3

Bert Jansch born in Glasgow, in 1943. A folk-blues guitarist, he formed Pentangle in 1967 and had considerable success with the group in the USA. It was an amplified acoustic band, combining traditional and contemporary folk music with jazz and blues influences.
Brian Poole born in London in 1941. His group The Tremeloes turned professional in 1961. "Do You Love Me" in 1963 was their UK No. 1.

Lulu (Marie McDonald McLaughlin Lawrie) born in Glasgow, in 1948. Enters charts in 1964 in UK with "Shout".

James Taylor and Carly Simon were married in 1972 at 6.30 pm, in her Manhattan apartment by a judge. Carly appeared on stage to take a bow with James at his concert that night at Radio City Music Hall.
The Crystals reach US No. 1 with "He's A Rebel" in 1962.
Stanley finds Livingstone in the jungle, in 1871.

NOVEMBER 4

The Beatles take part in the Royal Variety Performance at the Prince of Wales Theater, London, in 1963. "Those of you in the cheaper seats clap; the rest of you can rattle your jewelry"—John Lennon.

Bob Dylan plays at Carnegie Hall in 1961. His first major appearance uptown. The hall was badly attended, mostly filled with Dylan's friends, and he sang badly though talked at length to the audience. In 1971 Dylan records "George Jackson" single in CBS Studios, New York City, in protest of the Soledad Brother's death. It was arranged by Leon Russell with Ken Buttrey, drums; Ben Keith, steel guitar and with Joshie Armstead and Rose Hicks singing harmony.
Kathy Kirby enters UK charts with "Secret Love" in 1963.
Clinton Ford born in Salford, Lancashire. "Too Many Beautiful Girls" was his UK hit in 1961.

NOVEMBER 5

Guy Fawkes Day in Britain in celebration of the attempt to blow up Parliament.

Ike Turner born in Clarksdale, Mississippi, in 1931. The elder statesman of Southern R & B. After forming his band The Kings of Rhythm he auditioned for Sam Phillips in 1950. Moved to Sun Records when the label was formed by Phillips in 1952, and his band included his first wife Bonnie. He acted as a talent scout for Sun, discovering Howlin' Wolf and Little Milton among many others. Later had a world-wide hit (except in the US) with "River Deep And Mountain High" recorded with second wife Tina, and produced by Phil Spector. His career still continues successfully including record production. His backing group The Ikettes have spawned much new talent.

IKE TURNER.

157

ART GARFUNKEL / PHOTO: TOM SHEEHAN.

NOVEMBER 6

P. J. Proby (James Marcus Smith) born in Houston, Texas, in 1938. A country and western singer, his sister dated Elvis in 1952. As Jet Powers he moved to Hollywood in 1955 and made a demo for Elvis in 1958. He dated Elvis's girl friend while Presley was in the army. No more demos. Changed his name to P. J. Proby and was asked to play "Iago" opposite Cassius Clay's "Othello". In England appeared on "Meet The Beatles" in 1964, and "Hold Me" made UK No. 3

Art Garfunkel born in Forest Hills, New York. Grew up with Paul Simon and together they formed Tom and Jerry. Later as Simon and Garfunkel they had many hits beginning with "The Sound Of Silence". Made first solo album "Angel Clare" in 1973.

Gram Parsons born Winter Haven, Florida, in 1946. His father was the country singer Coon Dog (Conner). His country music influenced The Byrds when he joined them, particularly on their "Sweetheart Of The Rodeo" album. Left to form Flying Burrito Brothers. The boy friend of Emmylou Harris, he died on September 19th, 1972. She sang with him on his two solo albums, "GP" and "Grievous Angel".

Steve Miller born in Milwaukee, Wisconsin, in 1943. He formed the Steve Miller Blues Band in San Francisco, in 1966, and it was a highly regarded part of the West Coast musical scene. "Children Of The Future" in 1967 launched them, but Miller never managed to make the very top until 1974 with "The Joker".

Herman (Peter Noonan), of Herman's Hermits, born in Manchester. "I'm Into Something Good" introduced them to the No. 1 spot in the UK in 1964 (a cover version of the Earl Jean original). Huge success in the USA.

Johnny Horton dies in a car crash near Milano, Texas, in 1960. He was first in the US charts with his No. 1 hit "Battle Of New Orleans" in 1959.

Miss Christine, of The GTOs, dies of a drug overdose in 1972. She is the woman on the cover of Frank Zappa's "Hot Rats" album.

Roy Rogers born in Cincinnati. Ohio, in 1912.

Beach Boys enter UK charts with "Good Vibrations" which reaches No. 1 in 1966.

in July. His trousers split on tour in 1965 and he was banned by many theaters and television. His fourth disc "I Apologize" appeared in the charts in February 1965. He attempted a comeback in the early Seventies but with no success.

Doug Sahm born in San Antone, Texas, in 1942. He formed The Sir Douglas Quintet in 1964. In 1965 "She's About A Mover" reached the US Top 20 and in 1966 "The Rains Came" did the same. In 1969 the group released their highly acclaimed "Mendocino" album.

George Young, rhythm guitarist with The Easybeats, born in 1947. "Friday On My Mind" was a transatlantic hit in 1966, after they had a number of local hits in Australia.

Chris Glen, bass player with The Sensational Alex Harvey Band, born in 1950. "Delilah" was the first big

STEVE MILLER / PHOTO: SIMON FOWLER (L.F.I.).

hit for the SAHB in 1975.
Glenn Frey born in 1946. Together with other members of Linda Ronstadt's backing group he formed The Eagles in August 1971. They had instant success with their first album "Eagles" which included US chart hit "Take It Easy".

Joseph Pope, of The Tams, born in Atlanta, Georgia, in 1933. Their first hit was "Untie Me" in 1962, but they didn't enter the UK charts until 1971 when "Hey Girl Don't Bother Me" was reissued and made No. 1.

Jean Shrimpton born in 1942. The archetypal fashion model of the "swingin' Sixties in London. Now a photographer in her own right. Starred in the film "Privilege" with Paul Jones.

Ray Conniff born in 1916. His instrumental themes have taken him five times into the US charts.

Eugene Pitt, lead of The Jive Five, born in Brooklyn, New York City, in 1937. "My True Story" reached US No. 3 in 1961.

Mike Clifford born in 1943, in Los Angeles. "Close To Cathy" made US No. 12 in September 1962.

Billy Murcia, drummer of The New York Dolls, dies of accidental suffocation when a girl pours black coffee down his throat, after he nods out in her flat after coming home with her from The Speakeasy in London. He was 21.

Annette Kellerman, the "Million Dollar Mermaid", who shocked the world by wearing the first one-piece bathing suit in public, dies at Queensland nursing home in 1975, aged 84.

NOVEMBER 7

Joni Mitchell born in McLeod, Alberta, Canada in 1943. In New York City she entered folk circles. Judy Collins, Tom Rush and The Fairport Convention began recording her songs. "Song To A Seagull", her first album, was released in 1968. "Ladies Of The Canyon" gave her almost superstar status when it was released in 1970 and from there she went from strength to strength; her 1975 "The Hissing Of Summer Lawns" was heralded by critics as a masterpiece.

Mary Ellin Travers, of Peter, Paul and Mary, born in Louisville, Kentucky, in 1937. "Puff The Magic Dragon" in March 1963 was

JONI MITCHELL

MARY TRAVERS / PHOTO: GRAHAM KEEN.

thought by some to advocate drug usage. Bob Dylan's "Blowin' In The Wind" provided them with a hit single.

Dee Clark (Delectus Clark) born in Blythsville, Arkansas, in 1938. "Raindrops" made US No. 2 in 1961.

Johnny Rivers born in New York City, in 1942. "Poor Side Of Town" was US No. 1 in 1966. Ran Soul City record label.
Guitar Plucking. Steve Anderson became the new world champion in 1975, with a time of 114 hours and 17 minutes, beating the previous best by almost four hours. The record

attempt was part of a contest with over 200 competitors held in Los Angeles.
Lenin and the Bolsheviks seize power in Russia in 1917, during the "October Revolution" (October 25th, in the old style calendar).

A. P. Carter, of the famous Carter Family of folk singers, dies in 1960.

NOVEMBER 8

Roy Wood born in 1948. Leader of the Birmingham group The Move, who became famous in the London underground in late 1966, for their violent stage act. Wood wrote all the group's many Top Twenty hits. Prime Minister Harold Wilson sued them successfully over a caricature used in publicity for their first single. Wood launched The Electric Light Orchestra in 1972, but left to form Wizzard. Had a hit with their first single, and the second "See My Baby Jive" was a UK No. 1 in 1973. Wood developed a format for dressing up rock 'n' roll originals with Phil Spector style production, which paid-off in UK hits.

Bonnie Bramlett (Bonnie Lynn) born in Acton, Illinois in 1944. With her husband she toured with Eric Clapton, and introduced many musicians who are now top sidemen. Since their divorce in 1972 they have both developed solo careers.

Bonnie Raitt, born in Los Angeles of a musical family. On the East Coast she had initial success playing clubs, often sharing the bill with the blues singers who had most influenced her music; her first album "Bonnie Raitt" featured Junior Wells. She returned to Los Angeles and recorded "Taking My Time" with Lowell George and Bill Payne from Little Feat. "Street Lights" and "Home Plate" albums had both added to her growing reputation. She and her band frequently play community benefit concerts, political rallies and concerts for Pacifica Radio.

Chris Connor born in 1930. "I Miss You So" was her biggest US hit in 1956.

Patti Page born in 1927. Her first hit was "Confess" in June 1948.
Ivory Joe Hunter, great blues pianist, dies of lung cancer in 1974.

Cynthia and John Lennon granted Decree Nisi in their divorce case in 1968.
"Led Zeppelin" II enters the UK album charts in 1969, to stay for over a year.
Katharine Hepburn born in 1907. She made her first film in 1932, and starred in many others including "Adam's Rib", one of many with her close friend Spencer Tracy.

NOVEMBER 9

Roger McGough, of Scaffold, born. As well as comedy hits such as "Lily The Pink" he did the more serious album with Mike McGear, "McGough And McGear" featuring his poems and with backing by Paul McCartney, Jimi Hendrix, Jane Asher and her mum, and hosts of others.

Lee Graziano, drummer with The American Breed, born in 1943. "Bend Me, Shape Me" was the biggest of their five chart records, reaching US No. 5 in 1967.

New York City Blackout in 1965. The blind lead confused New Yorkers, candles cost $2.00 each and mugging, theft and rape run rampant.

Brian Epstein first sees The Beatles play, at one of their 1961 lunch-time sessions at The Cavern Club.

"Rolling Stone" magazine starts in San Francisco, in 1967. A free roach holder was a give-away with the first issue.

NOVEMBER 10

Screamin' Lord Sutch (David Edward Sutch) born in 1940. Even with a little help from his heavy friends Jimmy Page, Noel Redding, Nicky Hopkins, Keith Moon and Jeff Beck, he has never been able to get a hit. Amazing self-publicist, he ran against Harold Wilson for Parliament. Noted for his bizarre stage act.

Greg Lake, bass, guitars and vocals with Emerson, Lake and Palmer, born. Originally with King Crimson, he formed ELP with ex-Nice organist Keith Emerson in 1969, later adding drummer Carl Palmer. The trio, although showing great flair and dynamism, have suffered from criticisms of lack of feeling in their music.

Tommy Dorsey, famous bandleader with his brother, born in 1905.

Tommy Facenda born in 1939. "High School USA" reached No. 26 in the US charts in 1959.

Tim Rice, lyricist of "Jesus Christ Superstar", born in Amersham, England, in 1944.

Bill Graham first hires the San Francisco Fillmore Auditorium for the night for $60.00, in 1965. His first show featured The Grateful Dead, The Jefferson Airplane, The Charlatans, and Sam Thomas and The Gentlemen's Band.

NOVEMBER 11

Martinmas, Wine Festival.
St. Martin, patron of Germany, protector of Vineyards.
Bacchus, God of Wine.
Vinalia, the pagan wine festival.
St. Mennas, patron of Egypt, form of Menes, the first King of Egypt,
Demi-God.

Mose Allison born in Tippo, Mississippi, in 1927. Jazz-singer and pianist, sometimes trumpeter, he first recorded in 1957. His style and songs were a big influence on the Sixties rock groups. "Parchman Farm", "Seventh Son" and "I Love The Life I Live" all feature his unique vocals and helped build a cult following for him. The Who, Georgie Fame, John Mayall have all recorded his work.

Jesse Colin Young born in 1944. Originally on the New York City folk scene, and with two solo albums to his name, Young formed The Youngbloods. They reached the height of their success

with ''Elephant Mountain'' and ''Rock Festival'' albums and even started their own, Racoon, label. The group split in 1973 and since then Young has reverted to making solo albums.

Vince Martell, guitarist with Vanilla Fudge, born in 1945. They began in the New York area as The Pigeons, before becoming Vanilla Fudge in 1967, the first ''heavy'' group. Best known for ''You Keep Me Hanging On''. They broke up in 1970.

Pat Daugherty, bass player with Black Oak Arkansas, born in Jonesboro, Arkansas, in 1947. A successful southern blues funk band with an energetic stage act.

Chris Dreja, rhythm guitarist with The Yardbirds, born in 1946. They began as The Metropolitan Blues Quartet at Kingston Art School, and replaced The Rolling Stones at the Crawdaddy Club in Richmond when they moved on to greater things. Their first real success came in 1965 with ''For Your Love'' which reached UK No. 2. After they broke up in July 1968, Chris Dreja took up photography.

Berry Oakley, of The Allman Brothers, dies when his motorcycle hits a Macon City bus, in 1972. He refuses hospital treatment but dies later of a brain haemorrhage. The accident happened only three blocks from the spot where Duane Allman died.

Dave Stringbean Akerman, country singer, and his wife were beaten up, robbed then murdered in 1973.

Narvel Felts born in Keiser, Arkansas, in 1938. ''Honey Love'' was in the US Top 20 in February 1960.

Bob Dylan's ''Tarantula'' published in 1970, in New York City. The first extracts from it appeared in ''The Georgia Straight'' underground paper in October 1968.

Jim Morrison, of The Doors, jailed for ''interfering with the flight of an intercontinental aircraft and public drunkenness'', in 1969.

World's First Pinball

Tournament. The South Carolina Open Pinball Flipper Machine Championship was held in the parking lot of a restaurant in Winnsboro, before 1,000 people, in 1972.

World War I ended by Armistice which took effect at 11.00 am in 1918.

NOVEMBER 12
St. Nilus and St. Horus.

Neil Young born in Toronto, in 1945. Formed Buffalo Springfield with Steve Stills in 1966, after they had met when they collided in a traffic jam. He then went solo, recording with Crazy Horse, the backing group he assembled for his album ''Everybody Knows This Is Nowhere'' (1969). Joined Crosby Stills and Nash, and made the highly successful album ''Deja Vu'' with them. Many solo albums to his name since then, including the classic ''After The Gold Rush''.

Booker T. Jones born in Memphis, Tennessee, in

1944. The instrumental "Green Onions" established him in 1962, with his group the MGs (Memphis Group).
Jimmy Hayes of The Persuasions born in Hopewell, Virginia, in 1943. The group has moved through a large number of labels since they first formed in 1968.
Leslie McKeown, singer with The Bay City Rollers, born in Edinburgh in 1955.

Brian Hyland born in New York City, in 1943. "Itsy Bitsy Teenie Weenie Yellow Polka Dot Bikini" was his 1960 comedy hit.
John Walker (John Maus), of the Walker Brothers, born. "Love Her" was their first UK chart entry in 1966. It reached No. 20.
Bob Crewe born in Newark, New Jersey, in 1931. "The Wiffenpoof Song" was his US chart hit in 1960.
Bobby Jameson broke both legs when he slipped and fell, while being talked down from a suicide attempt from the roof of the Hollywood Theater. Frank Zappa wrote and played the backing track to his "Got My Roogalator Working".
Charles Manson born in 1934. Found guilty of multi-murder, including that of Sharon Tate. The leader of The Family, still on Death Row.

NOVEMBER 13
Today and tomorrow: Lamentations of Isis.
St. Serapion, Christianized form of Serapis, the Egyptian Jupiter.

Terry Reid born in Paxton

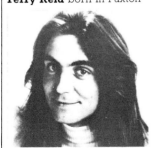

THE WHO
The prediction business (2)

Park, Huntingdonshire, England, in 1949. A number of solo albums including "Bang Bang You're Terry Reid" (1969). Toured with Cream. Made critically acclaimed "River" album in 1973.
"My Generation" by The Who enters UK charts in 1965 to reach No. 2. The Who's first world-wide hit.
"1-2-3" by Len Barry enters UK charts in 1965.
Timmy Thomas born in Evansville, Indiana, in 1934. "Why Can't We Live Together" reaches US No. 3 in November 1972.
Slade reach UK No. 1 with "Coz I Luv You" in 1971. They were managed by ex-Animal bassist Chas Chandler, who previously had done the same for Jimi Hendrix.

NOVEMBER 14
Keith Relf, former lead singer of The Yardbirds, found dead by his eight-year-old son, in 1976, at his house in Hounslow, West London. He was holding a live electric guitar. The

focal point of The Yardbirds, one of the pioneer groups of early British rock which acted as a proving ground for Eric Clapton, Jimmy Page and Peter Green. He later formed Renaissance with his sister Jane and ex-Yardbird Jim McCarty. In 1975 he formed Armageddon which recorded one single, but he never regained the success of his earlier years.
Freddie (Garrity), of Freddie and The Dreamers, born in Manchester, in 1940. "If You Gotta Make A Fool Of Somebody" was a May 1963

UK hit. An ex-milkman, he was managed by Brian Epstein.
"New Musical Express" the British music paper, begins printing record sales charts in 1942.
Moratorium Day, in 1969. Nearly half a million people

moratorium

marched in San Francisco and Washington to put an end to the Vietnam war.
BBC sent out the first daily radio program in 1922, from Alexandra Palace, London. The call sign of the station was "2 LO".
Queen's "A Night At The Opera" released in the UK in 1975. Said to cost between £30,000—£40,000 to make, it was one of the most expensive ever recorded in Britain. By January it had sold over 500,000 copies.
Budapest uprising in 1956.

NOVEMBER 15
St. Albertus Magnus, Magician and Scientist.
Bodhidharma, founder of Zen Buddhism.

Clyde McPhatter born in Raleigh, North Carolina, in 1933. "Seven Days" was his first solo chart entry after leaving The Drifters, which he followed up with over twenty more including the famous "Lover Please" in 1962.
Little Willie John (William J. Woods) born in Camden, Arkansas, in 1937. He had his biggest US chart success with "Sleep" in September 1960.

Petula Clark born in Rugby, England, in 1932. She had enormous chart success in the UK from the early Fifties onwards with hits such as "This Is My Song" which was No. 1 in February 1967. She has a large following in France where she now lives.

Howlin' Wolf suffered a heart attack in Chicago, in 1969. He pulled through, but died seven years later.

Janis Joplin arrested in 1969, for using "vulgar and indecent language" in Tampa, Florida. She was released on a $50 bond.

NOVEMBER 16

Pattie Santos, vocalist with It's A Beautiful Day, born in 1949. Their best known single was "White Bird", which also appeared on their first album "It's A Beautiful Day" in 1968.

Troy Seals born in Bill Hill, Kentucky, in 1938. Mostly works as a backing musician (for everyone from James Brown onwards), but recorded a solo album "Now Presenting Troy Seals" in 1973.

Toni Brown, vocals, keyboards and guitar with Joy Of Cooking, born in 1938. Formed by two women at the University of Berkeley, California, their first album was "Joy Of Cooking" in 1970. She left to go solo in 1973 and cut "Good For You Too" in 1974.

Mike Leadbitter dies in 1974. Foremost blues discographer. Founded the Blues Appreciation Society in Sussex in 1961, and in 1963, with Simon Napier, began to publish the magazine "Blues Unlimited". Based in Britain, it is regarded as the most authoritative of all the specialist blues magazines.

Alan Watts, author of "Beat Zen, Square Zen And Zen" dies in his Mill Valley, California home, in 1973. He was responsible for introducing Zen Buddhism to the American Beat community in the Fifties. Though British, he spent most of his later life in the USA. He was fifty-eight.

NOVEMBER 17

Gene Clark born in Tipton, Missouri, in 1941. Originally with The New Christy Minstrels, he joined The Byrds when they were still called The Jet Set in the summer of 1964 in Los Angeles. "Mr. Tambourine Man", their first single made US and UK No. 1 but McGuinn was the only Byrd playing on it. "Turn Turn Turn" in 1965 was Clark's

first true US No. 1. The Byrds lost their major songwriter when Clark left to go solo in 1966.

Gordon Lightfoot born in Orillia, Ontario in 1938. The only Canadian singer-songwriter to stay in his homeland, Lightfoot is one of the most prolific. His early work reflected the Toronto Yorktown scene, "Early Morning Rain" becoming a standard, even being recorded by Bob Dylan. His was the first recording of "Me And Bobby McGee" and in 1970 he had a No.1 hit with "Sundown".

Rod Clements, of Lindisfarne born, in 1947. The group had a great success in Britain with their album "Fog On The Tyne" in 1971-72; it was the biggest-selling album in Britain. But they never found success in America and split into two separate groups in 1972, disbanding in 1975.

Jean Owen, of The Vernons Girls, born in 1943. One of the all-girl groups of the early British TV rock and roll shows produced by Jack Goode.

Bob Gaudio, of The Four Seasons, born in 1942. "Sherry" was their biggest hit.

NOVEMBER 18

Danny Whitten, vocalist with Neil Young's old backing group, Crazy Horse, dies of a heroin overdose in 1972. He appeared on the first album "Crazy Horse" which also featured Jack Nitzsche. With Nitzsche and Whitten gone, they made more albums which were

not well received by the critics or the public. Neil Young's "Tonight's The Night" was recorded as a wake for Whitten.

Junior Parker dies in 1971, during an eye operation. He began as Little Junior Parker and His Blue Flames, in Memphis in 1952, cutting such tracks as "Bad Women, Bad Whiskey" and recording constantly from then on.

Hank Ballard born in Detroit, in 1936. He was discovered by Johnny Otis in 1954. "Work With Me Annie" was a hit and started the "Annie" records. In 1959 he wrote "The Twist", but Chubby Checker made it a hit a year later.

Long John Baldry's "Let The Heartaches Begin" enters UK charts in 1967.

NOVEMBER 19

Ray Collins (Raymond Eugene Collins) born in 1937. He was the vocalist with The Mothers Of Invention when they formed in 1965, and sings on all albums up until the line-up changes in 1970, when Zappa replaced most of the band.

Fred Lipsius, former alto sax and piano with Blood Sweat and Tears, born in New York City.

John Dummer, of the John Dummer Blues Band, born. One of the Sixties bands in Britain that contributed to the scene, but had no hits.

Joe Hill (Joel Emanuel Hagglund), Swedish union organizer in the US, author of "Casey Jones", and songwriter of "Pie In The Sky", used as a scapegoat in a 1915 murder trial, and murdered by firing squad in Utah State Prison. He was killed for his political beliefs. 30,000 people marched in his funeral procession in Chicago.

First newspaper color section appeared in 1893, in a Sunday newspaper, the "New York World".

NOVEMBER 20

Duane Allman born. One of the Allman Brothers Band and one of the most innovative guitarists of the turn of the Sixties. Played with Eric Clapton in Derek and The Dominoes, and on their single "Layla". He died in October 1971, in a road accident in his hometown of Macon, Georgia (Berry Oakley died in a similar crash near the same place a year later). "Eat A Peach" in 1973, was recorded back in 1971, and was the biggest selling and most successful album from the group.

Gary Green born in 1950. Lead guitarist with Gentle Giant. The group formed in 1969 but, as part of the new wave of "intellectual bands" from England, was approached with caution in the States and it wasn't until "Octopus" in 1973 that they had any success there.

Norman Greenbaum born in Malden, Massachusetts, in 1942, "Spirit In The Sky" reaches US No. 3 in February 1970.

Alan Sherman, Jewish comedian, dies of respiratory trouble, in 1973. Had a hit with "Hello Mudda, Hello Fadda".

Isaac Hayes gets to US No. 1 with his "Theme From Shaft" in 1971. Finally establishes him as a major pop composer.

General Franco dies in 1975. Prince Juan Carlos

was invested as King of Spain two days later. The slight relaxation in fascist control resulted in waves of strikes during the ensuing months.

US Senate Committee stated in 1975, that the CIA plotted to have Fidel Castro and Patrice Lumumba murdered.

Women's Liberation members arrested in London, in 1970, for throwing smoke bombs in the Miss World contest at the Royal Albert Hall.

NOVEMBER 21

Lonnie Jordan, keyboard player with War, born in 1948. In the Sixties they had various names until as the Night Shift they joined Eric Burdon as his backing group. They became War and finally made it alone.

David Porter born in Memphis, Tennessee, in 1941. Together with Isaac Hayes he has written "B-A-B-Y" for Carla Thomas, "Hold On, I'm Coming" for Sam and Dave and many other soul hits.

Livingston Taylor, brother of James, born in 1950. After the huge success of brother James Taylor, both Livingston and sister Kate recorded albums. Their voices and delivery were so similar to famous brother that their albums went nowhere, though they deserved a better fate—both having sung and played all their lives.

The Beatles' double white album released in the UK in 1968. Each copy was individually numbered, and contained a poster designed by painter Richard Hamilton.

Jimi Hendrix reaches UK No. 1 with "Voodoo Chile" in 1970, on which Steve Winwood played organ.

Francois Marie Arouet Voltaire, French writer, born in 1694.

FAMILY MAN & BOB MARLEY / PHOTO: ADRIAN BOOT

NOVEMBER 22

Sun enters Sagittarius, ruled by Jupiter, but associated by the Romans with Diana, Goddess of Hunting. Pagan Greek festival of Music. St. Cecilia, Patron of Music.

"Family Man" Barrett, bass player of The Wailers, born in Kingston, Jamaica, in 1946. He and his younger brother Carlie joined Bob Marley's group in 1970.

The Johnny Otis Show, with Marie Adams, "Ma (He's Making Eyes At Me") in 1957 enters UK charts to reach No. 2. Unusual for the fact that it made no impression in the US.

The Beatles' second album "With The Beatles" released in the UK in 1963. A vital ingredient to any party, along with Beatle boots and collarless suits.

Hoagy Carmichael, songwriter and pianist, born in 1899.

J. F. Kennedy shot in Dallas, Texas, in 1963. It is now thought that at least three gunmen were involved.

PRESIDENT KENNEDY'S SHIRT / PHOTO: F.B.I.

Muhammad Ali TKO's Floyd Patterson in their championship fight, in 1965, at Las Vegas.

NOVEMBER 23

Freddie Marsden born in Liverpool, in 1940. Played drums in his brother Gerry's group, Gerry and The Pacemakers. They were the second group to be signed by Brian Epstein and like The Beatles were produced by George Martin. "How Do You Do It?" and "I Like It" were both transatlantic hits. They starred in the film "Ferry Cross The Mersey" but split up soon after, in 1966.

NICK EXPOSED WHITE LINING OF TIE

FBI LABORATORY

VIEW OF THE BACK OF PRESIDENT KENNEDY'S SHIRT WITH CLOSE-UP OF BULLET ENTRANCE HOLE. LOWER TWO PHOTOGRAPHS SHOW PROJECTILE EXIT HOLE IN COLLAR AND NICK IN RIGHT SIDE OF TIE.

EXHIBIT 60

First jukebox was installed in 1899, at the Palais Royal Hotel in San Francisco, by the Pacific Phonograph Company.

The Rolling Stones are banned by the BBC, after arriving late for "Saturday Club" and "Top Gear" radio shows, in 1964.

"No One To Love Me" by The Shaweez recorded in New Orleans, in 1952. This curious single, which was not a hit, has become one of the most sought-after collector's items. It was the group's only record.

Billy The Kid born in 1859.

Boris Karloff born in 1887.

NOVEMBER 24

Scott Joplin born in 1868. The king of ragtime piano at the turn of the century. Partly due to its use in the film "The Sting", his music made a big comeback in the early Seventies, notably "The Entertainer".

Robin Williamson, of The Incredible String Band, born in Glasgow, in 1943. Originally a folk trio, Williamson and Mike Heron moved to London and took on producer Joe Boyd, who made their most successful albums "The 5,000 Spirits Or The Layers Of The Onion" and "Wee Tam And The Big Huge". They had a considerable cult following in the hippie circles, but finally moved into a more standard rock format until they broke up in 1974.

ROBIN WILLIAMSON.

Michael Holliday born in Ireland, in 1928. "Yellow Rose Of Texas" was released in the UK in September 1955.

Gary Boyle born in Patna, India, in 1941. Dusty Springfield's guitarist for two years, and with Julie Driscoll and Brian Auger's Trinity during 1967-8. Joined Isotope on its formation.

Donald "Duck" Dunn, bass with Booker T and The MGs, born in 1941. "Green Onions" was released in 1962.

John Barry's "James Bond Theme" enters UK charts in 1962.

Manx Radio, Britain's first landbased commercial radio statio, began broadcasting in 1964, from a caravan.

NOVEMBER 25

St. Mercury, Christianized form of Mercury.
St. Catherine, martyred on the wheel, with which she is generally represented. Cosmic symbol of the pagans associated with Fortuna.
Thanksgiving Day in America.

John Lennon returns his MBE to the Queen, in protest against Britain's involvement in Biafra and Vietnam, and against "Cold Turkey" slipping down the UK charts in 1969.

Val Fuentes, drummer with It's A Beautiful Day, born in 1947. Their first album, "It's A Beautiful Day", featured their best known single "White Bird", which was a hit in 1969.

Albert Ayler, the avant garde saxophonist, found drowned in 1970, in the Hudson River. His body was taken home to Cleveland. Reason for death unknown.

Miles Davis makes his first recording in 1945, as a member of Charlie Parker's band.

Roy Lynes, organ piano and vocals with Status Quo, born in 1943. "Pictures Of Matchstick Men" was a UK hit in 1968. Their single "Almost But Not Quite There" was banned by the BBC for its title.

"Rock Around The Clock" by Bill Haley and The Comets makes No. 1 in the UK in 1955.

The Singing Dogs enter UK charts with a song of the same name, in 1955. (Tapes of dogs barking, arranged to make a tune).

Joe DiMaggio born, 1914.

Hugh Moore, inventor of the paper cup, died in 1972, aged 85. He left Harvard to found the Dixie Cup Company.

NOVEMBER 26

Tina Turner (Annie Mae Bulluck) born in Brownsville, Tennessee, in 1938. Although known as Little Ann, her first record was credited to Ike and Tina Turner, "A Fool In Love" released in 1960. It sold a million and resulted in the formation of The Ikettes (Merry Clayton and Bonnie Bramlett have both been members). She formed, with Ike Turner, one of the most dramatically successful rock acts of the Seventies, recording over thirty albums, with a stage act centered around her flaunting sexuality.

John McVie, bass player with Fleetwood Mac, born in 1945. When Peter Green, the band's founder, quit in 1969, his place was filled by McVie's wife Christine Perfect, who was formerly with Chicken Shack.

Olivia Newton John born in Melbourne, Australia. She was with a group called Tomorrow (not the British underground group of the same name), before going solo. "If Not For You" was her first US chart entry in May 1971.

Burt Reiter, bass player of Focus, born in 1946. The Amsterdam group have had a number of successful albums and two UK Top Twenty hits since their formation in 1969, including "Sylvis" and "Hocus Pocus".

John Rostill, of The Shadows, dies of electrocution in 1973. He replaced Brian Locking on bass, who had in turn replaced Jet Harris. The Shadows had over twenty instrumental hits in Britain, before disbanding in 1968.

Garnet Mimms born in Ashland, West Virginia, in 1937. With The Enchanters he had his million-selling hit "Cry Baby" in August 1962.

The Cream play their farewell concert at the Royal Albert Hall, London, in 1969. The BBC film called "The Cream" was a critical failure, but remains a record of a great gig and a great group.

Tommy Dorsey, big-band leader, dies in 1956.

Peter Kropotkin, Russian anarchist, born in 1842, in Moscow.

NOVEMBER 27

James Marshall Hendrix born in Seattle, Washington, in 1942. "My dad danced and played spoons. My first instrument was a harmonica which I got when I was about four. Next it was a violin. I always dug string instruments and guitars and pianos. Then I started digging guitars— it was the instrument that always seemed to be around. I was about 14 or 15 when I first started playing the guitar and I remember my first gig . . . we earned 35 cents apiece." "Sometimes I jump on the guitar. Sometimes I grind the strings up against the frets. The more it grinds, the more it whines. Sometimes I rub myself up against the amplifier.

Sometimes I play the guitar with my teeth or with my elbow. I can't remember all the things I do . . . "

Bruce Lee (Liu Yuen Kam), king of Kung-Fu, born in the Chinese Hospital in San Francisco, in 1940.

Al Jackson, drummer with Booker T and the MGs, born in 1935.

Jimmy Widener, lead guitarist for Hank Snow for ten years, and Mildred Hazelwood, mugged and then shot to death in 1973.

Dozy, of Dave Dee Dozy Beaky Mick and Tich, born. "Legend of Xanadu" was their UK No. 1 in February 1968. They had ten chart entries between 1966 and 1968.

The Beatles' album "Beatles For Sale" and the single "I Feel Fine" released in the UK in 1964.

Mick Jagger fined £16 for driving offenses in Tottenhall, Staffordshire, in 1964.

Drugs. First meeting of the UN Commission on Narcotic Drugs, held at Lake Success, New York, in 1946.

NOVEMBER 28

Randy Newman born in Los Angeles, in 1943. A major songwriter, his first (recorded) album (second released) "12 Songs" and his "Live" album are among his finest. Very much overlooked. Alan Price had a UK No. 4 hit with his "Simon Smith And His Dancing Bear", and Nilsson has recorded an entire LP of his songs.

Hugh McKenna, pianist with The Sensational Alex Harvey Band, born in 1949. "Delilah" was their first hit in 1975.

R. B. Greaves born in 1944. "Take A Letter, Maria" in 1969 sold over four million copies.

Gary Troxel, of The Fleetwoods, born in Centralia, Washington. "Come Softly To Me" was US No. 1 during March 1959.

Clem Curtis, vocals with The Fortunes, born in 1940. They had instant success with "Baby Now That I've Found You" when the group was launched in 1967.

Papa Lightfoot dies in 1971 "Papa George Blues", his first recording, was made in 1949.

Shangri-Las' "Leader Of The Pack" reaches US No. 1 in 1964.

Lord Rockingham's XI reach UK No. 1 with "Hoots Mon" in 1958.

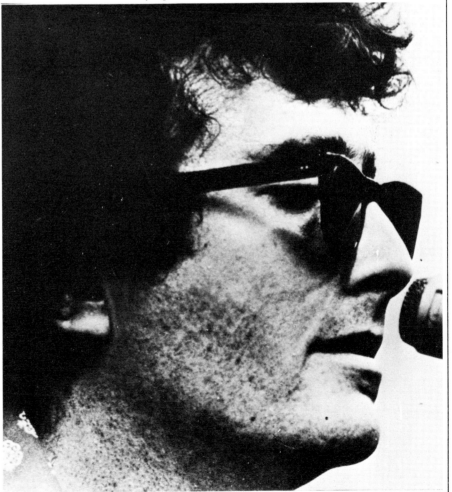

RANDY NEWMAN

JOHN MAYALL.

NOVEMBER 29

St. Saturninas, one of the days dedicated to Saturn, father of Jupiter, Neptune and Pluto.

John Mayall born in Macclesfield, Cheshire, in 1933. In 1963 he formed Blues Syndicate and then The Bluesbreakers, which Eric Clapton joined in 1965. Peter Green played with him before forming Fleetwood Mac. Mick Taylor played with the group until he joined the Rolling Stones. From 1964 he has released twenty albums, most of which have not received the attention due to them.

Jody Miller born in Phoenix, Arizona, in 1941. In 1965 her answer record to Roger Miller's "King Of The Road" called "Queen Of The House" was a hit. She later moved to the C & W area.

John Lennon's "Two Virgins" album released in 1968, on the Zapple label in the UK. American release was delayed because the cover photograph of John and Yoko naked had to be covered with a plain wrapper for the American public.

Rolling Stones records, as well as some by Elton John and others, valued at over $2000, burnt by officials in Tallahassee, Florida, after a Baptist Church had described them as immoral and "appealing to the flesh".

Felix Cavaliere, organist with The Rascals, born in 1944. Originally The Young Rascals, they dropped the "Young" on reaching the age of 20. "Good Lovin'" was a US No. 1 in 1966.

NOVEMBER 30

Noel Paul Stookey born in Baltimore, Maryland, in 1937. Originally brought together by manager Al Grossman, Peter Paul and Mary soon became a major force in the folk-protest movement of the early Sixties. They took "Blowin'

In The Wind" to the charts in 1963, and between 1962 and 1969 had nearly 20 chart entries including a US No. 1 with "Leaving On A Jet Plane" in 1969. In 1971 they disbanded and all three made solo albums.

Shuggie Otis born in 1954. One of the youngest blues-guitarists in the business. First recorded with his famous father Johnny Otis on their "Cold

Shot" album in 1969 has a number of albums to his name since then including one with Al Kooper.

Leo Lyons, bass with Ten Years After, born in Standbridge, in 1943. Met Alvin Lee in Nottingham and toured Hamburg with him. Later they formed Ten Years After. First album "Ten Years After" was in 1967.

Bonzo Dog Doo Dah Band enter UK charts with "I'm The Urban Spaceman" in 1968, produced by Paul McCartney.

Mark Twain born in 1825.

G. Gordon Liddy born in 1930. With Howard Hunt, he led the "Dirty Tricks" department the White House had set up under Charles Colson.

170

DECEMBER 1

St. Eloi. This Saint is given some of the legends of Wieland (Teutonic) and Vulcan (Roman), the Heavenly Blacksmith. Patron of Blacksmiths and Metal Workers.

John Paul Densmore, drummer with The Doors, born in Santa Monica, California, in 1944.
Billy Paul born in Philadelphia in 1934. He had a million seller in 1972 with ''Me And Mrs Jones''.

Gilbert O'Sullivan (Raymond O'Sullivan) born in Waterford, Ireland, in 1946. ''Alone Again, Naturally'' was US No. 1 in June 1972.

Aleister Crowley dies in 1947, of myocardial degeneration and chronic bronchitis, leaving beneath his pillow a parchment talisman in Enochian. ''The Great Beast 666'' survived many years of hard drug addiction, and persecution for his magical practices.
Magic Sam (Sam Maghett) dies in 1969, aged 32. Best known for ''High Heel Sneakers'' in 1964. Famous Mississippi blues guitarist and singer.
Carter Stanley, the bluegrass man, dies in 1966.
Lou Rawls born in Chicago. The first of his many hits was ''Three O'Clock In The Morning'' which entered the US charts in June 1965.
The Beatles' ''Magical Mystery Tour'' book and records package published in the UK in 1967. It was released as an album in the USA.

DECEMBER 2

Tom McGuiness, bass and guitarist with Manfred Mann, born, in 1941. Left the group to form his own band McGuiness Flint.
Jimmy Rodgers found in mysterious circumstances in his car with his skull fractured, in 1967. He recovers. His hit ''Child Of Clay'' had just left the US charts.
Taj Mahal gives a concert to the men on death row in Washington State Penitentiary in 1971.
Maria Callas born in 1923, in New York City.

DECEMBER 3

Rhea, a form of Earth Goddess.

John Wilson born in 1949. Drummer of Taste, formed by blues guitarist Rory Gallagher in 1968.
Ozzie Osbourne, vocalist of Black Sabbath, born in 1948. The band have maintained their image of doom-rock heavy metal since their first album in 1970, despite constant slagging by critics.
Reindeer roundup in Finland begins.
Ferlin Husky born in 1927. ''Gone'' reached US No. 4 in January 1957.
The Montreux Casino, Montreux, Switzerland, burnt to the ground in 1971, half way through a concert by The Mothers Of Invention, with the loss of all their equipment, valued at $50,000. The fire was started by a local hippie who was listening to the concert up in the roof.
Drugs. The premier British medical journal, ''The Lancet'' reports in 1887: ''Indian hemp, night and morning and continued for some time, is the most valuable remedy met with in the treatment of persistent headache.''
The Beatles' album ''Rubber Soul'' released in 1965 on same day as the single ''Day Tripper''/''We Can Work It Out''. In 1965 they begin their British tour at the Odeon, Glasgow.

DECEMBER 4

St. Barbara, given the tower legend of Danae. Patron of Arms and Fortifications, invoked against thunder and lightning. Minerva, Goddess of Wisdom, patron of Armor for the pagan Romans.

Dennis Wilson, drummer and vocalist of The Beach Boys, born in Hawthorne, California, in 1944. It was Dennis's addiction to surfing that gave the Beach Boys their initial identity. He suggested that they sing about his pastime and a song, written by brother Brian and cousin Mike Love, called ''Surfin''' was the result. Their father, also a songwriter, took it to his music publisher. The song was a local success and they appeared first of all as The Pendletones, before changing their name to The Beach Boys in late 1961.

Freddy Cannon (Frederick Anthony Picariello) born in Revere, Massachusetts, in 1940. ''Tallahassee Lassie'' was a May 1959 US hit, for him.
Chris Hillman born in 1942. He was on the folk scene, with The Scottsville Squirrel Breakers and then his own group The Hillmen before The Byrds—then known as The Jet Set. He changed from mandolin to bass guitar. He wrote some of the classic Byrds songs, co-writing ''So You Want To Be A Rock'n'Roll Star''. Hillman finally left to form the Flying Burrito Brothers with Gram Parsons.
Bob Marley shot at his home in Kingston during the Jamaican elections in 1976. One of his band and his manager were seriously injured but Marley was only hit in the arm. The attack was thought to be politically motivated; ironical as being a Rastafarian, Marley was a pacifist. He was to have topped the bill the next day at a concert put on by the Jamaican Prime Minister.

BOB MARLEY / PHOTO: ADRIAN BOOT.

Eddie Heywood born in 1926. "Soft Summer Breeze" was a 1956 summer hit in the USA.

Drugs. A report in the authoritative British medical journal "The Lancet" of 1971, claims that research workers in Bristol and Cardiff have found a form of brain damage that may be caused by the chronic use of cannabis.

Sly and The Family Stone get to US No. 1 with "Family Affair" in 1971.

Bob Dylan's "Rolling Thunder Review" reaches Montreal in 1975.

The Great London Smog begins in 1952. It lasts three weeks and was blamed for the eventual death of 4,000 people.

DECEMBER 5

Little Richard (Richard Pennimann) born in Macon, Georgia, in 1932. In 1951 he won a talent show and got a contract with RCA. In 1955 he sent a tape to Specialty and they bought out his contract and took him to the famous Cosmo studio in New Orleans. It was here he cut his first hit, "Tutti Frutti". He recorded a run of hits including "Long Tall Sally", "Lucille", "Jenny Jenny" and "Baby Face" through 'till 1959, when he retired into the church for a number of years. Little Richard is the author of some of the most characteristic and vigorous rock'n'roll of all time, inventing, among other things "A-Wop-Bop-A-Loo-Bop-A-Lop-Bam-Boom".

Jim Messina born in Maywood, California, in 1947. Ex-Buffalo Springfield, was in Poco, and then left to concentrate on record production. Almost at once got together with Kenny Loggins and formed the band Loggins and Messina.

John Cale born in Wales, in 1940. Went to the USA on a Leonard Bernstein scholarship, and in 1964 met Lou Reed. They began The Velvet Underground with Cale on bass, viola and organ. In 1968 he quit to go solo and

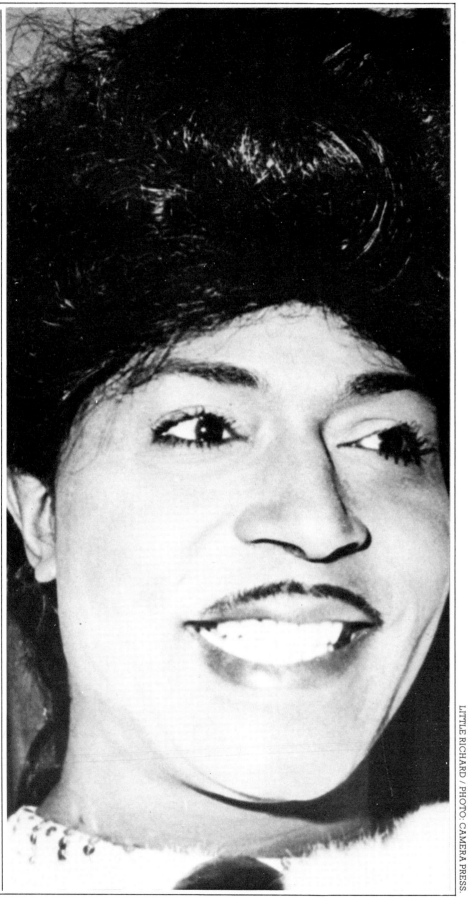

LITTLE RICHARD / PHOTO: CAMERA PRESS

JOHN CALE.

produce. In June 1974 he participated in a joint effort by himself, Eno, Rico and Kevin Ayers. Among his productions are Nico and the debut album by Patti Smith.

ALTAMONT / PHOTO: ASSOCIATED PRESS.

Rolling Stones hold a "Beggars Banquet" at the Elizabethan Rooms, London, in 1968 to mark the release of the album of the same name. Custard pies are thrown at the guests.
Adam Faith's "What Do You Want" reaches UK No. 1 and stays six weeks in 1959.
Walt Disney born in Marceline, in 1901. "There is a natural hootchy-kootchy to a goldfish".

signatures such as 7/4. Had hits with singles, notably "Take Five" and "Unsquare Dance".
Steve Alaimo born in Rochester, New York, in 1940. "Every Day I Have To Cry" was his US hit in February 1963.
Keith West born in Dagenham. Recorded the first "rock opera" "Excerpt From A Teenage Opera", Originally one of The In-Crowd and later the cult underground group

Tomorrow, best-known for "My White Bicycle". He released the album "Moonrider" in 1975.
Jonathan King born in London, in 1944. In 1965 his "Everyone's Gone To The Moon" was a UK hit.
Meredith Hunter killed by Hell's Angels at the Altamont Speedway, during the Rolling Stones Free Concert in 1969. The murder was filmed and shown to Mick Jagger as part of the Maysles Brothers' film "Gimme Shelter".
"Gimme Shelter", the Rolling Stones film, opens in New York City in 1970.

DECEMBER 6

Dave Brubeck, jazz pianist, born in Concord, California. Specialized in playing in unusual time

Leadbelly dies in 1949. Famous for "Ella Speed" and the classic "Goodnight Irene".
First sound recording made on a machine invented by Thomas Edison, in 1877. His first words were "Mary had a little lamb."

DECEMBER 7

Harry Chapin born in 1942. Temporarily a member of Brothers and Sisters with Carly Simon, pilot and film director, he began recording in 1972. He had a 1975 US No.1 with "Cat's In The Cradle".
Teddy Bears' "To Know Him Is To Love Him" reaches US No. 1 in 1958. Phil Spector wrote the song and sang on the record. Said to be the epitaph on his father's gravestone.
Apple, The Beatles' boutique at 94 Baker Street, London, opens in 1967.

The Beatles act as the panel on the BBC-TV show "Juke Box Jury" in 1963.
Japanese bomb Pearl Harbor in 1941.

(LIV 6) LIVERMORE, CALIF., DEC.9 (AP)-- MICK JAGGER (CENTER) DANCES ON STAGE CAUSING AUDIENCE MEMBERS TO RAISE THEIR ARMS AND HANDS DURING ROCK CONCERT SATURDAY AT THE ALTAMOUNT SPEEDWAY NEAR LIVERMORE. HELLS ANGELS FLANK THE STAGE DURING THE STONES' CONCERT. (AP WIREPHOTO) gr 1969

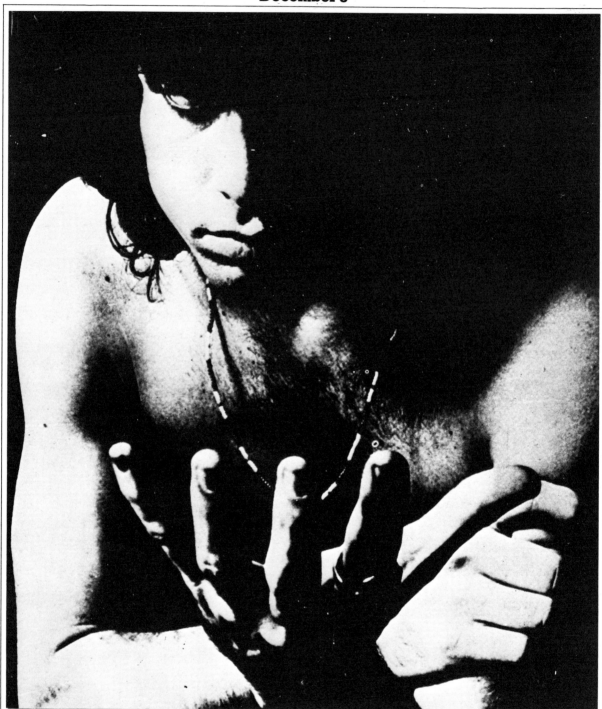

DECEMBER 8

Miraculous Conception of Juno, Queen of Heaven.

James Douglas Morrison born in Melbourne, Florida, in 1943. Died in Paris in 1971. The Doors were conceived in the spring of 1965 (using the idea from Huxley's "Doors Of Perception") and they released their first album in January 1967. Morrison was the "Lizard King" poet and singer of the Sixties underground scene.

Gregg Allman born in 1947. Began playing keyboards with his brother Duane in a Los Angeles group called Hour Glass which released an album on Liberty. When his brother signed with Capricorn Records in Macon, Georgia, Gregg returned from the coast to be in it. The deaths of both Duane Allman and bass player Berry Oakley changed The Allman Brothers Band sound and by the mid-Seventies Gregg had cut a solo album and

was moving on the celebrity circuit, marrying Cher Bono and sponsoring Jimmy

Carter for President. In July 1976, he and Cher had a son, Elijah Blue.

Jimmy Smith born in 1925. In 1962 he was teamed with an Oliver Nelson arranged big band and reached a wide audience with his jazz organ adaptations such as "Walk On The Wild Side". His cult followers tend to prefer his earlier small combo recordings such as the "Home Cookin'" and "Prayer Meeting" albums, which have been more influential.

Ray Shulman born in Glasgow in 1949. Together with his brothers Phil and Derek he formed Simon Dupree and The Big Sound. After line-up changes the brothers created Gentle Giant in 1969. Ray plays a wide range of instruments including bass, guitar, violin, drums and piano. ''Octopus'' in 1973 was their first hit in the US.

Graham Knight, bass player of Marmalade, born in 1946. Originally a Scottish group named Dean Ford and the Gaylords, they are best known for their UK No. 1 cover version of The Beatles ''Ob La Di Ob La Da''.

Jerry Butler born in Sunflower, Mississippi, in 1939. He wrote ''For Your Precious Love'' which he recorded with The Impressions and has had over thirty US chart entries.

Sammy Davis Jr born in 1925. All 'round entertainer and Nixon supporter. Member of the ''Rat Pack'', and one of rock'n'roll's earliest opponents.

Frank Sinatra Jr kidnapped at gunpoint in 1963, from a motel in Lake Tahoe. He was released after thirty-four hours.

Bob Dylan's ''Rolling Thunder Review'' arrives at New York City, to play Madison Square Garden in 1975.

Jean Sibelius, Finnish composer, born in 1865.

DECEMBER 9

Junior Wells (Amos Wells Jr) born in West Memphis, Arkansas, in 1932. He replaced blues harmonica player Little Walter in the Muddy Waters Band in the early fifties and cut his first solo record in 1953. That year he recorded his famous ''Hoodoo Man'' with Muddy Waters Band backing him. In 1972 he teamed with Buddy Guy and they have toured with The Rolling Stones, as well as releasing an album part produced by Eric Clapton.

Sam Strain, of Little Anthony and The Imperials, born in 1940.

Lou Handman dies. He wrote ''Are You Lonesome Tonight'' for Al Jolson, but died in 1956 before he could hear Presley's version.

Helen Reddy goes to US No. 1 with ''I Am Woman'' in 1972.

New York escapes total financial collapse, as President Ford bails the city out with a massive loan, in 1975.

DECEMBER 10

Johnny Rodriguez born in Sabinal, Texas in 1952. He emphasised his Chicano identity on country hits like ''Ridin' My Thumb To Mexico''. A strong balladeer in the Merle Haggard mold.

Otis Redding killed in 1967, together with three of the Bar-Kays, when their plane crashes into a frozen lake in Wisconsin, after leaving Cleveland, Ohio.

Frank Zappa thrown from the stage of the London Rainbow Theater in 1971 He breaks a leg, an ankle and fractures his skull. ''I did it because my girlfriend said she loved Frank'' said Trevor Howell, aged 24.

Chad Stuart, of Chad and Jeremy, born in Durham, in England, in 1943. Very much in the mold of Peter and Gordon, they were a British group who achieved success in the USA in the post-Beatles ''British Invasion'' but were virtually unknown at home. Chad wrote the music, the most complex and highly regarded of which was on their ''Of Cabbages And Kings'' album in 1967. They broke up in 1969 and Chad went on to write musicals.

''Good Vibrations'' by The Beach Boys reaches US No. 1 in 1966. The most expensive single ever made to that date.

Emily Dickinson born 1830, in Amherst, Massachusetts.

Arthur Rimbaud dies in 1891. French poet, admired by Bob Dylan, Patti Smith, and others.

Jimi Hendrix acquitted in Toronto, in 1969, of possession of heroin.

DECEMBER 11

Brenda Lee (Brenda Mae Tarpley) born in Atlanta, Georgia. ''I'm Sorry'' was a June 1961 hit. ''Speak To Me Pretty'' was her highest UK chart entry at No. 3 in 1962.

Sam Cooke shot three times in a Hollywood motel, in 1964, by a woman he was allegedly trying to rape. Heavy influence on Otis Redding, he wrote ''Twisting The Night Away'' among many others.

David Gates born in Tulsa, Oklahoma in 1939. An ex-rockabilly singer and producer, he went solo after leaving Bread, due to some conflict over the material they should use. Met with some success after his second solo album in 1975, especially in Britain.

Jermaine Jackson, of The Jackson Five, born in Gary, Indiana, in 1954.

DECEMBER 12
Rumi, Persian Poet and Mystic.

Dionne Warwick born in East Orange, New Jersey. ''Walk On By'' was her first UK hit in 1964, but ''Don't Make Me Over'' was her first US entry in December 1962. Later added an ''e'' to her name ''for luck''. Even later she dropped it again.

Paul Rodgers, lead vocalist with Free, born in Middlesbrough in 1949. The group's first album ''Tons Of Sobs'' was released in 1969. They disbanded in 1973, and he and drummer Simon Kirke went on to form Bad Company.

Francis Albert Sinatra born in Hoboken, New Jersey, in 1915. A teenage idol before the age of rock'n'roll, his interests extend beyond that of music.

Mike Smith, vocalist with The Dave Clark Five, born in London, in 1943. ''Glad All Over'' was a transatlantic hit in 1964 and paved the way for many more.

Jeff Lynne born in Birmingham, England, in 1947. After three years with The Idle Race he joined The Move in 1970, co-produced two of their albums, wrote their US hit ''Do Ya'' and helped form The Electric Light Orchestra. Albums such as ''Eldorado'' in 1974 and singles such as ''Evil Woman'' in 1975 helped keep him in the charts.

Mike Heron born in 1942. Founder member of the Incredible String Band, which began as a folk trio in Glasgow in 1965. Heron and Robin Williamson moved to London and moved away from the strictly folk sound, incorporating Eastern instruments and becoming a cult band in the London "underground" scene. Their first album "The 5,000 Spirits Or The Layers Of The Onion" in 1967 was highly influential. They moved further into rock, added to the line-up and finally broke up in 1974. Mike Heron went on to form his own group, Mike Heron's Reputation.

Ray Jackson, of Lindisfarne, born in 1948. The Newcastle group had a top-selling British album in 1971-72 with "Fog On The Tyne" and a memorable single "Lady Eleanor". They disbanded in 1975, having never got the acceptance they deserved in the USA.

Richard Betts born in 1943. First with Tommy Roe's Romans he joined The Allman Brothers Band as guitarist, when Duane Allman put the band together in 1969. The success of "Idlewild South" was the interaction between Betts' playing and that of lead guitarist Duane Allman.

Clive Bunker, drummer with Jethro Tull, born in 1946. A series of concept albums beginning with "Aqualung" in 1971, have contributed to the great success this band enjoys, particularly in the USA. Bunker left to form Jude.

Tony Williams born in Chicago in 1945. At the age of 19 he played on Miles Davis's "Miles In Europe" on drums. Made two solo albums before forming the Tony Williams Lifetime.

Connie Francis (Constance Franconero) born in 1938. "Who's Sorry Now" was a January 1958 hit and "Stupid Cupid" came in August 1958.

"Friends" Magazine starts publication in 1969, in London. It was formed by the London staff of "Rolling Stone" magazine after its sudden closure. One of the more serious underground news magazines, it lasted in various forms until 1973.

Marconi first transmits and receives a transatlantic radio signal, in 1901.

Picasso's estate estimated at $1 trillion in 1975, after his death in April 1973.

Edward G. Robinson born in 1893. The archetype of the Thirties and Forties tough-guy.

Brian Jones wins his drugs conviction appeal in 1967, and is fined £1,000 and given three years probation instead of nine months in jail.

DECEMBER 13

Davey O'List born in 1950. He has played with Attack, Nice (sometimes), Roxy Music (early on), on Bryan Ferry's solo efforts and Jet.

Tony Gomez, organist with the Foundations, born in 1940. The group had a million-seller with their first release, "Baby Now That I've Found You" in 1967.

The Beatles end their third British tour at the Gaumont, Southampton, in 1963.

Earliest sound on film picture, shown by Dr. Lee de Forest, in 1923.

DECEMBER 14

St. Viator ; this name is a title of Mercury.

Charlie Rich born in Colt, Arkansas in 1932. The country-pop superstar of the Seventies.

Joyce Vincent, one of the two lady singers in Dawn, born in Detroit in 1946. "Tie A Yellow Ribbon Round The Old Oak Tree" was a 1973 hit for them.

Dinah Washington (Ruth Jones) dies in Chicago, of an accidental overdose of sleeping pills, in 1963.

Mick Taylor announces that he is leaving the Rolling Stones in 1974, after playing with them for five years.

"The Red Flag" composed in 1889, by Jim Connell. "I was inspired to write 'The Red Flag' by the Paris Commune, the heroism of the Russian nihilists, the firmness and self-sacrifice of the Land Leaguers and the devotion unto the death of the Chicago anarchists".

The Who perform "Tommy" at the Colosseum Opera House, London, in 1969.

Rolling Stones Rock and Roll Circus filmed at Wembley TV Studios, in 1968. John and Yoko Lennon, Eric Clapton, The Who, Jethro Tull, and Mitch Mitchell were among the performers. It was never shown.

DECEMBER 15

Cindy Birdsong, of The Supremes, born in 1939. She replaced Florence Ballard who left in 1967. She was with them for such hits as "Love Child" (1968) and "Someday We'll Be Together" (1969) both of which made No. 1.

Dave Clark, drummer and leader of The Dave Clark Five, born in 1942. "Glad All Over" was UK No. 1 in December, 1963, knocking The Beatles from top position for the first time in weeks.

Carmine Appice born in Staten Island, New York, in 1946. First with The Vanilla Fudge, then the supergroup Beck, Bogert and Appice, and finally recording with KGB.

Jesse Belvin born in Texarkana, Arkansas, in 1933. "Goodnight My Love" was his biggest hit in November 1956. He also recorded under the name of The Cliques, overdubbing his voice to create a quartet. "Girl Of My Dreams" was an April 1956 hit.
John Hammond born in New York City, in 1910. Famous supporter of jazz through the Thirties, he finally became A & R at Columbia Records, signing Aretha Franklin, Pete Seeger and Bob Dylan (who was known as "Hammond's Folly" until his records began to sell).
Harry Ray born in 1946. He joined The Moments, the sweet soul New Jersey group, whose later hits feature his lead vocal.
Glen Miller's plane goes missing over the English channel, in 1944. As usual rumors spread that he was alive somewhere, crippled or in hiding. Attempts are being made to retrieve a briefcase from the wreck, supposedly containing unpublished music.

Fats Waller dies of alcoholic poisoning, on the Sante Fe Superchief train, in 1943. One of the all-time great boogie pianists.

Alan Freed born in 1922. He coined the phrase "Rock'n'Roll" and changed the name of his WJW radio show from "Record Rendezvous" to "The Moondog House Rock'n' Roll Party".
Rasputin murdered in 1916. After poisoning, shooting, being thrown into a freezing river, he finally died.

DECEMBER 16

Tson Kapa, fifteenth century Tibetan Lama who founded the Gelugpa Sect, (the first "Yellow Hat" school).

Tony Hicks, guitarist with The Hollies, born. Formed in 1963, they first entered the charts with "Searchin'" in 1963 in UK, and followed it with more than twenty more hits.
Joan Baez and the others in the party, invited to Hanoi by the Committee for Solidarity with the American People, arrive in 1972 just in time for the US bombing of the city. From the time the US broke off the peace talks until the party of Americans could leave, over two thousand civilians were killed in the city.
Margaret Mead born in 1901, in Philadelphia. Her books on magic and anthropology have been very influential in the growth of interest in mysticism in the USA.
"The Death And Rebirth Of The Haight-Ashbury And The Death Of Money" was the theme of a parade in 1966, organized by the radical "Diggers", led by ex-San Francisco mime troupe member Emmet Grogan.

Noel Coward, archetypal English sophisticate and brilliant lyricist, born in London in 1899. His first film appearance was in "Hearts Of The World" in 1918. Joe Cocker's "Mad Dogs And Englishmen" named after his song of the same name.
"The Music Of Lennon And McCartney" shown by Granada TV, in the London area, in 1965, and the same day The Beatles "Magical Mystery Tour" double EP and book enters UK charts in 1965.
"Boston Tea Party" in 1773, begins the American War Of Independence.

DECEMBER 17

Paul Butterfield born in Chicago, Illinois, in 1942. Playing in the black clubs in Chicago's South Side, he developed the technique which turned him into the white blues harmonica virtuoso of America. His first record was released in 1965, when his band featured Mike Bloomfield on guitar. The next year "East-West" was released, regarded as their best. In 1967 Bloomfield left to work with Bob Dylan. In 1969 Butterfield changed from white blues towards a mixture of jazz and soul. Later re-united with Bloomfield on the "Fathers And Sons" album, in 1971 Todd Rundgren produced a live double album. The Paul Butterfield Blues Band came to an end in late 1972, having recorded eight best-selling albums. In 1973 he formed a new group, Better Days, releasing two albums before going solo.

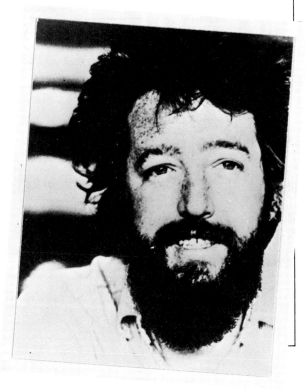

TOMMY STEELE WITH HIS PARENTS IN 1957 / PHOTO: CAMERA PRESS

Tommy Steele (Tommy Hicks) born in Bermondsey, London, in 1936. He was "discovered" at the Two I's in Old Compton Street, Soho, and launched as Britain's answer to Elvis and Bill Haley. "Rock With The Caveman" made UK No. 13 in November 1956. "Singing The Blues" went to No. 1 in January, 1957, replacing Guy Mitchell's original version at the top.

Carlie Barrett, drummer of The Wailers, born in Kingston, Jamaica in 1950. He joined the group with his brother "Family Man" in 1970, having earlier toured the UK in the Upsetters.

Eddie Kendricks born in Birmingham, Alabama, in 1939. Original member of The Temptations he went solo in 1971 and had a US No. 1 with "Keep On Truckin' ".

Jim Bonfanti, drummer with The Raspberries, born in 1948. "Starting Over", their final album in 1975, was the first one that the critics liked.

Karl Denver (Angus MacKenzie) born in Glasgow, in 1934. His first hit was "Marcheta" in the UK charts June 1961.

Dave Dee born. Together with Dozy, Beaky, Mick and Tich they had ten chart hits in the UK, beginning with "Hold Tight" in March 1966.

Radio North Sea, the only station to broadcast pirate TV as well as radio, boarded and closed down by Dutch authorities, even though it was outside territorial waters, in 1964.

Lynette "Squeaky" Fromme was sentenced to life imprisonment in 1975, for attempting to assassinate President Ford. She was a former member of Charles Manson's "Family".

DECEMBER 18

Keith Richard (Keith Richards) born in Dartford, Kent, in 1943. His father ran a dance band before the war. Keith was given a £10 guitar for his birthday and then, while attending Sidcup Art School: "So I get on this fucking train one morning and there's Jagger and under his arm he has four or five albums. I haven't seen him since the time I bought an ice cream off him and we haven't hung around since we were five, six, ten years old. We recognized each other straight off. "Hi, man," I say. "Where ya going?" he says. And under his arm he's got Chuck Berry and Little Walter, Muddy Waters. "You're into Chuck Berry, man, really? That's a coincidence." He said, "Yeah, I gotta few more albums. Been writin' away to this, uh, Chess Records in Chicago and got a mailing list thing and . . . got it together, you know?" Wow man!"

Chas Chandler (Bryan Chandler) born in 1938. Bass player of the Animals. In 1963 they were known as the Alan Price Combo playing in Newcastle beat clubs. In the wake of the Stones, they were immediately successful as the Animals and signed to EMI records and produced by Mickie Most. Their second single "House Of The Rising Sun" became a multi-million selling rock classic, and is said to have inspired Dylan to play rock; the song was taken from Dylan's first album. The Animals split in 1966, and the same year Chandler discovered Jimi Hendrix playing in The Cafe Wha! in Greenwich Village, New York. He brought Hendrix to England in 1966 and managed him until his death in 1970. Chandler then became manager of Slade.

Professor Longhair (Ron Byrd) born in Bogalusa, Pearl River, Louisiana, in 1918. One of the greatest influences on New Orleans' rock'n'roll, Professor Longhair's piano style can be felt in the work of Fats Domino and Little Richard, through to Lloyd Price. His "She Ain't Got No Hair" is a classic. A victim of unscrupulous showbiz businessmen, poor production and mistreated by promoters and club-owners, he has never been given the recognition he deserved.

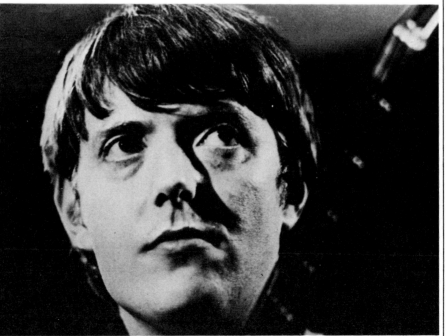

CHAS CHANDLER IN 1966 / PHOTO: GRAHAM KEEN.

Quetzalcoatl, the Aztec Feathered Serpent God.

Bo Diddley (Ellas McDaniels) born in McComb, Mississippi, in 1928. In 1955 he auditioned for Phil and Leonard Chess and cut "Uncle John". They didn't like the title so he named it after himself. It took 35 takes to get it right, but the final version was a hit and established his reputation. "Diddley Daddy", "Say Man Back

DECEMBER 19

St. Samantha, the Celtic Saint.

Alvin Lee born in Nottingham, in 1944. After gigs in Hamburg with Leo Lyons, the two of them formed Jaybirds. Changed name to Ten Years After, in 1966 and launched themselves at the Marquee and a fantastic showcase gig at the Windsor Blues Festival, where they drew a standing ovation. Lee is best known for his fast guitar work within the standard blues format.

became part of the Dylan, Dave Van Ronk, Tom Paxton crowd—publishing his anti-Vietnam War songs

in "Broadside" as early as 1962. His journalistic background tended to make his songs more literal than those of the other "protest" songwriters, and this placed him at a disadvantage when he tried to progress into other areas. His biggest hit song "There But For Fortune" was taken into the charts by Joan Baez, whereas Ochs remained tied to his cult following. In a fit of depression he hanged himself in New York, in the Spring of 1976.
John McEuen born in 1945. Banjo, guitar and mandolin player of The Nitty Gritty Dirt Band. The country-rock band had a surprise Top Ten hit in 1970 with "Mr Bojangles" and their album "Will The Circle Be Unbroken" was very well received.

Mick Jagger fined £200 and £52.50 costs, at Marlborough Street Magistrates Court, London, for possession of cannabis, in 1969.
Jean Genet born in 1910. Thief and convicted murderer, whose writing was regarded as so important that he was released from jail providing he signed his royalties over to the French state.

Conway Twitty (Harold Jenkins) reaches UK No. 1 with "It's Only Make Believe" in 1958.
Edith Piaf born in Paris, in 1915. The 4 ft. 10 ins. chanteuse who went from street singer to the darling of all France. International symbol during the world-weary Fifties, her best known song was "Je Ne Regrette Rien", and that is how she was.

Again" and "You Can't Tell A Book By The Cover" were all big hits and the April 1960 "Road Runner" became a classic.
Bobby Colomby, drums and vocals with Blood Sweat and Tears, born. One of the biggest jazz-rock bands of the Sixties, their second album sold over 3 million copies.
Bobby Darin dies during an operation to correct a malfunctioning artificial heart valve, in 1973. "Dream Lover" and "Mack The Knife" were two of his 1959 hits.
Peter Paul and Mary's "Leaving On A Jet Plane" reached US No. 1 in 1969.

DECEMBER 21

The Winter Solstice. Sun enters Capricorn, ruled by Saturn but associated by the Romans with Vesta. Birth of Horus.
Norse Freyr born, celebrated as Feast of Jul, whence comes Yule.

Frank Zappa (Francis Vincent Zappa) born in Baltimore, Maryland, in 1940. He later moved to Lancaster, California where he grew up with, among others, Captain Beefheart. Played with The Hollywood Pursuaders, The Heartbreakers and other such bands, did backing tracks, wrote "Memories Of El Monte" for The Penguins and had his own studio, before finally starting The Mothers Of Invention.

Phil Ochs born in El Paso, Texas, in 1940. After a spell in military academy in the family tradition, he quit to study journalism at Ohio State University. In Greenwich Village he

Liverpool, in 1963.
Ma Rainey, great blues singer and songwriter, dies in 1939.

DECEMBER 23

Plutarch.
St. Victoria, a virgin martyr who corresponds with the Roman Goddess of Victory.

Johnny Kidd (Frederick Heath) born in Willesden, London, in 1939. His group was called The Pirates and he wore an eyepatch. Their first release was ''Please Don't Touch Me'' in May 1959.

Jorma Kaukonen born in 1940. Began as the lead guitarist with The Jefferson Airplane and provided the characteristic San Francisco feedback sound on their albums, from 1967 until he and Jack Casady left to form the splinter group Hot Tuna. Most people were not aware that this was a permanent split and consequently didn't regard Hot Tuna seriously until it was too late. Hot Tuna degenerated into a very cliched form of heavy metal blues oriented guitar bass and drums. In the UK their sales depreciated so that their albums were no longer released but in the US a hard core of fans remain loyal.
Luther James Grosvenor, lead guitarist with Spooky Tooth, born in Evesham, Worcestershire, in 1949. One of the major late Sixties progressive groups.
Little Esther Phillips born in 1935. ''Release Me'' reached No. 8 in the US in 1962.

Carl Wilson, of The Beach Boys, born in 1946. As guitarist and vocalist he determined the group's sound to a large degree, always masterminded, of course, by Brian Wilson.
Jane Fonda born in New York City, in 1937. Her first film was ''Tall Story'' in 1960. Sex roles like ''Barbarella'' (1968) finally gave way to more serious acting, such as in ''Klute'' (1971). As a left-wing political activist she made a film herself about Hanoi.
Charlie Watts' book ''Ode To A High Flying Bird'' published in 1964. Written in 1961, it is a book of drawings and text about Charlie ''Bird'' Parker.
Beatles' Christmas Show appears at The Gaumont,

Bradford, in 1963. Also on the bill were Rolf Harris, The Barron-Knights, Tommy Quickly, The Fourmost, Billy J. Kramer and The Dakotas and Cilla Black.
LaVern Baker records her classic ''Jim Dandy'' in New York City in 1955. It was produced by Ahmet Ertegun and Jerry Wexler.
Augustus Owsley Stanley III's secret LSD factory was raided by the police in 1967. They found sixty-seven grams of acid in his lab, in surburban Orinda, California ; enough for 700,000 trips.
Rolling Stones play the Lyceum, London, in 1969.
Apollo 8 fired into moon orbit in 1968.
Josef Stalin born 1879.

DECEMBER 22

Rahilla, son and disciple of Gautama Buddha.

Robin and Maurice Gibb, of The Bee Gees, born in Manchester, in 1949. Family moved to Australia in 1958. ''New York Mining Disaster 1941'' launched them in the UK in 1967.
Steve Stills lost a paternity suit brought against him in 1973, by Harriet B. Tunis of Mill Valley, California. The child, Justin Stills, was born in 1971. Still's attorney attempted to discredit Ms. Tunis' testimony by asking the jury : ''How can you believe this witness who works in the record business ?''.
Beatles' Christmas Show appears at the Empire,

Night Tripper, the first appearance of London's UFO club, in 1966. Run by the staff of ''International Times'' (London's underground newspaper) and featuring progressive rock, light shows, movies and weirdness 'til dawn. The first show featured The Pink Floyd. The Floyd, The Soft Machine, Tomorrow and Arthur Brown appeared often, and developed their following there.
Tim Hardin born in Oregon. His first album ''Tim Hardin 1'' was released in 1966. Songs such as ''If I Were A Carpenter'' have been recorded by many artists, from Bobby Darin to Rod Stewart.
Radio London begins regular transmissions, in 1964. Closed down on August 14, 1967. One of the best of the mid-Sixties pirate radio stations in the UK.
Charles Atlas ''The strongest man in the world'' dies in 1973, aged 79.

DECEMBER 24
Yule Log burnt.

Lee Michaels born. The organ player who, backed only by a drummer, brought out an enormous number of fine rock albums from 1968 onwards.
Lee Dorsey born in New Orleans, Louisiana, in 1924. His hits began in 1961 when ''Ya Ya'' made US No. 7 Others from the mid-Sixties included ''Ride Your Pony'', ''Working In The Coalmine'' and ''Holy Cow''.
The Tokens ''The Lion Sleeps Tonight'' reached US No. 1 in 1961. Eno revived it as a single in summer 1975.

Jan Akkerman born in 1946. The guitarist for Focus, the Dutch group of four highly trained musicians originally formed for the Amsterdam production of ''Hair'' in 1969.
The Beatles open their Christmas Show at the Odeon, Hammersmith, London, in 1964, which ran until January 18. With them on the bill were Freddie and The Dreamers, The Yardbirds, Elkie Brooks, Jimmy Saville, Mike Haslam, and The Mike Cotton Sound.

Ava Gardner (Lucy Johnson) born in 1922. American leading lady who was once voted the world's most beautiful woman. Married at various times to Artie Shaw, Mickey Rooney, Frank Sinatra.
Tom Johnston, of The Doobie Brothers, arrested Visalia, California, in 1974, on a marijuana possession charge. The Doobies next album was ''What Were Once Vices Are Now Habits''.

DECEMBER 25
Birthday of Mithras, Osiris, Bacchus, Adonis, and many forms of Savior.

Noel David Redding, bass player with The Jimi Hendrix Experience, born in Folkstone, Sussex in 1945. The single ''Hey Joe'' shot the newly formed group into success in 1967.

Trevor Lucas, guitar and vocals with The Fairport Convention, born in Bungaree, Australia, in 1945. Former Fotheringay member he joined the Fairports in 1973, and produced the album ''Rosie''. He is married to Sandy Denny.
Billy Horton, lead singer of The Silhouettes, born in 1937. The group Sha-Na-Na took their name from a line in ''Get A Job'', the big January 1958 hit for The Silhouettes.

Alice Cooper (Vincent Furnier) born in Detroit in 1945. He formed The Earwigs in 1965 and later changed their name to The Spiders. Had a local hit with "Don't Blow Your Mind". As The Nazz they moved to Los Angeles. Apparently found the final name by contacting an Alice Cooper on a Ouija board. Zappa saw them playing on The Strip and signed them to his Straight label. The group grew in notoriety. Alice's chicken-killing and snake fondling gave them maximum publicity and albums such as "School's Out" became huge hits. After the three month 1973 tour he retreated, horrified at the violence of the audiences, becoming a personality on TV and magazines.

Henry Vestine, lead guitarist with Canned Heart, born in Washington DC, in 1944. Heavy blues-rock group, began in 1967 when their first album, called "Canned Heat" was released. "On The Road Again" was a big world-wide hit single.

O'Kelly Isley, of The Isley Brothers, born in 1937. The Beatles cover of "Twist And Shout" stopped them having a UK hit with it.

Kenny Everett born. English DJ specializing in pre-recorded tapes made at his own home studio. Works for London FM station Capitol Radio.

Humphrey Bogart born in New York City, in 1899. "The only thing you owe the public is a good performance".

Merry Clayton, session vocalist, born. Sang on Rolling Stones "Gimme Shelter", the "Performance" soundtrack and various Bobby Darin records.

Johnny Ace dies after shooting himself in a game of Russian Roulette, back-stage at City Auditorium in Houston the previous day

in 1954. His ''Pledging My Love'' went on to become a big hit of 1955.

W. C. Fields misanthropic alcoholic, comedian and juggler, dies in 1946. ''If at first you don't succeed, try again. Then quit. No use being a damn fool about it.''

Johnny Tillotson's ''Poetry In Motion'' reaches UK No. 1 in 1960.

Paul McCartney and Jane Asher engaged in 1967. McCartney had been living in the Asher household with the rest of Jane's family for nearly two years.

DECEMBER 26

Phil Spector born in the Bronx, in 1939. Creator of the ''wall of sound'' in his beautiful productions of The Crystals, The Ronettes, Ike and Tina Turner and so on . . . Later producer of The Beatles' ''Let It Be'' album and George Harrison's ''All Things Must Pass'' as well as work done with John Lennon. Married Ronnie, of The Ronettes.

Rolling Stones (as yet unnamed) play The Piccadilly Club in London, in 1962.

George Harrison's ''My Sweet Lord'' reaches No. 1 in the US in 1970, to stay there for four weeks. Produced by Phil Spector.

Fidel Castro and a handful of comrades, land in Cuba in 1956, to start the Cuban Revolution.

Steve Allen born in 1921. His TV talk show consistently featured rock artists.

Mao Tse Tung born in 1893.

The Beatles ''Magical Mystery Tour'' film has its world premiere on BBC TV in 1967.

Henry Miller born in New York City, in 1891. Author of the controversial ''Tropic Of Cancer'' and ''Tropic Of Capricorn'' as well as ''The Rosy Crucifixion'' Trilogy: ''Sexus'', ''Plexus'' and ''Nexus''.

DECEMBER 27

Tracy Nelson born in Madison, Wisconsin, in 1944. Piano and vocals with Mother Earth, their first album was released in 1968 ''Living With The Animals''. She has made a number of

solo albums the first of which was before Mother Earth was formed.

Pete Brown born in London, in 1940. Originally responsible for spreading modern poetry across the face of Britain with the New Departures traveling circus of modern poets, that he ran together with poet Michael Horovitz. Brown wrote extensively with Jack Bruce for Cream. ''Wrapping Paper'', ''Sunshine Of Your Love'' and other big hits assured his future and he formed a series of experimental jazz-rock groups, beginning with Pete Brown's Battered Ornaments.

Scotty Moore (Winifred Scott Moore) born in Gadsden, Tennessee, in 1931. Played guitar on the early work of Elvis Presley and was his first manager. Now leads the Nashville group What's Left.

The Beatles are hailed by ''The Times'' music critic William Mann as ''the outstanding composers of 1963''. He described ''With The Beatles'' as ''. . . expressively unusual for its lugubrious music, but harmonically it is one of their most interesting with its chains of pandiatonic clusters.''

''Welcome Home'' concert for The Beatles at Litherland Town Hall, Liverpool, in 1960, when they return from their second trip to Hamburg.

Mike Pinder, keyboards and vocals with The Moody Blues, born. He was one of the founders of the group in Birmingham in 1964. Their first album was ''The

Magnificent Moodies'' in 1965. In 1969 they moved to the village of Cobham in Surrey and ran their Threshold record label from there.

Les Maguire, piano and vocals with Gerry and The Pacemakers, born in Wallesey in 1942. They had three UK No. 1's in 1963 beginning with ''How Do You Do It''

Marlene Dietrich born in Berlin, in 1901. ''The Blue Angel'' created her as an erotic myth in 1930, from whence came ''Falling In Love Again''.

DECEMBER 28

Johnny Otis born in 1924. His first big hit was ''Willie And The Hand Jive'' in June 1958 in the US, but was recording for years before

that. The Johnny Otis Show has located and promoted many of the great artists of the Fifties who had . disappeared into obscurity At the Monterey Jazz Festival in 1970, he presented a show with Joe Turner, Roy Brown, Eddie 'Cleanhead' Vinson and his guitarist son, Shuggie Otis. Probably best known as a songwriter.

Earl ''Fatha'' Hines born in 1905. A jazz pianist, in the late Twenties he was briefly a member of Louis Armstrong's Hot Five. In the Forties he led a band including Charlie Parker and Dizzy Gillespie. A forgotten figure in the Fifties, he has recently made a comeback, appearing live

and on records, including Ry Cooder's ''Paradise And Lunch''.

Edgar Winter born in Leland, Mississippi, in 1947. With his group White Trash, he followed in his brother Johnny's footsteps to New York City. Had his first hit in 1971 with ''Keep Playing That Rock'n' Roll''. He hit the singles charts with ''Frankenstein'' in 1973.

Roebuck ''Pops'' Staples born in Winona, Mississippi in 1915. The Staples Singers consists of Pops plus his three daughters, Mavis (the lead singer), Cleotha and Yvonne.

JOHNNY OTIS / PHOTO: ROGER PERRY.

THE STAPLES SINGERS

RICK DANKO.

They worked for 15 years before finding success with Stax records, climaxing with "Respect Yourself", the million-selling single that brought them international fame as a soul/blues vocal group.

Dorsey Burnette born in Memphis, Tennessee, in 1932. He was with his brother's Johnny Burnette Trio until 1969, but had a solo hit with "Tall Oak Tree" in the US in February 1960.

Bobby Comstock born in Ithaca, New York, in 1943. "Tennessee Waltz" was his biggest US hit in October 1969.

Dick Diamonde, of The Easybeats, born in Australia, in 1947. They moved to Britain in 1966 and had a transatlantic hit with "Friday On My Mind".

"At The Hop" by Danny and The Juniors reached US No. 1 in 1957 and stayed seven weeks. A Philadelphia group who were unable to follow-up.

Drugs. The New York "Daily Worker" of 1940, in its Health Advice column, reports: "Smoking of the weed is habit forming. It destroys the willpower, releases restraints and promotes insane reactions. Continued use causes the face to become bloated, the eyes bloodshot, the limbs weak and trembling and the mind sinks into insanity. Robberies, thrill murders, sex crimes and other offenses result . . .''

DECEMBER 29

Rick Danko, bass player of The Band, born in 1942. In the late Fifties The Band came together in Canada as Ronnie Hawkin's backing group The Hawks. In 1965 they backed Bob Dylan for the first time on "Can You Please Crawl Out Your Window?''. They toured with Dylan in 1965-6, and when he was recovering from his motorcylce accident in Woodstock they recorded the legendary "Basement Tapes''. The Band's first album, "Music From Big Pink" was released in 1968, to much critical acclaim. It was followed by an album each year until 1973. They backed Dylan on his 1974 tour and his "Planet Waves", album.

Radio Luxembourg given permission to begin operations by the Grand Duchy government in 1930. Throughout the Fifties and early Sixties, this was the only commercial radio station broadcasting in English in Europe, and the only one playing rock'n'-roll. They featured Alan Freed's rock show as part of their Saturday night show.

Ray Thomas, of The Moody Blues, born in 1947. "Go Now" their first single, made UK No. 1 in January 1965 and reached No. 10 in the US.

Women's Rights. The Sex Discrimination and Equal Pay acts came into operation in Great Britain in 1975.

Bob Dylan's "Rolling Thunder Review" crosses over into Canada in 1975, and plays Quebec City.

DECEMBER 30

Monkees' Davy Jones, vocalist, born in Manchester, England, in 1945. Two years earlier, on the same day, guitarist Mike Nesmith was born in Houston, Texas. A very successful attempt to launch "The New Beatles" by Don Kirschner's ATV company who created the group for a regular TV show based on The Beatles' films. The Monkees finally made a weird psychedelic film called Head and lost much of their teeny-bopper following.

John Hartford born in 1947. Glen Campbell recorded "Gentle On My Mind" written by Hartford and made his reputation. Hartford played banjo and fiddle on The Byrds "Sweetheart Of The Rodeo".

Del Shannon born in Grand Rapids, Michigan, in 1939. "Runaway" was the UK No. 1 in April 1961.

Andy Williams born in Wall Lake, Iowa, in 1930. "Butterfly" and "I Love Your Kind Of Love" were both 1957 hits for him. He had over forty US chart entries and is a big selling album artist.

Skeeter Davis (Mary Francis Penick) born in 1931, in Dry Ridge, Kentucky. Her recording of Carole King's "I Can't Stay Mad At You" reached US No. 7.

Andy Stewart born in Glasgow in 1933. In August 1959 he released "Donald Were's Your Trousers?" and has kept in with TV appearances ever since.

Jeff Lynne, guitar and vocalist with The Move, in its final line-up, born in Birmingham, in 1947.

THE KINKS WITH PETER QUAIFE (SECOND LEFT) / PHOTO: CAMERA PRESS.

DECEMBER 31

Vesta, Goddess of the Hearth. Hogmanay in Scotland.

Peter Quaife, of The Kinks, born in Tavistock, Devon, in 1943. Bass player with the group when they started in 1964, and stayed with them until 1969. Played on all their early hits such as "You Really Got Me" and "All Day And All Of The Night".

Odetta born in 1930. Folk and gospel singer, friend of Bob Dylan and integral member of the Greenwich Village scene in early Sixties.

Rex Allen born in Willcox, Arizona, in 1924. "Don't Go Near The Indians" made the US Top 20 in September 1962.

Jimi Hendrix's Band of Gypsies play their debut gig at the Fillmore East in New York City, in 1969-70. Featuring Buddy Miles on drums and Billy Cox on bass.

Beach Boys, first concert under that name at the Richie Valens Memorial Center in Long Beach, in 1961. Previously they were Carl and The Passions.

The Monkees' "I'm A Believer" reaches US No. 1 and stays there for seven weeks in 1966. The Neil Diamond song later gave ex-Soft Machine drummer Robert Wyatt a UK hit in 1974. It sold 65,000 copies in a couple of weeks, then sales suddenly stopped. When asked what this meant he replied, "It means that the 65,000 people who bought it are now enjoying it."

David Bowie receives a plaque in 1973, for having five different albums in the charts at the same time for nineteen weeks running.

Bob Dylan joined The Band onstage for their encore at the New Year concert at New York Academy of Music, in 1971. He did four numbers in a 20 minute impromptu set. The Band's set was released as the live album "Rock Of Ages".

John Denver born in 1943. Son of an Air Force pilot, composed "Leaving On A Jet Plane" for Peter, Paul and Mary. A clean-cut kid and he's been to college too; he majored in architecture at Texas Tech. In the Seventies he found great success with solo albums backed by TV shows.

JOHN DENVER.

atter how small.
ı marijuana could
ender up to
ırs jail.

alker (Gary Leeds),
ıalker Brothers, born
ıdale, California, in
When the Walker
ərs split in 1967, he
ted to his real name
ıormed a group called

ce Harrison, keyboards
Spooky Tooth, born in
. When the band broke
ıade an unsuccessful
album before reforming
wo more albums.

n Brewer, drummer of
ıd Funk Railroad, born
ı8. The group had 10
ı albums before
ır to producers such
Rundgren and
ıppa.

ıd Owl" Wilson, of
Heat, found dead
ıottle of downers in
group member Bob
ıarden, in Topanga
ı, Los Angeles,
ıia, in 1970. He

ıain , ıuuı ırıdwıu
nit.

Pearce Marchbank born
in Farnborough, England in
1948. After receiving an
honours degree in design,
he art directed
"Architectural Design"
magazine. Via the UK
edition of "Rolling Stone" he
moved to the underground
press, art directing
"Friends", "Time Out",
"Oz", and many other
publications in the early
seventies. Since he has
designed and edited
mainly music books,
including editions for The
Beatles, Rolling Stones,
David Bowie, Eric Clapton,
Jimi Hendrix and Bob

Marley. His work has been
internationally exhibited
and he is often a jury
member of the Design and
Art Directors Association of
London. At present he is
working as a freelance
publishing editor and
designer.

_y Rider".
They disbanded in 1972,
but re-formed in 1974.

Miles (Barry Miles) born in
Cheltenham Spa, England,
in 1943. In 1966 started
Indica Bookshop in London
and from there founded
Europe's first underground
newspaper "International
Times" (IT). His rock
interviews have appeared
in over sixty newspapers
including "Rolling Stone",
"Oz", "Village Voice",
"Vogue", "The Sunday
Times", "LA Free Press" and
"Fusion". In 1969 The Beatles
sent him to US to produce
spoken word albums. He
worked for two years with
Allen Ginsberg and then as
bibliographer to William
Burroughs. Since 1975 he
has written regularly for
"New Musical Express".